Treading the Mill
Workings in Traditional Witchcraft

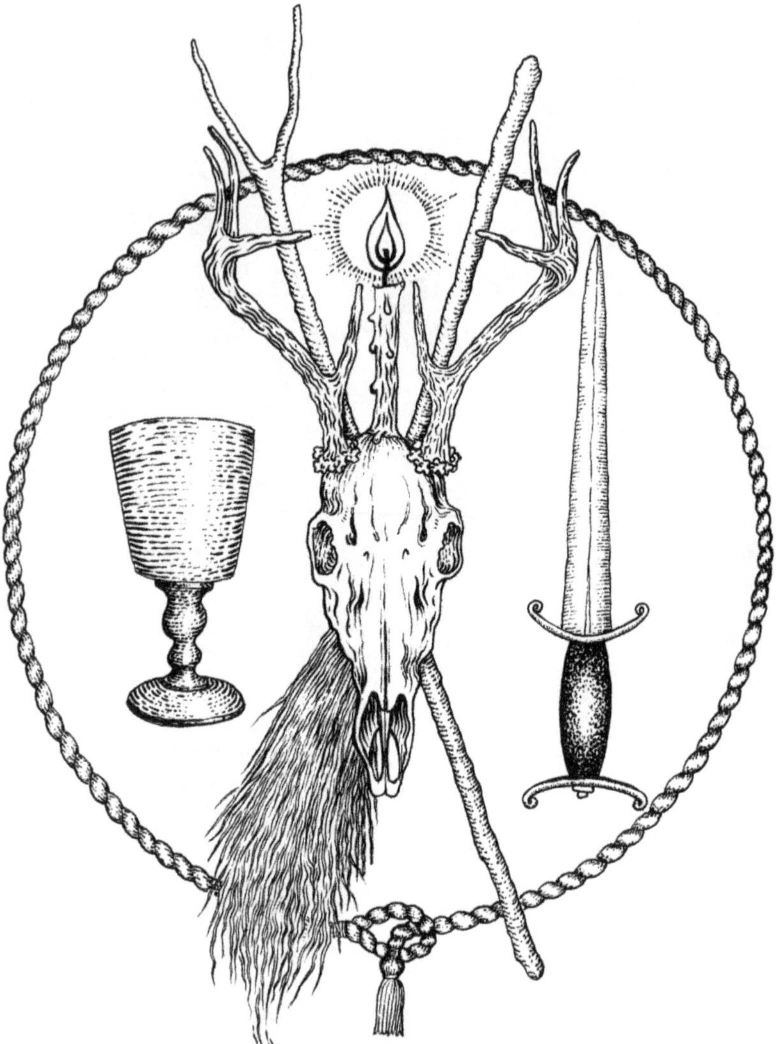

Treading *the* Mill
Workings in Traditional Witchcraft

by

Nigel G. Pearson

TROY BOOKS

First printing in paperback April 2017

ISBN 978-1-909602-21-2

Revised and expanded from the first edition
published by Capall Bann in 2007

Published by Troy Books
www.troybooks.co.uk

Troy Books Publishing
BM Box 8003
London WC1N 3XX

Cover & dust jacket design: Gemma Gary

Printed and bound in Great Britain

Dedication

This book is dedicated with devotion and respect to;
The Hidden Master, the Secret King
and to the Pale Goddess beyond and behind it All.

Acknowledgements

Debts of gratitude are owed to the following;

Jean and Lawrence Tebbott, who started me off in the Craft and gave me my first lessons, so long ago. Blessings to you in the realms of the Ancestors.

Jane Cox and Gemma Gary of Troy Books for encouraging me in my work and taking on this second edition.

All those teachers and mentors in the Craft that I have had over the years and who have imparted their knowledge and wisdom to me. Especially to the late Michael Howard, who was a great help and encouragement in many weird and unusual ways.

The people who have read my work and appreciated it enough to ask for more!

And, as ever, to my beloved husband Anthony, who still puts up with me after all these years.

Contents

Photoplates

between pages 128 – 129

All Photography by the author

INTRODUCTION
to the Second Edition

I find it hard to credit that it is now ten years since I finished writing the first edition of Treading the Mill: Practical CraftWorking in Modern Traditional Witchcraft. At that time, there were relatively few serious books on Traditional Craft and very few written with a view to giving the relative newcomer an insight into some of the workings of, what was then, a still unknown and murky area of magical Craft. Since that time, there has been a veritable explosion of books in the genre, some good, some not so, but it was ever so. One of the leading lights in the field of Traditional Witchcraft in recent years has been Troy Books, leading the way with the writings of Gemma Gary, in particular. I am therefore very pleased that Troy have agreed to publish this second edition of my work and hope that it is a worthy addition to their stable.

My original intent with this book was to try to write something that I would have liked to read when I was first looking into this field; something useful, informative, practical and relatively easy to understand, without too much deep, theoretical background but giving the rationale that underpinned the actions. I also tried to include something for the more experienced practitioner as well and give a sample of some of my experiences, the better to illustrate the practical applications of the Craft. From the feedback I have received in the ensuing years since it's initial publication, Treading the Mill seems to have fulfilled that brief fairly well, and to have been well received in many areas. However, nothing is ever perfect and, in the realms of an authors work, ever finished either - it can always be bettered.

In this second edition, I have attempted to address some of the valid critiques that were levelled at my initial work and, to that extent, have revised some areas of the original text. The first chapter on Hallowing the Compass has been fairly extensively re-written, in an attempt to better explain the concept and practical applications of this very important technique. The original chapter on the mysteries of the Cup and the use of wines and winemaking in the Craft has been removed, it being deemed not highly relevant in this context. I have replaced this with a chapter on the use and creation of magical Incenses and related areas, which I hope will be of more relevance and interest. The final chapter, Approaching the Powers, has been much revised and expanded, the better to develop some deeper concepts that were either little addressed or left out of the original text. It also includes added techniques for creating the compass, something that was much needed to further explore this important concept and practice. The other chapters remain essentially the same, although I have not been able to resist "tweaking" here and there, having been given the opportunity to do so.

I hope that, in this second edition, I have addressed the points that people felt needed addressing and have perhaps given a further insight into the workings of a more Traditional method of practical Witchcraft. Much of my work here seems very simple, especially when compared with the works of other modern writers on the subject. However, I maintain my original premise that, at its core, the Craft is a simple, practical and natural/Land-based practice, how ever far and deep those practices may ultimately lead. These workings – and those similar – have served me very well for many years and, from feedback received, I know that many other people have worked successfully with them as well. So, to any other sceptics out there I would say, just try the techniques given here with an open mind and heart and maybe they'll work for you too, no matter what your background or previous training.

I have resisted the strong temptation to revise the original Introduction and it is included here following, as both a small historical testament as to what I was trying to do and to show how far this second edition may have travelled from the premise of the first.

Nigel G. Pearson,
Suffolk, England.
Michaelmas, 2016.

INTRODUCTION
to the First Edition

The intention of this volume is to give an idea, however brief and incomplete, to both the relative newcomer and maybe the more seasoned practitioner in this field of study, of an alternative to the Wiccan/Pagan practices found in most books. This volume aims to present some of the methods deriving from an older stratum of belief and practice, albeit in a modern context, which generally come under the heading of Traditional Witchcraft, Old Craft or simply Craft. I do not profess to be representing all aspects or paths of the Craft, as they are many and very varied, but I do hope to give some fairly detailed explanations of some of the methods used by some Witches or Crafters.

Before proceeding further, I feel some explanations and definitions are in order. What exactly do I mean by "Traditional Witchcraft", as opposed to modern Wicca or other Neo-Pagan traditions? By this term I mean a practice or practices that predate Gardnerian Wicca in origin, whether that be decades or centuries, that have been passed on in continuous transmission outside of modern, known traditions and that do not derive from or have any connection with the modern, Neo-Pagan belief systems. I realise that this is not as tight a definition as some Traditionals would wish, but it is such a wide field that I risk alienating many Crafters were I to draw it any tighter. Having discussed this question with many people, one of the defining things about Traditional Craft apart from anything else, is its "feel". This type of Craft is definitely of the Land and the Powers and People who live with it. Although some Crafters may use techniques derived from grimoires and other learned tomes, it is not essentially a literary or learned tradition, whereas modern Wicca draws heavily from both theses sources. Traditional Craft stems directly from personal encounters with the raw and undiluted powers of the natural world and the knowledge and energies that flow there from. These encounters become encoded into a corpus of knowledge over a period of time, the individual adding from their own experiences. It is a living, growing and vibrant path, fuelled both by ancient lore and individual expression.

Other than a few well-known practitioners, the Craft has no "founding fathers" either. Unlike Gardnerian or Alexandrian Wicca, or other traditions initiated by well known "names", Traditional Craft cannot point to any individuals as their source of inspiration or knowledge. For however long, the Craft has been passed on from individual to individual – sometimes within a "coven" structure, very often not – with no knowledge of where it came from and no more desire than that it should be passed on and continued. Individuals will change a bit here and there, but the core remains the same as it is not derived from a single source but from personal experience and realisation of the Craft as a living reality. You either "get it" or you don't and if you don't, then you're not practising Traditional Witchcraft. Sorry, but that's the way it goes!

The question also arises as to whether Traditional Craft is a religion or not; some practitioners would say yes, some would say definitely not. On the surface it appears that it is, especially if one takes the meaning of "religion" at root value, meaning "to bind" to one's gods. However it is, the essential thing to remember – which sets Crafters apart from most modern Wiccans – is that they do not worship their gods. Honour, respect and devotion are given freely and it is at the core of all they do, but worship? No, I don't think so. There is too close a bond of energy, knowledge and partnership in working for that relationship to happen. The gods, as discussed later, are not put on a pedestal but are seen as different patterns of energy in an energetic universe that we all partake of; therefore worship is impossible to the true Crafter.

Finally, on this point of explanations, it is important to remember that Traditional Witchcraft begins and ends in the Land around us, however far it travels in between. This is not said as an emotional, ideal concept of how nice the Earth Mother is, but firmly grounded in a practical knowledge and experience of the physical and energetic levels of the Earth itself. Most Crafters will always work outside, unless it is too dangerous or the weather is just too bad. This brings with it an intimate knowledge of the tides, rhythms and energies of the Land on which we live and of the myths and folklore, which it gave birth to; no comfy sitting room with the chairs pushed back for a Traditional Witch! The definition of Land in this context means not just the physical soil and earth alone, but the powers and forces which animate it and bring it alive; the web of intricate detail that joins all life into one rich cloth of living flesh, of which we are an inherent part. Again, this is not said in any sentimental way, as part of this shining life of the Land is the knowledge that death waits just round the corner and that, too, informs the knowledge and actions of the Traditional Witch.

The rites, techniques and methods given in this book are not drawn from any one path in Traditional Witchcraft, but are taken from the various teachings I have received from different people, from varying traditions, over the years. I do not claim that any are hundreds of years old or even decades, merely that they are a valid part of an ongoing, magical stream that works and has its roots in some distant past. If you wish to work with any of the techniques given here please use them with respect and genuine feeling for the Craft and its adherents.

As this is essentially a practical workbook, I have not attempted to give any more than basic theoretical, theological or historical backgrounds in any of the sections. I give what I hope is a full and rounded bibliography and reading list at the end of this book and direct the interested reader there for further and deeper understanding.

Nigel G. Pearson
Suffolk
Midsummer 2007.

HALLOWING *the* COMPASS

Unlike many other spiritual traditions, the Witch, or Crafter, rarely has a designated space set aside permanently and consecrated purely for their work or practice. Therefore, this space must be freshly created or brought into being, whenever it is considered necessary for the work in hand (for not all witches will consider it needful to work in a compass for every operation). This space is almost invariably circular in shape (although there are variations) and is generally orientated to the natural directions, or compass points, of North, East, South and West; hence the generic name of "Compass" used by most Traditional witches. The reason for thus orientating the space is to take advantage of and work along with, the flow of the natural forces within the Earth on which we stand. Once hallowed, the compass is "set aside" or lies just outside of, normal reality and within this space the Crafter will feel confident in performing their work, safe and secure from interruption. Once the work has been completed, the compass may be "dismantled" in one of a number of ways or, once thanks have been given, simply walked away from (if outdoors) and left to dissipate naturally. The compass way be created either indoors or out but most Crafters prefer to work outside wherever possible, considering the contact with the natural forces, spirits and Powers to be stronger *au naturel.*

There are many different methods of hallowing the compass (conjuring the circle, laying the round, ploughing the furrow or creating sacred space, as it is variously called) and not all traditions will use this space for the same purposes, or view it in the same way. Some methods can be quite lengthy, usually when there is a gathering of a group or coven of witches, involving various invocations and calls to the spirits and Powers, the better to create a group "mindset". At the other end of the scale, for you as an individual worker, hallowing the compass can involve little more than "walking" around the edge of your working space to delineate the physical area in which you will work and to set up the non-physical space. Different methods may be more appropriate to different occasions and workings and these will need to be decided upon in advance, so remember to be flexible in your approach.

On one level, the compass is there purely and simply to mark out the space you are going to work in, to delineate your working area; this is the most traditional form of compass and the one that most paths recognise and work with. It is there to *set aside* that space from the everyday world and its energies and make that space, for a time, something *other* for you and your work. This type of compass also has the added function of warding or preventing any unwanted or uninvited "guests" from intruding and disrupting your work. The words you use to create your compass will reflect the use to which it is to be put to and also who, or what, is to be allowed to join you in your work. It is normal and common for other Powers and spirits to be invited to work with you and this will be reflected in the form of setting up your working area.

On another level altogether, the compass acts as a kind of portal to different realms. Sometimes called "The Wood between the Worlds", this compass is used as a "halfway-house" between this world and whatever realm we wish to journey to. We stand with one foot in each realm; so to speak, as do the entities in the different worlds we wish to contact. Our working space becomes a no-man's land or neutral area, in which to experience other dimensions and beings. Further than this, we may safely leave our bodies in this warded area whilst we send our spirit/fetch/astral body out into other worlds, perhaps to acquire further knowledge or communicate with other beings in their own realms, secure in the knowledge that it will come to no harm whilst we are journeying. This is the original meaning of the term "Hedge Witch" or "Hedge Rider" - the person who rides the boundary or hedge between this world and the next, to bring back knowledge and magic for use in this world.

The different types of compass are decided upon before creation and are then brought into being accordingly. The main ingredients in the construction of a compass are always the visualisation and energy you put into it; if you don't have that, then there is no "dimensional shift" and hence, no compass. This last point cannot be stressed too strongly; it is not the words you use that create your compass – although they will shape its reality – it is the effort and energy that you expend, the focused concentration and aimed visualisation, that brings it into being. If you do not expend the energy, then you have not created a compass and hence will have not created a place set apart.

Whilst some traditions would disagree strongly with this point, it should be mentioned here that, although it is invariably referred to as a "compass" and is seen as a flat, circular area in which to work, outside of everyday reality, what *some* paths create is actually viewed as a sphere or a bubble. (This concept of a sphere is more usual in the modern, Wiccan traditions but also occurs in at least two Traditional paths that I know of, so is worth mentioning here, I feel). In this format, the ritual area extends above and below the Crafter, as well as from in front, behind and from side to side and so they are to all intents and purposes, enclosed in a psychic bubble. The Crafter is at the centre of his/her own magical universe and acts as creator and sustainer therein. This is what is used to travel into the different "realms", inside of which the individual remains safe and in control.

Other traditions or paths would consider this to be totally irrelevant or not needed, in that the standard compass is used as a space to travel in anyway. Unlike more modern paths, within Traditional Craft, rather than calling the Powers and spirits *into* the compass, the compass is used either as a portal to other worlds, there to meet other Beings face to face, or is used to journey in itself, rather than filling it from outside.

In addition to the above, there are also differences in the way Crafters refer to this space. Some refer to this area as a "circle" and reserve the word "compass" for the powers and forces that they may invite to work with them. Others refer to the whole thing as a "compass" and never use the term "circle" at all - some even considering it anathema! The terms "Ring", "Bloodacre", "Castle" and "Crossroads" are also used, each having a slightly or greatly differing meaning to the others, but basically used for the same purpose. I shall here continue to use the word "compass" as this is the term most Crafters will use and understand. However, as this is such a rich area of symbolism and practice on its own, irrespective of what takes place within the space, I would like to give basic examples at the end of this chapter and develop the concept and symbolism of the compass with further examples in a later chapter (see "Approaching the Powers").

At the simplest (or on a different level, the most complex), level, there is no actual need to use any "tool" or "weapon" to hallow or create your compass. However, it is traditional to use at least one to aid you, both as a psychological aid and to incorporate the symbolism inherent in the tool itself into your work. We will now examine some of the tools you may wish to use in constructing your compass.

Tools

The Stang

What is a Stang? The word 'stang' comes from the Old Norse *Stong* or *Stange* and literally means "Pole". It is a wooden staff, normally somewhere between waist and head height, although shoulder height is more usual. More often than not, it is cleft in some way at the top, either by naturally branching into a "Y" shape, or sometimes simply split along the grain near the top. Horns or antlers are often fixed to the top if it is not naturally forked. The wood is more often than not Ash wood, but different regions will have their own variations and other types of wood are used for specific purposes. The end is normally "shod" with one or more iron nails, the number depending on the particular path of the Crafter. Some Traditions "shoe" their Stang with a miniature horseshoe, the better to reflect one of the traditional aspects of its nature, which is that of a steed, used to carry the witch to different dimensions during certain rites.

Traditionally, you would go out into the wild and ask for your own Stang from the spirits of the Land. They will give it when they are ready and it is suitable to you; a Stang would not normally be bought from someone else. It is said that there is Stang for everyone, waiting to be found, you just need to find it. In the past it would have been a natural object to have about oneself, especially if one was going on a journey. It would act as a support, a defence against attack and a prop for a tent or shelter.

It is used to hallow the compass, and generally direct energy, becoming an extension of your own energy system. In Traditional Craft belief, all things have an axis and the Stang can be seen as a symbol of this axis. There is a pole of energy that runs up the spine of the human being and the Stang is the expression of this. This energy is often represented in Craft symbolism as a serpent, but is not the same as the Eastern "kundalini". 'Pole' also has the meaning of the Pole Star, the Nowl, or Nail of the heavens, around which all the constellations circulate and from which the Crafter derives knowledge, energy, information and understanding. In this manner, the Stang also represents the *axis mundi*, the World Tree and is used to journey up or down, in the quest for knowledge and experience. It is the centre, foundation and base upon which the working methods are planned and I will speak more on this subject in the final chapter of this book. Part of the symbolism of the top of the Stang is that the fork represents both the horns of the god and the lunar curve of the goddess, although rarely, if ever, representing the goddess in actuality. To ascend the pole is to aspire to that state of being where one may speak with the gods.

It is usual for the Stang to act as an altar in ritual, in which case it will be stuck in the ground with the horns pointing upwards, usually in the North, to embody the energy and presence of the Horned One. At different times of year it may be moved around the compass to stand at different "stations" and be decorated to represent the season or a different aspect of Himself. The fork, or split, at the top of the Stang, as well as representing the horns of the God and possibly the lunar crescent in some instances, also represents the flowering and fountaining of the vital energy within the human frame. The lighted candle that is sometimes placed between the horns in ritual echoes this. During ritual, apart from any other usage, the Stang is seen and treated as the very embodiment of the Old One and, because of this, is given honour and respect. It is the physical manifestation and presence of the actuality of the Ancient One and is never, ever, just a forked stick!

TheWand

This can sometimes be viewed as a smaller counterpart to the Stang, which may or may not also be forked at one end, although it is more often – and usually – viewed as a working tool in its own right. I have covered the subject of Wands in depth in the next chapter – "WandCrafting" – and would therefore refer the reader to this for further information. This chapter also covers the cutting, fashioning and preserving of wood used for magical practices and this would also apply equally to the Stang.

The Knife

The knife is essentially a practical tool in Traditional Craft, although it also has symbolic values and uses as well. On a practical level, the knife is used for what it was invented for – cutting. If gathering herbs for use in magic or medicine, cutting wood for a wand or staff, or fashioning a tool that needs carving, all these would employ the knife. It may be of any design that is comfortable to the user; single or double-sided, long or short and with a colour hilt or binding of their choice. The one thing it must be is sharp – no room for a knife that can't cut in Traditional Craft!

On a symbolic level it has various functions. It is a symbol of the Will of the user and is used to project that Will into manifestation. It is sometimes used to control and/or direct spirits that are worked with and that are a bit "recalcitrant". As a thrusting tool, it is also a male, phallic symbol and is used in various hallowing rites, most notably in the dedication of the wine in the cup/chalice. In keeping with the ancient, fertility associations of the Craft, the Cup and the Knife represent the conjoining of the male and the female, to create Life in the form of the mysterious liquid within the womb of the Cup. The knife may also be indicative of the "lightning flash" of power, deriving from the sky gods and the fiery energy born from the heat of the forge of the divine Smith-Gods and is used as a channel for these energies within the rites. It can be used to direct the accumulated force during ritual in the compass and, in this case, is similar to the Wand. It is also, and frequently, used to delineate the edge of the compass when working outdoors, if so desired. In this instance, the symbolism can be likened to that of the iron-shod plough, which creates the furrow that divides one world or realm from another.

The Cup

This is a tool of singular importance and use within Traditional Craft and I will try here to convey some of the more essential meanings and use of this vessel.

The Cup as used today by most Crafters derives in essence from those ancient Cauldrons, spoken of in myth and legend. As a feminine symbol it is supreme and it is the singular most important representation of the Goddess and Her Mysteries usually found within a Crafter's workings. In its shape and design it contains a resume of the lore and magic associated with the various aspects of the Goddess.

As a Cauldron symbol or substitute, it represents the fecund womb of Mother Nature, the potential of possibilities, the blessings of Her fertility and the manifestation of the same. In this potent symbol, it also represents the opening to that same womb, and hence the deeper sexual mysteries of the Craft. In this case, the symbolism is often combined with that of the knife or rod and the ritual proceeds in token or actuality. In certain branches of Craft, just as in a metal Cauldron, a certain "elixir" can then be "brewed" in this manner and shared by the two Witches involved. However, this is deep lore and something that I cannot cover here. Suffice it to say that, in this case, as a symbol of inspiration and exhaltation, the "Cup" equates specifically with the Cauldron of the Welsh goddess Kerridwen and the distillation of what is commonly known as the "Awen" – Divine Inspiration. It is in this aspect that the Cauldron came to be identified with the Christian cup that held the blood of Jesus and hence gave rise to the whole corpus of lore surrounding the Holy Grail. An examination of the Grail lore in depth would richly reward any Crafter in their search for knowledge of this subject.

But, just as in Life, so in the Craft and its Mysteries. As the Cup/Cauldron is a symbol of potentiality and abundance, bestowing wisdom and illumination, so is it also its reverse, a symbol of sacrifice and death (again, tying in with some of the Grail lore). The opening of the Cup is often spoken of as the entrance to the tomb and in times gone by, the Cauldron was used to catch the blood of those offered to the gods. This may be seen graphically in the figures modelled on the side of the famous Gundestrup Cauldron, which are actually being plunged into the vessel whole (or should that be being extracted from the Cauldron reborn?). Both sides of this example can be seen played out in the story of Branwen, sister to the god Bran, in the second branch of the collection of Welsh tales known as The Mabinogion. This sacrifice – actual or symbolic – admits the supplicant once again to the deeper levels of knowledge of the Goddess and here we are dealing with those realms and levels that go beyond our known time and space. As an entry into the Otherworlds of the Goddess, alive or dead, the Cup can again bestow the blessings of divine knowledge and inspiration, or it can lead us out of this worldly realm entirely and into a new stage of existence. It is the portal to the outer reaches of the starry wisdom of Time and Fate itself and these Mysteries are held very close to the bosom of the Dame, bestowed only upon Her 'most favoured'.

On a lower level, the Crafter can use the Cup without passing through the "supreme doors". It can be filled with any number of aqueous substances and used as a scrying medium. Using a solution of Vervain herb during scrying in the Cup may access the Lady's starry wisdom, or the darker realms may be approached by using a black ink. The addition of various essential oils to the "brew" may further aid the shift in consciousness, as scent is a powerful aid in this respect.

As a vessel however, the Cup acts not only as a symbol, but also as a practical working tool. It is in the Cup that the Crafter may brew some of his/her most potent spells and philtres and I have gone into this in more detail in the chapter entitled "SpellCrafting". Although not used as a vessel for heating in the same way as a Cauldron, the Cup is still used as a vessel of alchemical transformation, affecting both the Crafter and object of the spell alike. How ever one views the Cup, the most usual usage is to hold the beverage for the feast, either communal or solitary and it is this aspect that often gives the most pleasure, joy and access to divine Mysteries!

The Besom

A besom is a broom that has a straight, wooden handle, with twigs bound at one end. Indeed, just as you see them in the picture books with a Witch astride. Apart from its very practical use as a brush to sweep away dirt and rubbish – both physical and non – the besom is essentially a symbol of boundaries and crossings, hence its symbolic and actual use in flying and projection and also sometimes marking out and clearing away the edge of the compass. It is the liminal nature of the besom that makes it so important in Craft rites, as much of the Witch's work is to do with "crossing over" into the unseen realms. In those Traditions that utilise a Sword in their rites, the Broom and Sword are often laid crossways on the ground at the edge of the compass, forming the liminal gateway over which the company step, to gain access to the hallowed ground.

The besom is usually created from three types of wood, although there are nine wood versions and, like all things in Traditional Craft, there are many regional variations. In the three wood versions, the handle is normally made from Ash wood, being indicative of straightness and flight (one of the reasons it was favoured for spear making and from whence it gets its name; "Aesc" is Anglo-Saxon for Spear). The brush or broom part is usually made from Birch twigs, representing purity, cleanliness and fresh beginnings. It is also the female counterpart to the male Ash; many besoms have the Ash handle terminating in a carved phallus, which is bound into the Birch brush. Unlike shop-bought besoms, a traditional broom is never bound with wire or any metal, the usual binding being made from Willow withies. This tree is sacred to the Dame and represents the lunar side of Her nature – hence, in the symbolism of the besom reflecting the night-flight of the Witch and the nocturnal mysteries of the dark.

As a liminal symbol par excellence, the besom is frequently used at traditional marriages to represent the crossing from one state of life to another. The besom is either jumped or skipped over by the couple and to trip or stumble on the way is seen as a very bad omen indeed.

The Cord

Both a practical and symbolic "tool", the cord has various uses, both within and without the compass. Unique to the individual, the cord is dedicated at the commencement of the Crafters magical career and ideally stays with them all their life, being buried with them at the end. The cord can be of various colours, depending on the path of the user, and is usually the length of the person's height – the traditional *measure* and a representation of the individual.

Essentially, the cord has two symbolic meanings, which can be seen as the two sides of one coin. Firstly, it represents the link between the individual and the gods, specifically the Goddess; it is a kind of spiritual umbilical cord. Secondly, it can be seen to evoke the darker side of this relationship, in that it was used in the past, as a garrotte, to return the Crafter to the Goddess, should they betray their fellow People, or should a willing, voluntary sacrifice be needed. It is usually worn round the waist, during ritual and at certain other times, and hence represents the cycle of birth, death and rebirth and all that comes between them. At other times, it is worn as a halter around the neck, stressing the ties to the Mother and the fact that the Crafter is always subject to Her decrees and laws.

It is common to tie a certain number of knots into the cord, usually nine or thirteen depending on the path of the individual Crafter, these representing significant points in the person's magical career, such as initiation, handfasting, etc. These knots can also be used for spell workings and meditations, such as using the knots in a manner similar to a rosary. The cord itself can be used in hallowings (consecrations) – where the power is bound into the object and to the owner – and can act as the measure of the radius of the compass whilst being cast. This last use links it more closely with the individual Crafter, the resulting compass having a direct relationship with the body of the Crafter and being unique to them alone.

The cord is invariably made of a natural material such as linen, cotton, jute or hemp and is traditionally woven or plaited by the owner, to whom it is even more directly linked.

Calling the Directions

Once you have physically and "energetically" hallowed your compass, using one, or more, of the tools discussed above, it is usual to "anchor" your circle in the physical realm and orientate it according to sacred geometry in the other realms. This is normally done by calling upon, or opening up to, energies/Powers/spirits originating from different sections of the compass and these are the four directions; North, East, South and West. Some form of spiritual being that embodies the energy of a particular element may also be called upon at each direction and these are then considered to mediate the energies, or qualities, of that direction throughout the duration of the rite. (In actuality, these energies are always already present; what you are doing is bringing them to the forefront of your awareness, the better to communicate and work with them, if they so please). Many Crafters see these compass directions as actually being "roads" or pathways, either leading up to, or away from, the edge of the Compass itself. It is along these roads that the Witch may travel to other realms, to have communication with their inhabitants, or may "Call" the denizens of those realms to join them in their rites, in their own otherworldly compass.

In many modern-day practices the directions are usually allocated Elementally as follows; North – Earth (black/brown), East – Air (yellow), South – Fire (red/orange), West – Water (blue/green/ grey). This format basically comes from the mediaeval magicians and their scholarly books of magic, which derive, ultimately, from the Greek and Roman translations of ancient Middle Eastern texts. They, therefore, come from a culture that is not only far in time from us, but in distance, ideology and orientation, amongst others. If you stand in Jerusalem, say, then, yes the greatest body of Earth appears to the North, the desert winds come from the East, the burning sun is to the South and the refreshing waters are to the West; but what of Britain, or elsewhere? In Traditional Craft, these correspondences may or may not be followed, depending on where you are in the country and if, indeed, the four "classical" elements are even called at all (see chapter 6, "SpiritWorking", for further discussion on this topic of elementals). For example, in East Anglia, the nearest, large body of water is to the East. The hottest place is admittedly to the South, but the strongest wind come from the North and the bulk of the land mass is to the West. If you are elsewhere in the country, or world, then obviously other correspondences will hold sway. Alternatively, if we go back in time, an English schematic, illuminated manuscript, dated to c.1080-90, showing astrological and elemental charts, gives the following correspondences; North – Fire (red), East – Earth (blue), South – Water (green), West – Air (white).

Further to the above points, is the consideration of how the individual's own energy-field equates/corresponds with the energies of the place where they are working and what effects that will have on/for them. Equally, in traditional lore and those traditions that use such correspondences at all, the elements of the air and atmosphere are seen as arcing above (North?), fire and light (Sun & Stars) are seen as originating in the East before finally setting in the West, a place of mythical and watery horizons, observed by the Moon, whilst Mankind observes from an Earthly base (in the South). All this is located within greater macro and microcosmic levels, which have little to do with the individual's immediate geographical location on *terra firma.*

So, where does that leave the individual Crafter in calling the directions and orientating their compass? What does one call on and where? Does one always need to have the same calling routine, or can it be tailored to what one is actually doing? Can deity or other spiritual beings be called at the directions as well as/instead of purely elemental energies?

The answer to these questions very much depends on where you are and what you wish to hallow your compass for in the first place, as mentioned above. There is no need, or even desire, to stick to a rigid format every time, as this does not allow for any flexibility in your focus of work, or room for expansion and exploration. What you call upon at the 4 directions of your compass will determine and be determined by the type of work that you are going to perform. In Traditional Craft, there are certain, acknowledged energy forms, or guardians, that are associated with each direction. However, each particular path within the Craft looks at them slightly differently and may call upon them in a different manner, depending on how it views them. Unless you are associated with a particular Traditional lineage, this would not necessarily work for you.

I offer here a visionary journey to help you decide what is appropriate for you to call upon at each direction and at your position in the Land. The results will not be the same for everybody and will probably not correspond with what you read as being the "correct" correspondences in other books. However, they will be right for you and you will derive more benefit from using them, than you will in slavishly following someone else's correspondences.

(N.B. As previously mentioned, in many Craft traditions, the directions are viewed as "roads", both leading up to the edge of the compass and, obviously, away from it in the other direction. It may help if this concept is kept in mind when performing this journey and when actually working in the compass).

A Visionary Journey to determine Individual Directional Correspondences

Seat yourself somewhere comfortable, where you will not be tempted to fall asleep and will not be disturbed for at least half an hour. Make sure you are warm enough and have not eaten recently. You may choose to read through the exercise and follow it in your mind's eye as you go, or record it on to some medium and play it back to yourself. However you do it, take a few full, deep breaths before beginning, then sit back and go with the imagery.

Create in your mind's eye the image of a large, oaken door, set into a solid, stone wall. The door is studded with large iron knobs and has ornate iron hinges. Ivy curls around the edges, softening the outline and the door seems to shimmer, as if it was almost transparent, but you cannot see through it. A breath of wind comes from behind you, seeming to push you forward and, as it does so, you step through the door in reality and find yourself on the other side.

You are standing in a square, wooden chamber, with a round table located in the centre; a single flame burns in a holder at the centre. You walk forward to the table and place both hands, palm down, on the surface. Looking around you,

you see that the room is bare of decoration and any other furniture, but that the wooden panelled walls gleam with a lustre of their own, their grain highly polished to a brilliant shine. There appears to be no ceiling that you can see but neither can you see the sky, only gently rippling patterns, high up, in the place of a ceiling. In each wall, set squarely in the centre, is an intricately carved archway. The archway does not seem to lead anywhere, but appears to be filled with the same, semi-transparent material that composed the oak door you have just stepped through. Each archway faces one of the cardinal directions, which are indicated by a carved letter above each arch: N for north, E for east, S for south and W for west.

You will now call the powers that are most valid for you from each direction.

Moving round the table until you are facing the North archway across it, the flame between you, raise your arms together and make a motion as if you were pulling apart a pair of curtains, at the same time saying; "Powers at the North I call to you; may you reveal yourself for me." Lower your arms and wait patiently.

The shimmering in the archway gradually begins to clear and a scene starts to appear. Watch closely and take careful note, as you will see those beings/guardians/spirits that have most relevance for you, for this direction. Do not attempt to interact at this point. (Pause for observation).

As the scene begins to fade, raise your arms once more and make a gesture as if closing a pair of curtains, at the same time saying; "Powers at the North, my thanks for appearing to my call." Lower your arms. Remember what you have seen.

Now move round the table until you are facing the East archway across it, raise your arms and make the opening gesture, at the same time saying; "Powers at the East I call to you; may you reveal yourself for me." Lower your arms and wait patiently.

The shimmering in the archway gradually begins to clear and a scene starts to appear. Watch closely and take careful note, as you will see those beings/guardians/spirits that have most relevance for you, for this direction. Do not attempt to interact at this point. (Pause for observation).

As the scene begins to fade, raise your arms once more and make the closing gesture, at the same time saying; "Powers at the East, my thanks for appearing to my call." Lower your arms. Remember what you have seen.

Now move round the table until you are facing the South archway across it, raise your arms together and make the opening gesture, at the same time saying; "Powers at the South I call to you; may you reveal yourself for me." Lower your arms and wait patiently.

The shimmering in the archway gradually begins to clear and a scene starts to appear. Watch closely and take careful note, as you will see those beings/guardians/spirits that have most relevance for you, for this direction. Do not attempt to interact at this point. (Pause for observation).

As the scene begins to fade, raise your arms once more and make the closing gesture, at the same time saying; "Powers at the South, my thanks for appearing to my call." Lower your arms. Remember what you have seen.

Now move round the table until you are facing the West archway across it, raise your arms together and make the opening gesture, at the same time saying; "Powers at the West I call to you; may you reveal yourself for me." Lower your arms and wait patiently.

The shimmering in the archway gradually begins to clear and a scene starts to appear. Watch closely and take careful note, as you will see those beings/guardians/spirits that have most relevance for you, for this direction. Do not attempt to interact at this point. (Pause for observation).

As the scene begins to fade, raise your arms once more and make the closing gesture, at the same time saying; "Powers at the West, my thanks for appearing to my call." Lower your arms. Remember what you have seen.

Place your palms once more on the table and take a few, deep breaths, whilst gazing into the flame. You step back from the table and as you do so, you feel a breath of wind in your face pushing you backwards. Step back and find yourself standing once more before the shimmering oaken door where you began. Let the door fade gradually from your inner vision and, in your own time, take a few more deep breaths and open your eyes.

Make notes immediately, in as much detail as you can remember; you may have perceived multiple beings at each direction, be that deities, guardians, spirits or guides. Record them all.

You may find that you do not achieve any understandable contact on the first attempt, in which case it is perfectly acceptable to try again until you are comfortable in your own mind that you have established your own correspondence/s for each direction. (And do bear in mind that it will be up to you, as to which you call and when, depending on the purpose of your rite). However, once you have reached this point, do not perform this exercise again until you have worked your compass with the correspondences that you have established for some time. Individual directional attributes can and do change over a period of time, particularly as you progress and become more experienced on the magical path, but to continually chop and change in the early stages will only confuse both yourself and the powers with which you are supposed to be working and with which you are building up a relationship. Continue with those that you have initially experienced, until such time as your intuition or experience tells you that they are changing and then perform the visualisation again. Or, alternatively, you could just be receptive and open to what changes naturally.

As an alternative to performing a separate calling at each direction, it is also possible to compose a chant of *all* the entities you wish to invite (as long as there are only one or two per direction), and to recite this whilst pacing the inside of your compass. This shows no disrespect to the entities themselves (as long as it is performed in a respectful attitude of mind), and has the benefit at the same time of creating a vortex of force with which to perform your magic (if that is the aim of the ritual), as and when you are ready. (The pacing or circumambulating of the compass is normally performed prior to magical work anyway, so all you have done is to combine two possible actions in one).

Content of the Rite

What is performed within the compass once hallowed is an entirely personal thing; there will be as many different rites performed within its sphere as there are Crafters hallowing one. I have attempted to give some idea of the kind of work a Traditional practitioner would use a compass for in the following chapters, so I shall not attempt to go into that aspect in depth here. Suffice it to say that once created, the compass is a world unto itself, hopefully in harmony with the Crafter and the Universe at large, within whose space the simplest or the greatest of magics may be wrought. It becomes for the Witch their own, unique macrocosm inside of which they may create, travel, divine, heal or just about anything else that can be apprehended. It is outside of normal time and everyday rules, so use it as you see fit to progress your work.

Closing Statement and Thanks

This dual-purpose declaration is used on two levels. The Closing Statement is the beginning of the "shutting down" process for both the powers and yourself. By making a statement that the ritual is now ending, or about to end, it begins to diffuse any remaining forces that are left over, particularly if it has been a magical, as opposed to a mystical or celebratory rite. It should never be assumed that all the energy accumulated has been used in the ritual, as it may well not have been. Any excess power left unaccounted for can easily lead to imbalances in the individual/s taking part, or in the atmosphere and ambience of the ritual area. At the least this could result in headaches or minor accidents, at the most it could result in personality disorders or poltergeist activity, depending on the amount of force used in the rite.

On a human level, the closing statement cues the individual that they are now coming down, or back from, the exalted levels they, hopefully, achieved during ritual. It is not wise to suddenly switch from one state of consciousness to another, as the shock could prove injurious to the individual psyche – a bit like going from fourth to first gear in one go whilst driving a car - so the closing statement warns the mind of the individual of what is about to happen, i.e. "back to normal" awareness. I am aware of more than one Crafter who, closing down their rite too quickly, has had an accident driving home, purely because of the power still floating around!

The giving of Thanks at the end of a ritual is not just a matter of common politeness, although I'm sure that is appreciated also! Power has been taken from those beings that have given it freely and a reciprocal gesture must be made. A genuine statement of thanks is an outpouring of energy, that gives back some of what was taken; you may even like to give back or dedicate any remaining force to the beings that have given it. Never assume that energy is yours by right – nothing ever is, it must be earned – so a giving back is always required to maintain a harmonious relationship on all levels. (Within Traditional Craft, there is always a reciprocal "arrangement" with the Powers; what is taken is also given back. What is received has to be paid for in some way. This is in no way meant to suggest there is bargaining between the Crafter and his or her gods – if you do this for me I'll give this back to you – it doesn't work like that. It is simply a matter of the bond between the Witch and the Powers he or she works with. If something is given, something must be given up in return and this is a mark of that intense bond). It is at this point that some form of "feast" is often performed, as a communion between yourself and the Powers that Be. If this is so, thanks and energy can be given in the form of a libation as part of the "feast", dedicated to those that have helped you. This theme will be developed and expanded upon in future chapters.

Honouring the Directions

Although thanks may have been given in the section above, to all beings present that have aided in the ritual, the Powers of the directions have previously been called upon specifically and should therefore be thanked, or honoured, specifically. The form of honouring will reflect the manner in which they were called, depending on the Powers requested. It is patently ridiculous to "dismiss" an Ancestor, a Deity or Elemental King, as they are always present – you would be in trouble if they weren't – and could easily ignore you if they willed it, anyway. A simple statement or acknowledgement of their presence and help is sufficient, along with a parting gesture or salute if felt needed by the individual. The Powers do not then depart to some other realm, they are ever present, but their force is withdrawn from your immediate perception and use. It's a bit like deliberately drawing a veil or curtain over a window, to block off your view of the outside world for a while – the outside world is still there, it doesn't go away!

Opening/Dismissing the Compass

Opening the compass is as significant as hallowing it to begin with, but obviously in reverse. Having hallowed your compass initially to separate you from the world of normal reality and maybe to go visiting other realms, it is the final step to returning you to that world which you left when you began your ritual. Opening the compass can be as simple as walking in the opposite direction to that in which you hallowed it. In which case you would simply re-absorb the force you expended in its creation, maybe by breathing in deeply and feeling the energies returning to you. Beware – they will be changed, as you yourself now are! If you hallowed the compass in a more "ceremonial" manner, then maybe you would reverse circumambulate clearing away what you created, and/or then ritually open it with stang, knife or wand. Some Crafters simply sweep their compass away with a broom and a few whispered words. Whatever method you use, they are all symbolic actions for a return to normal consciousness. Yes, you will now be subject to different energies than a few moments ago, but these are the energies of your everyday life and you should by now have re-attuned yourself to them.

Place of Working

Just a word here on *where* you will actually be hallowing your compass. In Traditional Craft, it is always preferable to work out of doors. There are various reasons for this, not the least of which is to get away from the ties and associations of humanity. Working indoors, or in a built-up area will constantly remind you of everyday things, such as work, domestic issues and worries and suchlike; these are best avoided in magical work, unless they are to be worked on magically. The other main reason is that the natural forces with which you will be working are much more likely to be contacted in a natural, wild area, that is - as far as possible these days - unmolested by man. Try to find somewhere out of doors that is reasonably secure and safe; by that I mean somewhere that is not overlooked by anyone who is likely to object to your "activities", or so far away from civilisation that you are unlikely to be disturbed by the casual rambler or mugger. This last is something that must be considered in today's society, so be aware of it. If you are in any doubt, take a friend along who does not mind hanging around nearby for some time, out of sight but within earshot, who can aid you in an emergency. Of course, groups can be a little more secure in their own minds about this, but it is a consideration nonetheless.

Some people prefer heathland, some beaches, some woods or forests, but wherever you choose to work, ensure that you have the permission of the local spirits or natural guardians before you begin. How would you like it if someone just marched into your living room, without a by your leave, and started enacting all sorts of weird goings on? No, you wouldn't, so be considerate to the "people" who live outdoors as well. The simplest way is to visit the site sometime before hand with an offering of something like bread and milk, or milk and honey. Out loud, or mentally, ask permission of the natural guardian/s to use the site as a working place and pour the offering out on the ground, on a tree stump, rock or a hole in the sand. Sit quietly and open your inner senses for a reply. It may take some time, so be patient, but you will get an answer if you trust your intuition. You may feel a warm gust of air, hear a bird singing brightly, find an animal is staring at you in an appraising kind of way, or any number of things. Let your feelings be your guide; does it feel right or wrong? Do you feel welcome or not? Be honest here, as there is no sense in lying to yourself as, if you try to work at a place where you are not welcome, or do not have permission, then you will soon know about it! If you do not feel welcome, rise, give your thanks and walk away, to try somewhere else another day. If you feel the answer is 'Yes', give your thanks and feel grateful that you have been accepted. You are now ready to use the place as your special, magical site and perhaps begin a relationship with its guardian/s. Remember, however, always to ask before entering and always give thanks and leave an offering on leaving the site. Politeness goes a long way in magic and is much appreciated by the unseen world.

If, for whatever reason, you are not able to work outdoors, then indoors is perfectly acceptable. If possible, try to set aside a room especially for your magical workings, which you keep clean and tidy at all times, decorated to your own tastes. If not, then clear an area of floor space wherever you can, sweep/vacuum /brush it clean and sprinkle a little salt water around to get rid of any intrusive energies before you begin. Try to keep the atmosphere clear of "unhelpful" energies at other times and this will help you to work there in a better frame of mind. One of the most traditional places to work is at the hearth of the house, if you are lucky enough to have one these days. The main fire of the home is very potent in certain workings and should never be ignored as a place to work. You may have to alter your normal format slightly to work there, but flexibility is one of the hallmarks of the Crafter. I shall speak more of the hearth later on.

Examples

I will now give a couple of example compass hallowings and dismissings. These you can use as they stand or, once you are a bit more experienced, adapt them to your own needs based on your increased knowledge having used them. Never be afraid to experiment and find out what works best for you. There *are* set formats for hallowing a compass within Traditional groups, but if you are working on your own, you need to feel comfortable with the way in which you, personally, work; there is no use slavishly following some format that you just can't get on with, so make sure you develop your own way, but based on solid, traditional principles and you won't go far wrong. As previously mentioned, I will go further into this topic and give a few more, slightly, advanced techniques, later in this book.

The first example is suitable for indoor or outdoor work, although outdoors is always preferable in Craft work, depending on the weather; there is no magical virtue in being drenched to the skin or frozen stiff!

Compass Hallowing 1

On arrival at your place of working, (although ideally you should already know this from previous visits to ask the spirits for permission to work there), firstly determine the compass directions north, east, south and west. This can be done with an actual compass, or by observing the rising and setting points of the sun beforehand; the sun rises due east and sets due west at the spring and autumn equinoxes, north and south obviously being in between these two points. Do note what time of year you are observing your directions if using this method, as the sun will rise and set further north in summer and further south in winter. Most people like to mark these directions in some way, a stone maybe, or a lantern (or candle indoors). You may even like to incorporate an appropriate offering to the powers of the directions into your hallowing. In any case, you must be aware of where each direction is located, as the orientation of your compass will depend upon this.

Place your Stang upright in the ground (or in a holder indoors), at the north and lay anything else you may need for your rite at the base. Tie your cord around your waist. Locate the rough centre of your compass area and go to stand there, facing north. Close your eyes and take a couple of deep breaths, "feeling" the energies of your surroundings and becoming comfortable with them, tuning in to them, whether indoors or out. When you are ready, go to the north and take up your Stang with reverence and begin to trace the compass edge, visualising it with all your force. See the magical light, like a blue fire, come from the end of your Stang as you trace the line along the ground, from the north to the east, then to the south, the west, then back to the north again, to complete the compass. As you go, you may choose to recite a chant to reinforce what you are doing and to delineate the boundaries out loud. The following can be used, or serve as an example for you to compose your own:

"Compass edge by Stang create,
Warding light flows in my wake.
Raise the Hedge as I do pace,
Secure within this hallowed space".

Make three circuits of your compass, reciting the chant once for each circuit. When you reach the north point for the last time, replace your Stang upright in the ground (or holder), once more. (If you choose to, you may create your compass with your wand, in which case leave the Stang at the north, replace "Stang" with "wand" in the chant and replace your wand at the foot of the Stang when you have finished).

It is now time to set your compass aside from normal reality and make it "other". From the north, pace the inside edge of your compass, in the same direction that you hallowed it, chanting the following, or similar, words

"From the Castles, four in all,
As the compass edge is paced,
Are the ancient powers now called,
Are the wardings strongly placed.

Round about and bound around,
Spirits of the elements four,
Powers I call from hill and mound,
From rock and forest, beach and moor.
Ward this compass as I tread,
Make the serpent power race,
Sisters as you spin your thread,
Hallow all within this place."

Continue to pace the compass as many times as you feel necessary, repeating the chant over and over until you feel the atmosphere become "sticky", begin to "thicken" or crackle. You will know when it is time to stop. If this is done as an outdoor rite, as you pace you may notice shapes begin to gather on the outside of your compass – do not worry or stop what you are doing. You have called the powers of elemental nature and they are attending – if only to see what you are up to – so do not be surprised if they appear! This part of the rite is similar to the actual technique known as 'Treading the Mill' and this will be discussed in more detail later in this book, in the chapter entitled, “Entering the Twilyte”.

(A note on the symbolism used in the chant above. In the first verse, the “Castles” referred to are similar to the better-known “Watchtowers” of more modern practice. They stand at the four directions and are considered by some Crafters to be the “homes” and gateways for the elemental and higher forces of the particular direction. The second verse refers to the powers of the four elements and the powers and forces of the different types of sacred Land. The “serpent power” stirred in the third verse is at one and the same time the power inherent within the Land beneath our feet – sometimes called the “dragon” power, or “ley” energy – and the corresponding energy within our own bodies. This is not the same as the Eastern Kundalini power, but the divine Fire gifted by the gods; more on that later. The “Sisters” are the Norns, the Wyrd sisters of northern mythology, who hold the powers of life, death and all in between within the threads that they spin; the controllers of our destiny).

Once you have completed your calling of the powers and setting aside your compass, return to the centre of your space. Stand with your feet shoulder width apart, your arms outstretched and your eyes closed. “Feel” the compass edge around you, beginning in the north, tracing round to the east, south, west and back to north again, pulsing with a magical light of its own. When you are secure with that feeling, envisage a line running from above you, through the top of your head and continuing down into the ground beneath you, as if you were “skewered” through the top of your head, with a line of pulsing light. Next, envisage a line running through your hips, from side to side, then a line going through you from front to back, intersecting with the other lines at a point just below your navel. Envisage the ends of these lines as touching the edge of your compass, now turned into a three-dimensional globe with you on the inside, and extending further outwards into infinity in all the directions. You are now connected with the four directions, above and below and are connected to your own magical sphere, of which you are a vital and living part.

It is now that you may perform the actual work of your rite, secure in the knowledge that you will not be disturbed, and only those whom you have called will be able to join with you in your charged and hallowed space. In Traditional Craft, paraphernalia is kept to a minimum and, if used at all, will normally be everyday or natural objects that would not arouse suspicion if seen out of context. If you use candles in your ritual, try to make them yourself, beeswax being the best and most natural choice. Always remember, however, whether indoors or out, to clear up after you and collect up any paraphernalia you may have used. It is a well-known saying that the site should change you – you should not change the site, and this is even more applicable in a Traditional Craft rite; no blobs of beeswax left on tree stumps or stones and definitely no buried crystals!

Once your work is finished, return to the centre of your compass, stand with feet shoulder width apart and arms spread, with eyes closed as you did originally. See once more the lines connecting you to your globe/sphere and beyond, but this time; draw them back into your body. See them gradually shortening, the ends coming closer to you, until they are pulled back to your centre. Once you have done this and it feels right and complete to you, open your eyes and say:

> *"I give thanks to those who have aided me and return part of that which I have taken as an offering of good faith between us."*
> (Or words to this effect. If you have invoked any beings specifically, then name and thank them).

Lower your arms now and as you do so, visualise all excess force draining out of you and the compass, into the ground beneath you. As you set aside your compass to begin with, you now need to "re-connect" it to the outside world once more. Make three circuits in the opposite direction to that in which you started and as you go, softly chant:

"This compass now I set aside,
With grateful thoughts I end this rite,
All who have been on my side,
Fade now from my inner sight.

The powers returned from whence they came,
I waken now to earthly life,
Until we all shall meet again,
Be peace 'pon us, no fear or strife.

The compass done, away and gone,
Spirits take flight for now,
All's returned from whence they come,
For we have worked enow."

When you have finished, return to stand in the centre of your space. Clap your hands or stamp your feet three times and say, "It is done."

Clear away any tools and paraphernalia you used for your rite and leave your working area without looking back.

Compass Hallowing 2

This example is suitable only for outdoor working, as you will see. On reaching your working site, sweep the ground clear of any obstructions. If you do not have a special besom for the purpose, a leafy/twiggy branch will suffice. The leaves, etc. that you have swept may form the outside perimeter of your compass in this instance. Note: you are not here clearing any "negative energies" away, as this is a natural site, empowered by a natural guardian; you are merely clearing a space to work in and, if you wish, mentally preparing your area for your work. As usual, locate the four compass directions, so that your compass is correctly orientated and place any items you may need for your ritual at the north. Now, take your stang, knife and cord and go to stand in the centre of your working area and face north. Plant your stang firmly in the ground with both hands, so that it will stand upright by itself and lean your forehead against the fork at the top. Mentally "merge" with the stang in the ground, until you feel yourself to be rooted and part of the central axis around which your compass will be cast. Allow yourself to feel this for a few moments, until the sense is well established. Gently withdraw from the stang and take up your cord. Loosely tie one end around your stang and wind the other around the handle of your knife.

Walk towards the north, to the fullest extent of your cord and lightly place the tip of your knife in the ground, so that it just breaks the surface. Ensure that any items that you need for your rite – including yourself! - are within the radius of your cord! Now, with full concentration and visualisation, inscribe your compass lightly into the ground as you go round, using your stang as the central axis and your cord as the length of the radius. Using your cord here is not only a practical measure, but ensures that you, yourself, are intrinsically incorporated into (the creation of) your compass, as it is your very measure that determines its ultimate size. (A small note here. Although modern-day traditions always insist that the direction of circling is to the right, called deosil or sunwise, this does not necessarily have to be so. As we know, the Sun does not go round the Earth, but vice versa and it is the turning of the Earth on its own axis that creates the impression of the Sun moving to the right, from East to West. To do this, the Earth actually spins widdershins, or *anti-clockwise!* So, to insist that turning to the right is sunwise is totally inaccurate, what one is actually doing is going counter-sunwise, or Moonwise. However, since the current generated by circling is alternating, it makes absolutely no difference to the moral or ethical orientation of the energy whether you circle to the left or to the right. Most Crafters will circle clockwise or to the right for a rite of celebration or non-magical work and widdershins if they wish to perform some specifically magical or "energetic" work - the choice is up to you). So, go round the edge of your compass to inscribe it and do this three times, concentrating fully as you do so – the line on the ground is no threshold, it is what you put into it that makes it so. Visualise a shallow moat or channel in the earth, which actually separates you off from the ground/world beyond and outside its perimeters. See this as a boundary ditch, inside of which you will perform your work in a separate reality.

Once you have returned to the north after your third circuit, untie your cord from your knife and stang, re-tie your cord around your waist and replace your stang in the north. You may wear your knife in a sheath on your cord if you wish, or lay it to one side at the foot of your stang, whatever is appropriate for you. Now you need to call the powers and enliven your compass. Take a step or two backwards from your Stang, facing north. If you so wish, you may raise your arms at this point to aid you in calling the powers. Call with conviction and force upon those powers and forces that you perceived when performing the visionary journey described earlier. If they have names, then use them, if not, use respectful terms, but above all, visualise them at the compass point as strongly as you can and in the way that you originally perceived them. You may use the following or create your own, but remember – be appropriate, only call upon those powers that you will actively be working with during your rite:

"Powers and Spirits of the North, X (name/s), You to whom I turn at this direction, be with me now. Honoured ones, join me in this work of X (magic/celebration/meditation/journey...) and empower my rite."

Pause a second or two for any response that may be given to you, then continue on to repeat the calling at the east, south and west.

Once you have finished and returned to the north, it is usual to pace the inside of your compass edge, both to reinforce the boundary separation and to immerse yourself in the otherworld that you have set aside. It is usual to pace widdershins in this instance, so begin at the north with a slow pacing, focussing on drawing to yourself those energies that you wish to work with in this case. (This again, is similar to the technique of 'Treading the Mill', which will be discussed later). Once you feel sufficiently calmed and otherworldly yourself, you can stop pacing and begin your work. Be respectful to those entities and powers that you have called or may call later in your rite and remember – you do not have the right to call or summon them - it must be earned.

When you have finished any rite, it is traditional (and I always feel, very enjoyable), to end with at least a token communal "feast". This is usually a cup or chalice of wine, ale or mead and a plate of cakes or bread, which are shared with all present – seen or unseen. This can sometimes be quite a complicated and stand-alone rite in itself, but here I will give a simplified version that can be performed by a single person or with others, that will act as a conclusion to a rite, as a thanksgiving, a general earthing and a communal feast all in one.

Go to stand before the stang in the north and take up the cup of wine/ale/mead and your knife, which you have previously placed at the foot of the stang. With the cup in one hand and your knife in the other, place the tip of your knife into the liquid in the cup. With full conviction, state these words:

"Master to Dame, Man to Woman, Sky to Earth; may this wine (ale/mead) be hallowed in the Old Ones names."

Put down the cup and take up the plate. Place the tip of the knife on the food and state clearly:

> *"Grown by Earth, ripened by Sun, hallowed by rite in the Old Ones names."*

Sit down now and drink some of the wine and eat some of the food - relax. Do this in the knowledge that you are not alone in this place and that the Gods and spirits of the place are with you, in a communal sharing that joins all of you at some deep level. Take your time, but make sure you leave some of the food and drink. When you are ready, mix the remains of the food and drink in the cup, then pour it out on the ground at the base of the stang, saying:

> *"As I have taken from the Gods, so do I return a portion of the feast in thanksgiving. We are wed in a mystical union that cannot be denied and therefore are we Hallowed."*

When you are ready, turn and go to the west of your compass. Visualise strongly those powers that you originally called upon at this direction. If they have names, use them in your thanks and farewell. Raise your arms in salute if you wish and say:

> *"Powers and Spirits of the West, X (name/s), You who have aided me from this direction, I give my thanks. All Hail."*

Lower your arms and your head for a few seconds. Await any response that may be given, then continue round to repeat your salutations at the south, east and north.

When you have finished at the north, take up your besom. Starting at the north, begin to sweep away your compass in the reverse direction to that in which you hallowed it. Go round three times, seeing the moat or ditch that you initially created being filled in and your compass once again becoming part of everyday reality. Gradually realise that there is no difference anymore between the "inside" and the "outside" of your space.

When you have finished, quietly and carefully clear everything away, leaving nothing behind. Walk away from the site and do not look back.

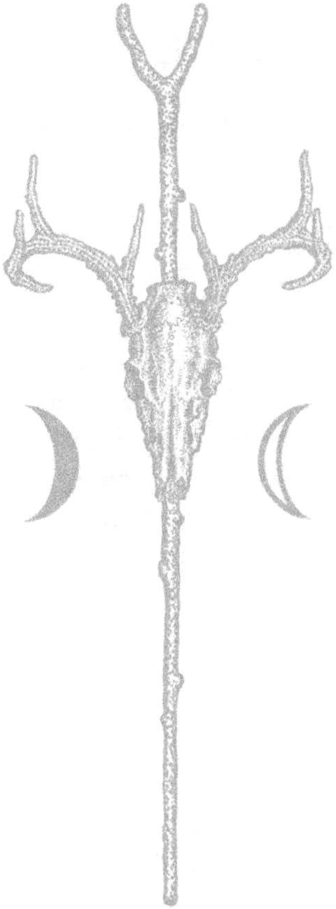

WANDCRAFTING

What is a Wand?

Simply put, a wand is an implement used in magical practice to project the virtue or force of the Witch; to direct power to a desired end or purpose. The force derives from within the body of the Witch, or is called from the wider Universe, spirits or deities and then channelled along the arm and out through the wand. (See "Entering the Twilyte" for more information on raising and directing power). It is basically an extension and substitute for a "pointing finger", but with some advantages that a finger doesn't have, which I shall come on to later. It can be made of practically any material; glass, crystal, metal, stone, wood, or any combination of these. However, it is wooden wands that a Traditional Crafter would usually employ, so I shall limit myself to a description of these only.

The traditional length of a wand is from the Witch's elbow to the tip of the middle (longest), finger, measuring along the *outside* of the arm. However, they can practically be of any length that is usable to the individual up to this size and many are of palm size, what is termed a "pocket wand" or "keppen". There are many advantages to using a wooden wand, as opposed to any other material, not the least of which is that it can more easily be cut and shaped to the individual's desired style. Wands come in many different forms, from simply a straight stick, bark on or off, to intricately carved pieces with extra items added, such as natural crystals, precious metals or magnets. They can be painted, stained, burnt or left plain. They can be bent into different shapes, left straight, or have grown in a natural, spiral form - the latter being especially prized by the Crafter for its innate "virtue" or inherent power.

Perhaps one of the greatest advantages of a wooden wand, is that it can encapsulate into it some of the energy and magic of the tree it was taken from, hence adding its own special meaning to the work being undertaken with it. I will now briefly look at some of the history and aspects of traditional tree lore; I say briefly, as tree lore is a vast field in itself and can take a lifetime to study and understand well.

Aspects of Traditional Tree Lore

When the last Ice-age ended and the ice-caps left the land, around eleven to twelve thousand years ago, the vacant space was rapidly colonised by the smaller, then the larger forms of plant life. Trees, in particular - Birch, Pines and Oak, were one of the earlier colonisers and quickly spread to create vast forests, covering practically the whole of the British Isles. Little is now left! When Man first arrived here some ten thousand years ago, he found a thickly wooded landscape, with little clear earth (other than the chalky uplands which would support few large trees) on which to erect temporary shelters as he was then still, primarily, a hunter-gatherer. At that time, the woods and forests were heavily populated with game, Man's major source of food. Deer, Bear, Boar, Wild Cattle (Aurochs) and various other dangerous forms of life, all lived in the vast forests, which had to be penetrated if he were to hunt and survive. Reverence for Trees then was a very early religious impulse, both as protector and as foe.

Trees were seen as representatives of the living Earth, being the largest living things and growing directly from Her. They were seen as being intermediaries between Man and the Earth and as such were treated with respect and awe, tinged perhaps, with not a little fear. Although most everyday items were made from bone or ivory, being stronger and more hard-wearing, many religious and magical items were made of wood. The reasons for this were (and are), various, but the most important being that wood had a life and spirit of its own; it could be seen to be alive all around, independent of any other living being, unlike bone, horn or ivory and had a direct connection to the Earth, the Land - the focus of magical and religious devotion. The leader of the tribe or clan was also very often the religious or spiritual leader and his or her ceremonial trappings had to be seen to be both impressive and powerful. The ceremonial staff or sceptre, which later came to be the Crafter's wand, was one of the most important of these items; hence, it had to be fashioned from some innately powerful material i.e. wood. Carving, perhaps incorporating the clan's totem or protective spirits, deities and sacred signs could also further enhance this and this tradition is continued today by modern practitioners of the Craft.

In some traditional lore, it was considered that the Dead, instead of passing into the Under/Otherworld, or being immediately reborn in another life, passed in spirit into trees, there to await their future lives. In this guise, they became the Guardians of central places, such as groves and sacred areas, protecting them from those who would cause harm. They could also be petitioned for favours, particularly by their descendants, or those that held the place sacred. There are many stories of dead lovers having trees planted on their graves and the trees growing together and embracing over the graves. In Northern European mythology, the gods are said to have made the first Man and first Woman from the Ash and Elm trees respectively. All of this demonstrates the close bond between humans and trees that has grown up over the millennia and which is eminently applicable to magical practice.

It may surprise most people to learn that only thirty five species of tree are actually native to the British Isles. Blackthorn and Elder, which are actually classed as shrubs, bring the total up to thirty seven, so the variety that we are used to seeing today would be completely alien to our ancestors. Amongst the indigenous number are Alder, Ash, Aspen Beech, Birch Blackthorn, Box, Cherry, Crab Apple, Elder, Elm, Hawthorn, Hazel, Holly, Hornbeam, Juniper, Lime, Maple, Oak, Pear, Poplar, Rowan, Scots Pine, Strawberry Tree, White Beam, Wild Service Tree, Willow, Wych Elm and Yew. (I will be looking at some of these trees in greater detail later on).

By the end of the Roman Age, much of the forested areas in these isles had been cut down and turned into farm or moorland. In later centuries, many thousands more acres were denuded, until we have the situation today where only a fraction of the original percentage still remains. However, pockets of original wildwood remain here and there and Nature is very good at quickly re-establishing a presence if left to Her own devices. Tree planting schemes are also gaining momentum and there are moves afoot to re-establish the great Caledonian forests of yore.

Trees were seen as having their own indwelling spirits, which were considered to be neuter, neither male nor female, or possibly both. These were (are) nothing like the modern concept of nature spirits, which have more to do with Victorian romanticism than anything approaching fact. In the early days, we are told, these spirits (and perhaps the trees themselves), were called the "Hooded Ones". This surely came from the feeling of being watched by hidden beings as the first hunters to walk the woods made their way through the near impenetrable growth of the dark forests. Later, the name became the "Many Eyed Ones" or the "Many Handed Ones", possibly due to the fact that the tree spirits are capable of what we would today call "multi-tasking". These titles may have fed into the lore of people like Robin Hood and their close associations with the wildwood, which have been passed down to us in myth and legend.

These days the term generally given to the spirits of the trees is "Dryad", although other, specific terms are used within particular traditions.

Dryads

The term Dryad is actually the Ancient Greek word for the spirit of the Oak tree, seen by the Greeks as being female. However, it has now come to be used for all tree spirits and is said to be favoured by them because its vibration is similar to the word they use for themselves. Like us, they have a physical part (the tree) and a non-physical part (the Dryad); however, their spatial concept and ability is completely unlike ours. One Dryad can occupy many bodies (trees) at the same time where there are groupings of the same species, or in the case of lone trees, there can be one Dryad per tree. They can also intermingle; in a wood for instance, where there are different species of tree, all with their own Dryad, they can all occupy the same space at the same time. It is almost like the Dryad is expandable and can occupy different space, but needs to anchor itself in one place (and time - as their time-sense is also different to ours), to draw sustenance and feed its physical reality. This has recently been borne out by scientific discoveries of the way trees grow and communicate on a physical level. They are joined by an intricate pathway of fungal connections below ground, so much so that, for all intents and purposes, a whole wood of trees is, in actuality, one tree, with different physical manifestations above ground. There would appear to be only one thing we can do that they can't and that is move around physically. This is where the magical use of trees comes in, particularly the magical use of Live Wood.

A small note here; tree spirits are NOT Faeries! They are of a completely different kind of life form altogether. I shall discuss the Faerie Folk at a later stage, but for now, it is better that this distinction is made.

Types of Wood

Magically speaking, there are basically three types of wood - Dead wood, Green wood and Live wood. Dead wood is wood that the Dryad has withdrawn from for whatever reason (disease, pests, lightning strike, etc.) and no longer has life or "virtue" in it - it's dead! It may stay on the tree for a while, but usually falls off. Green wood is freshly cut wood that still retains some "life-energy" in it, before drying out and basically becoming the same as Dead wood, if not used for magical purposes. Live wood is wood that still retains a piece of the tree's Dryad in it. Because of the Dryad's different spatial concept, under certain circumstances and with the full co-operation of the Dryad, it can "split" a bit of itself off from the "parent" Dryad and stay in the piece that is taken. It has all the knowledge and abilities of the parent and the added advantage that it can move around. This is why Dryads can sometimes be persuaded to split themselves. It's a bit like a horse (Witch) and rider (Dryad); the horse gains direction and information from a "higher" source, the rider gains mobility and a different perspective on life. This does not happen without a deep rapport being established between the horse and rider and magic will not take place until this rapport is established.

Some Native Trees

There are many books dealing with both the natural history and more esoteric aspects of British trees, including their folklore and traditional usage, so I will not duplicate the work of their authors here. I give a few suggestions for further reading in the bibliography at the end of this book. However, there are some trees that always seem to be left off the more common lists and I would like to take a short look at some of them here.

Beech *(Fagus sylvatica)*
Much used by the Iron Age peoples of Europe, Beech is a strong, hard and durable wood. It is useful both for burning and for crafting, producing excellent bowls, spoons and other utensils. Magically speaking, the word "Beech" comes from the same root as "Book" and it is therefore associated with knowledge and learning. A wand or staff made of this wood would be of great value to those employed in uncovering lost knowledge or in furthering their studies in the esoteric fields. It is said that the Druids of old employed Beech leaves as "pages" to mnemonically record their lore.

Box *(Buxus sempervirens)*
Although now mostly used for hedging and topiary, Box was for centuries used as a prime wood for fine carving and engraving. Left to its own devices, this large shrub will grow up to 35ft. in height, but is today exceedingly rare in this state, there being few remaining Box woods left. All parts of the Box are poisonous if taken internally in large enough amounts, although small doses have traditionally been used as a substitute for quinine in cases of the ague (malaria) and for the treating of intestinal worms. Magically, little is recorded, but one traditional use of a wand or staff of Box is to invoke the shades of past Crafters, during necromantic rites to the ancestors.

Crab Apple *(Malus sylvestris)*
The original, indigenous apple, the fruit of this tree is much smaller and tarter than later, cultivated varieties. It has a beautiful, pinkish-white blossom in the spring, which, added to the Roodmass fire, will sweetly scent the whole rite. One of the main "Goddess" trees of Britain, the Crab Apple has mainly been associated with love and romance, although, like the Dame Herself there is always the side of death to ponder. It is considered to be the fruit of Avalon, the "Isle of Apples", one of the names of the British Otherworld. The medicinal and healing properties of the fruit and bark link it strongly to the life-giving spirits of traditional lore, however, and it is also the famed "silver-branch" of British mythology. A wand or staff of this wood would not only have great healing and comforting powers, but is also traditionally used to gain access to the Otherworld, or to invoke the spirits that reside there.

Hornbeam *(Carpinus betulus)*
Similar in appearance to Beech, with exceptionally hard yet light and flexible timber, Hornbeam is indigenous to the south of Britain. Because of its similarity to Beech it is often overlooked in favour of its better known companion, yet it has admirable qualities of its own. It is a surprisingly tough wood, often used in the past for agricultural tools and equipment that had heavy-duty uses and was also incorporated into pianos, cogs and pulleys. On an esoteric level, traditional lore values it for its toughness and it is used for its qualities of endurance, steadfastness and support in mystical ordeals. It is most definitely a Faerie wood and should only be taken after permission from them is granted.

Lime *(Tilia cordata)*
There are three species of Lime, *Tilia cordata* being the only indigenous one to Britain; the small leafed variety. The broad

leafed and silver barked varieties are, however, also now grown extensively and have, to some extent, interbred. One of nature's de-stressers, the medicinal benefits of Lime are large. It is a nerve relaxant, a sedative, an anti-spasmodic and also reduces hypertension and hardening of the arteries. The flowers must be picked early in spring as they develop strong narcotic properties when older. It is a "Marker" tree, once planted at the centre of villages to represent the world axis, on boundaries and along geomantically important "earth lines". Once the bark is peeled it has a beautiful shiny, white wood, much prized for fine carving. The glowing whiteness speaks of Annwn and a wand or staff of this wood makes a fine underworld steed to go travelling along the spirit lines on or to aid in astral flight.

Poplar

Often confused with the somewhat familiar Aspen, the Poplar shares a lot of folkloric healing properties in traditional remedies. It is used to relieve aches, fevers, inflammation, arthritis and gout. Externally it was applied to piles, sprains and infected wounds. The timber is light but highly shock absorbent and was used in past ages for making shields. Poplar buds and leaves were sometimes listed as ingredients in traditional flying salves and the wood is said to give protection from all forms of disease and death therefrom. For these reasons a wand or staff of this wood is used when making defensive magic, similar to Rowan, or communicating with astral entities, like Willow.

Wild Service Tree

This much neglected tree is a very old, native denizen of the British Isles. As the name implies, its wood, which is very fine grained, was used in the past for a multitude of purposes. As one of our indigenous trees, but left out of later magical tree lists, it is likely that it was venerated as part of Faerie lore and later suppressed or replaced to hide its value; it would therefore make an ideal wood with which to contact the Good Folk. In autumn the leaves look like living fire and the brown berries can be used as a cure for colic, whilst the flaming leaves aid in consumptive disorders.

Cutting Wood for Magical Purposes

Traditionally, any wood you may want to cut for magical purposes should be "lopped" off with one stroke of a specially prepared and consecrated knife. To do this, the knife should be exceptionally sharp and quite heavy, else there is a danger of damaging the tree and ripping the bark; something that would anger the tree spirit and render any wood taken, magically invalid. I actually use a pruning saw and cut swiftly and carefully, doing as little damage as possible. Different traditions say different things about when you should cut your wood, e.g. dawn, midday, dusk, when the Moon is in a certain phase. Personally I prefer a waxing Moon, waxing Sun and at dawn or dusk. Make your own mind up and ask the tree!

If you are going for Live wood, it is imperative you get into a rapport with the tree first and this can take a long while, usually months before both you and the tree are ready. Touch, listen, feel, ask briefly and wait for as long as it takes. The tree will tell you. *don't* talk to it and *don't* hug it! Wait for it to accept you - if you take the wood before permission is given then the Dryad will not be present. It will tell you when and where to cut, which piece you may take. Cut quickly and surely, doing as little damage to the tree as possible and do *not* let the wood touch the ground once cut. If you do, this will earth the energies, return the Dryad to the tree and both your efforts will have been wasted. Now you must begin to build up your relationship with the Dryad - it's a bit like getting to know a new friend. Just take your time and listen a lot. Don't start making magical demands of it straight away; remember, it knows a lot more about the magical side of things than you do and will tell you when you are both ready.

Whatever type of wood you have taken (Green or Live), permission must always be asked and thanks given. (Of course, you can always use Dead wood for your wand if you wish – it will still have the same attributions - and many people prefer to do this, rather than cutting from a living tree). Thanks include an offering. This can be a libation to the tree (wine, water, milk, honey), some of the wood bark offered back and buried at the roots, a silver coin, cake, bread or in some traditions, a little of the persons own blood is left. (If offering blood, ensure that you are well - it is disease free and if you are not, it is an insult, will offend the tree and render the wood magically invalid - especially if Live wood was sought). Essentially, what you are doing is offering back some energy for that which you have taken; a life for a life so to speak.

Creating your Wand

Once you have chosen (or been chosen by!) your wand and cut it carefully, the next step is to season it. This means to dry the wood out so that it is suitable for cutting and carving; fresh/wet wood does not lend itself very well to carving, as the water content is too high and you will not be able to carve it cleanly. Of course, you may wish to leave it as it is and use it "au naturel" and this is perfectly acceptable.

The traditional length of time to leave your wood to dry for is one year for every inch of thickness. This may seem like a long time to wait, but it is worth it, as at the end of this time you will have a dry and hard piece of wood, which will readily take to the knife and give good results. However, if you need the wand before this and have not left enough time, I find a minimum of six to eight weeks is just about long enough for the wood to have dried sufficiently to carve. Leave it in a place with a moderate temperature – not too hot or too cold. Too hot and it will dry too quickly, warp and possibly crack (it's a good idea to tie your chosen wand to a strong piece of wood to prevent this); too damp and the wood can rot and destroy your efforts. If you wish to have a peeled wand, i.e. without the bark on, then this needs to be stripped whilst the wood is still fresh and wet, otherwise the bark will dry on to the wood and be next to impossible to remove cleanly. Use a sharp knife to make an incision just down to the underwood and then peel it back like a banana; most bark will come off easily if the wood is freshly cut.

How you carve your wand is entirely up to you - the end intention of the wand and your artistic and carving skills – there is no set way that it *has* to look. You need to consider deeply what it is going to be used for, any deity or spirit that it is to be dedicated to, the type of wood it is made from and any particular attributes you wish it to have. The natural wood shape itself may suggest one or more of these, but if not, they will have to be incorporated into the carving and shaping, or even attached later, such as a stone or metal wire. A few descriptions of the parts of a wand may be useful, however.

A wand obviously has two ends and a longer bit in the middle. The end that you hold in your hand – usually the thicker end - is called the "Base", "Butt", "Heel", "Foot" or "Hoof". The long bit in the middle is called the "Shank" or "Shaft". The other end is called the "Toe" or sometimes the "Head".

The Butt

The butt end of the wand, the thicker end, is often left just flat, or sometimes is rounded, or even carved into the shape of a Hoof, which gives it one of its alternative names. It is quite usual, although not essential, for a hole to be bored into the butt end. This is sometimes used to personalise the wand, or create a link between it and the Witch, by inserting some hair, nail parings, blood, or other body fluids. The hole is usually sealed by wax or a wooden plug. Sometimes the hole is used to place a small piece of paper or parchment inside, which states on it the intent of the spell that is to be performed. Obviously this is changed each time you do a different spell. It is also quite common to place a small lodestone (natural magnet), into the hole and seal it in, as a way of charging the wand with magical energy. In fact, some Crafters drill a hole all along the length and insert a copper rod, which is then (or previously) rubbed with a magnet along its length to achieve the same effect. The choice is up to you. Butts can also be a separate piece of material that has been added to the shaft, perhaps of a different type, such as clay or metal.

The Shaft

Although the shaft can be completely plain and straight, this is the part of the wand that is usually the most carved or styled. If not already grown in a natural spiral, the shaft can be carved into such a form, which is called a "Vine" or "Snake", depending on the style. The shaft can be carved into a series of balls, cut square, star or any shape you like really. It can be stained, painted, burnt, lettered, "runed", or any combination of the above and others. It can also have metal wires run around it in a spiral, or other pattern; this can be for beauty's sake, or to enhance its "magnetic" properties. The choice is that of the owner. Like the butt, the shaft may also be smeared with any of the owner's body fluids, to further enhance its connection with them.

The Toe

As with the butts the toe can be of a different material to the main wand, such as a naturally found crystal, stone, metal, bone, ivory or indeed a different piece of wood. This is joined to the main shaft by the "Binding" and is called the "Point", although it is actually the toe proper. If not adding a toe, then the end of the shaft can be left flat, like the butt, but is more often carved. Again, this can take any form you like, but the most usual would be a phallic toe, a "Cone" toe or a "Moon" toe. A cone is where the shaft suddenly narrows to a point and the moon is where it is gently rounded; a phallic toe is obvious, if not a somewhat strange description! Of course, the whole wand, from butt to toe could be gently tapering, along the shaft, like the pointing stick of an Australian aboriginal shaman or a snooker cue.

Finishing off your Wand

Once you have created a shape that is pleasing to you – and the spirit of the wand itself in the case of Live wood – you need to finish it off. Of course, the wand can just be left as it is, but this is going to be a tool that you will be working with, probably for many years, so it needs some care and protection, just like any working friend would.

Firstly, it needs to be sanded down, to smooth off any roughness left by any carving that you may have done, or just from stripping the bark and to refine the carving. Start with a rough grade of emery paper (also called wet & dry paper), and work up to a fine grade, to give the wand a really smooth finish. The starting grade of paper you use will depend on the relative hardness or softness of the wood you have chosen, so practice on a piece of waste wood first; using too rough a piece to start with could well erase any fine carving and make the wood rougher than it was to start with. I find that three, progressively finer, sandings is usually sufficient.

Finally you need to apply a few coats of varnish, beeswax or oil. The idea is to seal the wood, to stop any moisture and/or other harmful substance getting into/on to it and spoiling all your hard work. Some Crafters will work up a good sweat at this point and use their own secretions to rub into the wand, either before or instead of any other finish, the better to attune it to themselves. Depending on the choice of finish, it also feeds and enriches the wood and brings out the beautiful grain, depending on the species used. The choice of finish is up to you, but I find that beeswax is probably the nicest and certainly the most natural. This said, if you have a naturally spiralling wand, or have done some intricate carving, then getting a beeswax polish into the small crevices is very difficult, whereas applying varnish with a brush is much easier. A good linseed oil also does a good job, but this needs to be applied continuously throughout the wand's life to stop it drying out, whereas you will only need to give the wand three coats of varnish and that's it. Sand the wand down again, with the finest grade of paper, between coats of varnish, making sure that the varnish is completely dry, to remove any little surface imperfections that the varnish may have raised. The rule with beeswax is – once a day for a week, once a week for a month, once a month for a year and once a year for life. Buff up with a soft cloth immediately after each application of wax and you will soon develop a beautiful, smooth, silky finish to your wand. Do the same with the linseed oil, but continue with this throughout the life of the wand.

(N.B. Whilst the information given in this chapter is primarily concerned with the crafting of Wands, Stangs and similar tools, it is also appropriate for other types of wooden items as well. If requiring wood for the making of a sacred image, such as an altar or other statue, then the principles explained here should also be born in mind. Likewise when fashioning a doll or poppet for magical working, then the lore outlined here would be of value in crafting the object. The other obvious use of wood is in the crafting and forming of talismans and talismanic images. Using Live wood would be of immense value in this skill and, if not using Live wood, then bearing in mind the instructions given here for the cutting and taking of wood could easily add extra virtue or power to the final talisman or charm).

A Hallowing Rite

Once you have finished creating your wand, before it is used in any work of magic, it must be "Hallowed", or consecrated to your particular path. This is done both to set it aside from everyday life and activities and to give it an extra charge for the work it is to do. You may also chose to dedicate it to the deities you are used to working with.

It is better if you can perform this rite outside, but indoors will suffice if this is not possible. You will need your cord, a small fire (beeswax candle if indoors), a small bowl of spring or river water and a bowl of fresh earth, if indoors.

Set up your working area as you are used to and hallow your compass in your usual manner.

When you are ready and have called on the spirits and Powers that you habitually work with, pass the wand through the flames of the fire (or candle) three times. These flames burn away all that is past and purify the wand. Say this as you do so.

Sprinkle the wand three times with the spring water. These are the waters of forgetfulness which wash away all that is negative and unclean. Say this as you do so.

Scratch a small hole in the ground (or bowl of earth). Lay the wand in it and lightly, partially cover it with soil. This is the womb of the Earth our Mother, who will now give birth to the new wand. Say this.

Take up the wand after a moment and breathe three times upon it. This is the vital breath of life – the "virtue" – which endows the wand with its own spark of life. Say this.

Next mark three X's on the wand with your own saliva. This binds the wand to you for its magical life. Say so.

Now wrap your cord around the wand three times, thus sealing and binding the new life and power within. Say this. Finally raise the wand on high and, in your own words, make a heartfelt dedication of the wand to the Old Gods, the deities you are used to working with.

Close down your working in your usual manner, wrap up your wand securely and store it in a secure place, away from everyday life.

And there you have it – your very own magical friend, cut, crafted, created and hallowed by you, which, treated well, will give you a lifetime of friendship and service.

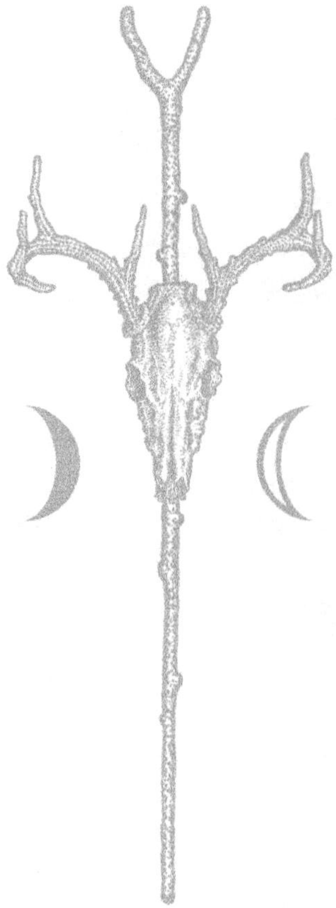

SPELLCRAFTING

What is a Spell?

There will be as many answers to this question as there are people answering it – and they will all be right! Spells, particularly for the Traditional worker, are a very individual type of magic and what works for one person will not work for another. Likewise, how one person casts a spell will be completely the opposite way to another. In this chapter we are concerned with what may be called "Natural Magic"; using the powers, forces, elements and objects of the natural world around us, to bring about the transformations or changes that we require. We are essentially dealing with what is sometimes called "Low" or "Kitchen Magic", the realm of the village Wise Woman or Cunning Man. However, make no mistake, the use of the term "Low" in no way implies any inferior status or lesser power to this type of magic, as its effects can be, and often are, just as powerful and profound as any other type. The term is used to differentiate it from the more ceremonial or "High" forms of magic, using "grimoires", or books of magical ritual, originally used more by the scholarly class than the village Wise Woman – although they *both* overlapped in history and still do today. The Traditional worker has never been averse to "borrowing" and will use whatever works for their purposes, often no matter what its origin. This does not mean of course that total eclecticism rules – as in much modern practice – as the Crafter is always concerned to work within the spiritual environs and traditions of the Land that they are in and of.

So, to answer our original question, what is a Spell? I will be discussing the use of the powers and inherent properties of words, herbs, trees, stones, oils, colours, etc. both singly and in combination, to bring about those changes in ourselves, others and the outside world that are considered needful at the time.

Where does this "power" come from? It is a combination of the natural energies of the items used in the spell, their correspondences with the wider powers of the universe, any deity or spirit chosen to help, all focused and directed by the Will of the Crafter performing the spell, to bring about the desired result. This brings in an interesting point. It is quite possible to tell someone how to perform a spell, tell them the ingredients to use, the timing, etc., what it is not possible to do is give someone the *ability* to perform the spell; this must come from the individual themselves. This is why so many spells do not, or appear not, to work; the "operator" has not focused, concentrated or otherwise prepared him or herself properly to perform it successfully. SpellCraft, like any other craft, is a skill and the more you apply yourself to learning the "tricks of the trade", the better you will be at your craft. Sloppy application will lead to sloppy spells, which will either not work at all, or not in the way you wanted them to. The end result lies already in the person performing the spell, not the spell itself!

This brings us on to the consideration of whether or not to actually perform a spell in any given situation, as the end result is always the responsibility of the spell caster, irrespective of whether they have been asked to do the spell by, or for, someone else or not. I am not speaking here of some vague form of New Age morality, nor am I harking back to the strict forms of patriarchal dogma. I am speaking of "Natural" morality; purely and simply, would it be right to do this spell, considering what will happen? What will the effects be? Will the knock-on effects be worse than what the spell was meant to change? Will it harm more than heal? These are the ramifications you need to consider before any act of magic, spell or otherwise. Obviously we cannot see every single effect of our actions, but we need to consider as many as possible. Although there is no one watching us with a big book, ticking down all our good and bad actions, which will eventually decide if we go to the nice or nasty place, it is not in the personal interests of any magical practitioner to deliberately, or even inadvertently, cause harm. It is detrimental to our magical and spiritual progress and the results will have to be faced and paid for at some point. Again, I am not speaking of any popular "three-fold return law", but "what goes around comes around". Our morality is our own to decide, and can be very specific to each individual situation, so consider it *before* you cast that "whammy".

However, although I am not advocating indiscriminate cursing, if you consider a well delivered hex to be appropriate in the situation, and justified, then go ahead and deliver a bit of "natural justice" - just be prepared for the consequences. Traditional Crafters do have their own code of ethics and do meddle in affairs if they consider it justified, independent of currently fashionable magical, morality.

So, let us move on to the practical aspects of SpellCrafting.

Verbal Charms and Chants

Both the word "Charm" and "Chant" come from the Latin word *carmen* – a chant, and so we can see that it originally meant a verbal formula. In a more modern context it is much more widely applied, being used to cover an object that is charmed also. For example, a pendant, a spell pouch, a dried bird's foot or hagstone; all these can be considered "charms" in themselves. In this section, however, we will be looking at the verbal formulas only.

Although not absolutely essential to a spell, a fairly integral part, and one which most people would normally think of as "the spell" proper, is the spoken part. This involves the use of words, usually in some form of rhyme, alliteration or meter, to state what the Crafter wishes to bring about. The Charm form of words is usually not overlong, but states what is desired to happen, who or what, if anyone, the Crafter is calling on to aid the spell (deities, spirits, elements, herbs, etc.), and also acts as a "lens" to focus and sharpen the mind. It is sometimes whispered, or muttered, under the breath and is frequently repeated X amount of times to increase its efficacy. This also has the added benefit of creating a light trance state (see chapter five, "Entering the Twilyte"), if you are using the charm as a focus for a rite as opposed to a spell on its own. It is often said that the most effective Charms are created on the spur of the moment, and while this is frequently undoubtedly true, there are some that are traditional that will serve for examples for us here.

This is an Anglo-Saxon charm for blessing the fields:

"Erce, Erce, Erce, Mother of Earth!
May the All-Wielder, Ever Lord grant thee
Acres a-waxing, upwards a-growing
Pregnant (with corn) and plenteous in strength;
Hosts of (grain) shafts and of glittering plants!
And of white wheat ears waxing,
Of the whole earth the harvest!
Let be guarded the grain against all ills
That are sown o'er the land by the sorcery men
Nor let the cunningwoman change it nor crafty man."

In the original Old English, the rhythm and meter are much tighter.

Here is another, from the Witches of Italy, to be used when sewing a charm bag together;

"This bag I sew for luck for me,
And also to my family;
That it may keep by night and day
Troubles and illness far away!"

And another to gain a prophetic dream of one's future true love, a sprig of the mystical Ash tree should be plucked with these words;

"Even Ash, even Ash, I pluck thee,
This night my true love for to see;
Neither in his rick or in his rear,
But in the clothes he does everyday wear!"

Finally, a modern day charm for general healing purposes;

"By powers of night and witchery
No ill in mind or body be
With herbs and stones and trees virtue
Expel disease and cleanse him through
Create the balm his health to stay
To put him on the healing way
By old ones names and ancient might
Make this person come aright!"

From these few examples it can be seen what the essential ingredients are.

Firstly, and most importantly, decide what the charm is for, e.g. healing, blessing, calling, protection, etc. This may sound obvious, but if it is not stated clearly, you will not get the desired effect. And it is amazing how often this is forgotten!

Next, who is it for? If it is for a specific person, try to get the name in, or else it may misfire and affect the wrong person.

Next, who or what, if anything, are you calling on to help you? Again, be clear about this; if you call on the wrong thing, you will get the wrong result.

Finally, set the conditions. This may be a time scale, or for the effect to happen in a certain place or duration, or even to exclude certain people, times, or places.

When you have decided on the above, weave your charm into a form of words that has a certain rhythm or pace that is easily verbalised, almost so it says itself. You are not trying to write wonderful poetry here, so a certain "tumpty, tumpty" feel to it, although bad verse, may actually make it a better charm.

Herbal Magic & Wortcunning

Herbal magic in itself is a vast field and can take many years of study to master, so here it is only possible give an idea of the art. Wortcunning is the Anglo-Saxon term meaning "Knowledge of herbs", a "wort" being any leafy plant, as opposed to a vegetable or tree and the "cunning" part referring more to the esoteric knowledge of same. This term is often applied to herbal medicine, but covers the wider field of magic and spellcasting also.

We will continue the use of charms, as examined in the previous section, and now apply this to the use of herbs. We have seen how a charm can be composed and now we will include the use of herbs in this, in the form of creating magical pouches or charm bags, using the herbs themselves.

Obviously, when creating any magical pouch, you first need to decide what it will be for; necessity should always dictate this, not desire. Never create a pouch for fun! (This is a cardinal rule in the wider field of spellcrafting in general too). Having decided what you are making the pouch for, you need to select the herbs that will help you. All herbs and plants have their own abilities and associated correspondences and you need to pick the ones that will aid you in your particular work. There are many books listing the attributes and magical correspondences of herbs, many of which contradict each other. Try to find one or two with which you feel confident and stick to these only, as confusion will only arise if you keep swapping your correspondences. After a while you will begin to learn the uses of each herb to your own satisfaction and can dispense with the books. You may even find some new correspondences for yourself - so much the better. Also, if a book prescribes a certain plant for a certain use and your intuition suggests another, go with your own intuition. It is this skill or ability that you will come to rely on increasingly in your work; a good witch always trusts their own intuition above all else.

Once you have decided on the herbs to use, you need to obtain them. There are two main ways of doing this; you can either collect them from the wild (or your garden), yourself, or you can buy them. There are advantages and disadvantages with both of these methods. If collecting the herbs yourself, you have the benefit of knowing that they have been collected correctly i.e. right moon/sun phase, time of year/day, correct attitude to the plant, etc. (see the final section at the end of this chapter), but the plants you need may not always be available or in season. This is why many Crafters become inveterate collectors of empty bottles and jars; collect the plants in their correct season, dry them and keep them for future use. You will swiftly find that you build up a sizeable collection for all uses! The alternative is to buy them ready picked and dried, from a reputable supplier. This has the advantage of ease of access when a plant is out of season, rare, or otherwise unavailable, but you have not collected it yourself; therefore you do not know when and how it was collected, or how old it is. The choice is the individual's, but I find it much more beneficial to collect my own, only using shop-bought ones when it is a rare or hard to find ingredient.

Having now decided upon and obtained your herbs for your specific purpose, you need to infuse these with magical energy and instruct them in their work. As an example, I will use a traditional spell that has been passed down to me, with slight adaptations for modern use.

A Spell for Protection in the Home

Assemble your herbs and chant the following, as you circle round and cast them into your cauldron or pot of fresh spring water;

"Round about the cauldron go,
In the herbs of magic throw,
Elfwort, Trefoil, Goats Leaf, Bour,
In the pot the magic four.
Goatweed, Basil, Graveyard Dust,
Thrice about it go we must.
Elfleaf, Dilly, Juno's Tears,
Driving off all mortal fears,
Witchbane, Bats Wings, Deadmens Bells,
Together bind a magic spell.
Thrice about the cauldron run,
Dance the dance and be it done."

Now, scoop the mixture into a small cloth or leather pouch and hang it up somewhere in the home, out of sight. It will gradually dry out, but the magic will remain.

(Elfwort – Elecampane, Trefoil, Goats Leaf – Honeysuckle, Bour – Elder, Goatweed – St. Johnswort, Basil, Graveyard Dust – Valerian/Mullein, Elfleaf – Rosemary/Lavender, Dilly – Dill, Juno's Tears – Vervain, Witchbane – Rowan, Bats Wings – Holly, Deadmens Bells – Foxglove).

Another example, for personal protection on a long journey, will show an alternative to how this method can be used:

A Spell for Protection on a Journey

Assemble the required herbs, fresh or dried, in an earthenware bowl. Run your fingers through them to mix them all well, whilst reciting the following charm;

> *"Knitbone wards from breaks and sprains,*
> *Flax preserves the purse,*
> *Elfdock guards from shafts and barbs,*
> *Huran circles round.*
> *Trefoil keeps the wearer safe,*
> *Eryngo brings the luck,*
> *Bind them all with good intent,*
> *And seal this safe road's charm."*

Hold your hands over the bowl for a few moments and infuse the herbs with power. Separate into two parts. Place one part in a red, cloth bag, tied with red thread and keep about the person on the journey. Grind the second part down and use as an incense. Cense the person going on the journey as they depart.

(Knitbone – Comfrey, Flax – Linseed, Elfdock – Elecampane, Huran – Horehound, Trefoil – Clover, Eryngo – Eryngium).

You will see from both these examples that the traditional, folk-names for the herbs are used, instead of their modern, technical names. This gives the charm a much more magical feel, at the same time as recalling the magic of our ancestors, which we are trying to emulate. From these two examples you can adapt the method for practically any purpose you like. Healing, Blessing, Love, Success, or whatever it is you desire. The magic, as always, comes from your desire and intention, coupled with the energy you raise, working in partnership with the inherent powers of the plants themselves.

Simples, Potions, Oils & Lotions

Having seen how we can use the powers of herbs in their natural, or dried and preserved, state we can now look at using them in other than their "raw" condition.

Simples

As the name implies, a "Simple" is the use of a single herb, in an infusion, to bring about a certain end. These are often used medicinally, such as chamomile tea to aid sleep, but they can also be used magically to great effect. A Simple to aid clairvoyance can be made either from Mugwort, Yarrow or Willow bark. Infuse a heaped teaspoon per cup of boiling water, for ten to fifteen minutes. Reciting a charm of your own devising over it, strain and drink before using the tarot, runes, crystal, or similar. Try a Simple of an infusion of Vervain, taken just before scrying in the flames of an outdoor fire – this releases the mundane mind to wander in the realms of the Otherworld; treat with caution!

Experiment with different Simples for different purposes. Not everyone will obtain the same effect from the same herb; some people may find one herb better than another for the same purpose. If using the fresh herb for a Simple, use twice as much as you would for dried.

Potions

We have already seen an example of a magical Potion above, in the spell for Protection of the Home. A Potion is a combination of two or more herbs, used for their magical influences, infused in some form of liquid, usually water, but sometimes alcohol or vinegar. These are usually drunk, but can be rubbed on to something, scattered or sprayed, poured out in a line or protective circle, or, as we have seen placed into a pouch or sachet and left to dry out.

One example of a magical Potion is "Thieves Vinegar", also known as "Four Thieves Vinegar". This was supposedly devised at the time of the Black Death, to enable thieves and vagabonds to enter houses, without detection or fear of infection, and rob the dying of their valuables. It has long been a 'stock-in-trade' of the village herbalist and cunning person and was probably taken from them. Here is a traditional recipe originating in the eighteenth Century, from East Anglia:

> *"Take Rue, Sage, Wormwood and Lavendar – a handful of each. Infuse them in a gallon of white wine vinegar in a stone pot covered close. Set on wormwood ashes for four days, after which strain the liquid through a fine flannel and put it into bottles well corked. Into every quart bottle put a quarter of an ounce of Samphire, the herb the liquor is made from."*

Obviously if you were making this up today you wouldn't need so much, so alter the measurements according to how much you're making. Alternatively, a simpler method – and one slightly more practical for today – is to infuse crushed garlic, rosemary and juniper in organic cider vinegar for eight days, strain off, bottle and use as normal. Thieves Vinegar is used for cleansing magical equipment (put a few drops in a bowl of water), banishing negative atmospheres by sprinkling or spraying it around, protection and purificatory baths and washes.

Another example of a Potion, is this traditional recipe for an Amatory Philtre. Take dried leaves of Periwinkle, Mercury Herb, Cinquefoil, Vervain and Rose Petals. Grind them all together into a fine powder with a mortar and pestle that you keep for nothing other than spellcrafting. Repeat as you do so a charm of your own composing, including the names of the two people you wish to "get together". Then take two small pinches of the powder and mix them with fresh spring water in your magical chalice or Cup, infusing it with the full force of your magical Will. Leave the potion to steep for twelve hours. Strain through fine muslin or other cloth and introduce it secretly into the food or drink of the people mentioned in the charm.

As with any other spell, you must first decide on your purpose, then chose your herbs appropriately. You must then decide what type of Potion would suit you best. Do you need to introduce it to food or drink? Then make your Potion with water. Would it be better sprayed or rubbed? Then maybe alcohol or vinegar would be better. The type of spell will determine the exact kind of recipe.

Oils

Magical oils have always been an important part of the spellcaster's armoury. They are used to concentrate the very essence of a herb, tree, flower or root and are very powerful when used correctly. More than this, they can retain the full scent of the plant and scents have a profound effect on the psyche, especially in combination with the magical intent.

The main method of making an oil is known as *enfleurage*, or infused oil. Having gathered your plant material correctly (see final section), pack a screw topped jar with the fresh material and top up the jar with a pure, vegetable oil, such as Sunflower - which oil to use as a "carrier" will depend on the desired outcome of the spell, or the end use of the magical oil. Check in the lists of correspondences for the appropriate oil to use. Screw on the lid tightly and put away in a warm place, out of direct sunlight. If making an oil purely for the magical or healing attributes of the plant, leave for ten to fourteen days, shaking daily. If you need the oil for its aromatic properties, leave for three days, strain off the oil, refill the jar with fresh leaves or flowers and pour the same oil back in. Repeat this every three days, shaking daily, until you have achieved the desired concentration of fragrance. Finally, with either type of oil, filter through fine cloth into a clean, dark glass jar and stopper tightly. Store it out of direct sunlight until needed. You can add a couple of drops of Benzoin essential oil as a preservative if you wish.

These oils can be used by themselves, for their individual properties, or combined with others, either for their magical, medicinal or fragrant attributes. The most powerful combine all of these aspects. Obviously it is up to the intended outcome of the spell as to which you combine and this will follow the same rules as we have already looked at in the previous sections.

The main use for oils is for anointing and this can be for or on an individual, a magical pouch, a candle, or anything else you can think of. Another use is in a bath, prior to a magical ritual or other important event. They can also be used as protective measures, by smearing them around door-frames and windowsills, or to obtain magical dreams by placing a few drops on the pillow at night. Below are some recipes for oil blends, but it is always best if you can devise your own, as they are more personal and tend to work better. Remember, when blending or using the oils, to always state their use and intent with some form of charm or chant.

General Purpose Anointing Oils

Using Sunflower oil as a base, blend equal parts of oils of; Lavendar, Frankincense & Lemon Balm or Cinnamon, Rose & Bay leaf or Cedar, Yarrow & Juniper. Create a blend that appeals to you personally; the magic is inherent in the herbs and the charms that you will use when creating the oil/s.

Protection Oil

Again using Sunflower oil as a base, mix together four parts Vervain oil, four parts Frankincense oil, two parts Clove oil and two parts Thyme oil. Blend together in your Compass, under the stars, two nights before the Full of the Moon.

DreamSeeker Oil

On a night of the Dark Moon blend together the following oils; Clary Sage, Nutmeg, Cinnamon, Myrrh, Chamomile and Valerian. Use equal portions of each, or alter each a little until you get the right "feel". This is a strange one and should be used with caution; no more than two drops on your pillow at night.

Satyrion

The name of this oil is quite widely known, but the recipes vary markedly. Here is one that has been handed down to me and that I find works to great effect. Blend the following oils together, for "whenever you feel the need"; one part Oakmoss, two parts Patchouli, one part Blackthorn blossom, three parts Pine resin and one part Ginger. If you don't know what it's for then you've no business using it!

Prosperity & Abundance

We could all do with a little of this and it is, after all, part of the Witch's stock in trade! On a Wednesday evening under a Waxing Moon, blend equal parts of Basil, Cinquefoil, Mint, Flax (Linseed) and Borage oils. Anoint your wallet or purse with this oil and it should never become empty.

As with all else above, work out what you need the oil for and blend accordingly. If you do not have the appropriate oil at the time, you can use a *pure essential oil* instead but remember, these are highly concentrated and should not be used neat on the skin. Blend at about 10% dilution in a base oil which you have chosen for its appropriate correspondence and use as normal.

Lotions

This should really be entitled ointments or salves, but Lotions rhymes with Potions – and you can always water it down a bit! These salves are basically a thicker version of the Oils, but have the advantage of being spreadable, particularly on the skin, and hence more readily absorbed into the body. Along with the magical intent you have put into creating them, they can be powerful aids to spellcrafting. An ointment or salve also has the added advantage of including Beeswax, which is a highly magical item in itself and can also add its beautiful aroma to the overall spell or charm.

There are many different ways to make a magical salve, some complicated some less so, but here we will look at a simple method that has served me well and has the benefit of being traditional. You need to know the *maximum* size of pot you are going to use for the salve (obviously the pot doesn't need to be full), to work out the different proportions of the ingredients. For convenience sake we will take an imaginary pot of 100ml. size/capacity. Your liquid contents (i.e. Oils or Potions), need to total 90% of the capacity – in this case 90ml. – and your solids (i.e. Beeswax), need to total 10% - in this case 10gms by weight. Using a double boiler – or a glass bowl over a pan of boiling water – first add the Beeswax. Once this has melted, carefully add the liquid ingredients so as to avoid any spilling or splashing – remember it will be very hot. *Blend* together well (do not whisk) and finally add any drops of essential oils you feel that you need (you do not have to count them into the liquid volume as they are so small) and stir well. Finally, carefully pour the liquid into the pot and leave to cool, capping immediately. (Some Crafters like to add the essential oils once the liquid is in the jar, to minimise the risk of evaporating off the volatile oils they contain). Shake to mix after capping. The Beeswax will cause the liquid to set as it cools, producing a smooth cream or salve. If it does not set to your satisfaction, simply reheat and add a bit more Beeswax for a thicker salve, or a bit more Oil for a thinner one. This will probably be easier to understand if I give an example, still using our imaginary 100ml. pot.

Recipe for a Divination Salve

10gm. Pure Beeswax
30ml. Wormwood Oil
30ml. Valerian Oil
30ml. Cinquefoil Oil
3 drops Cinnamon Pure Essential Oil.

Melt the Beeswax as detailed above. Add the herbal Oils and blend well. Add the Essential Oil, mix gently and pour into pot, or pour into pot then add Essential Oil. Cap immediately and shake. Leave till set. This ointment can be used by rubbing into the brow area and temples before any acts of scrying, tarot reading, rune casting or attempt at clairvoyance.

When making an ointment that includes a Simple or Potion, things are slightly more complicated. Because they usually contain water, the Simple or Potion will not mix with the Beeswax or Oils. So, when adding them to the other liquids you need to whisk them in briskly and continue to do this whilst pouring out into the pot to prevent them separating out. Another example will help.

Recipe for "Binding" Ointment

10gm. Pure Beeswax
45ml. Vervain Oil
45ml. Comfrey Simple
2 drops Frankincense Pure Essential Oil.

Melt the Beeswax as above and blend in the Vervain Oil. Add the Comfrey Simple whisking strongly all the while and continue for some moments. Continue beating whilst adding the liquid to the pot and immediately add the Frankincense. Cap straight away and shake forcefully to blend all the ingredients well. Leave to set. This salve can be smeared on anything you do not wish to lose, or that is important to you. For instance, when lending something to someone, add a touch of salve with a whispered charm to ensure its return.

If you know that you are going to use a Simple or Potion for an ointment when you are making it, it is better if you make a warm infusion in a pan and simmer it down until most of the liquid has been evaporated. This then creates a very strong infusion, which is easier to beat into the ointment as it contains much less liquid. Of course, all this beating, blending and stirring provides you with ample opportunity to add the magic into your preparations, by intently whispered charms and chants as you stir.

A small note of caution at this point; do be aware of what type of herbs and oils you are using; some can be toxic, although you are safe with the recipes given here. If giving them to someone else, either to drink or put on the skin, check the person's condition first. For example, during pregnancy, particularly the first trimester, no essential oils should be used at all. Certain herbs and oils can cause an allergic reaction in some people, so always do a patch test first.

Finally in this section a little historical curiosity that you might find of interest. It is taken from a manuscript, dated 1600, in the Ashmolean Museum at Oxford.

A Salve to Enable One to See the Faeries

> *"(Take) a pint of sallet-oyle and put it into a vial glasse; and first wash it with rose-water and marygolde water; the flowers to be gathered towards the east. Wash it till the oyle becomes white, then put into the glasse, and then put thereto the budds of hollyhocke, the flowers of marygolde, the flowers or toppes of wild thyme the budds of young hazle, and the thyme must be gathered near the side of a hill where fairies used to be; and take the grasse of a fairy throne; then all these put into the oyle in the glasse and sette it to dissolve three days in the sunne and then keep it for thy use."*

Elemental & Nature Magic

At first sight, separating out these two "functions" may seem unusual to those used to modern, pagan magic, as they are usually seen as one and the same thing. However, to a Traditional Witch, there are big differences between specifically elemental and purely Nature orientated magic. I will deal with a different type of elemental working in chapter six, SpiritWorking, but will here focus on a concentrated application of the classically understood four-element system.

Elemental Magic

We are dealing here with the four elements of the ancient world; Earth, Air, Fire and Water. All have their own attributes and correspondences, directions, and items that they govern; this is generally known and understood. Witches often work with a given element at a time and also combine them in their magic. There is a way of focusing and concentrating the powers of each element and this is known as the use of "Fluid Condensers". A Fluid Condenser refers to the non-physical (fluid) energy that is the essence of each element, which is incorporated into a liquid that can be used in the work of spellcrafting. It is similar to a Potion in construction, but is much more potent and utilises plant material that is governed by a single element only. There are various construction methods, all equally effective, but here we will look at one of the simpler ones.

On a waxing Moon, when the Moon is in one of the astrological signs governed by the element you are working with (failing this, use the Full Moon), gather together the appropriate herbs. Into a clean pot that you use only for your magical preparations (or cauldron if you are lucky enough to have a "workable" one), place two handfuls of herbs (this can be one herb only, or a combination, but if so, use an odd number), and cover with cold spring water, not tap water. Cover the pot, bring to the boil and simmer for about twenty minutes. Remove from the heat and leave to cool for fifteen minutes, keeping the pot covered. After this time strain the liquid off and return it to the pot. Dispose of the solid remains in a way that is in accordance with the element (e.g. for Earth, bury in some natural area; Water, place in some swift flowing river or stream; Fire, dry out and burn; Air, cast from some safe, high place for the winds to disperse). Boil the remaining liquid in the covered pot, until half the volume remains. Leave this to cool and then add the same quantity of strong, high proof spirits (gin/vodka/brandy) and shake vigorously – obviously with the lid on! Strain through four layers of linen or muslin and bottle in a dark glass container, making sure the lid is on firmly. Keep this somewhere dark and relatively cool until you need it. (Some Crafters like to add a little of one of their own bodily fluids with the spirits, to increase the potency; the choice is yours). And there you have your Fluid Condenser, ready to use. We will look at ways to use these Condensers shortly, but first here is a list of suggested plants to use for each element. This is by no means an exhaustive list, but will get you started and you can add to it at your leisure if you so desire.

Earth: Cedar, Cinquefoil, Cypress, Fern, Honeysuckle, Horehound, Pine, Sage.
Air: Broom, Comfrey, Elder, Eyebright, Hazel, Lavendar, Marjoram, Mugwort.
Fire: Alder, Basil, Cinnamon, Clove, Garlic, Holly, Nettle, Pepper, Rowan, Rue.
Water: Apple, Ash, Burdock, Elecampane, Hawthorn, Ivy, Meadowsweet, Rose.

There are many ways in which each condenser may be used and it is always a good idea to invent or devise your own, as these are more personal and, hence, more potent for you. However, below are some methods for each element that may give you some additional ideas.

Earth
From a natural site, collect some soil to use. Place this in a ceramic or earthenware bowl that you use for magic only and onto it place a few drops of your Earth Condenser. Recite a Charm of your own devising for the result that you desire, whilst stirring the condenser into the soil. See

in the bowl the spell coming about. Take the bowl back to where you got the soil and, whilst reciting your charm once more, re-bury the earth. Turn around and walk away without looking back. *Know* that your spell will work.

Anoint any charm pouches that come under the element of Earth with your Condenser to give it some extra power. Add the Condenser to any Potions or Salves that come under Earth (Use this Condenser for works of stability and balance, justice, wealth, jobs or promotion, etc.).

Air

Take a small, metallic bowl or ceramic saucer that you use for magic only and pour some pure spring water into it. Add 3 drops of your Air Condenser. Stir it around whilst reciting a charm of your own devising to bring about your desire. See in the bowl your desire being manifested. Then, either take the bowl to some – safe – high place on a windy day and cast the liquid into the air, repeating your charm with force as you do so; *or* place the bowl over a live flame and let the liquid evaporate whilst reciting your charm, until it has all gone. *Know* that your spell will work.

Anoint any charm pouches that come under the element of Air with your Condenser to give it some extra power. Add the Condenser to any Potions or Salves that come under Air (This Condenser is good for works of intelligence and learning/knowledge as well as communications).

Fire

On a clean piece of virgin paper or card, write out in *red* ink what you wish to come about (or your own charm of the same). Let fall a few drops of your Fire Condenser on it whilst reciting your charm and allow it to dry out, seeing the success of your spell as it dries out. Light a *red* candle and burn the paper completely (and it must all be consumed by the fire), whilst reciting your charm. Allow the candle to burn out in some safe place and *know* that your spell will work.

Anoint any charm pouches that come under the element of Fire with your Condenser to give it some extra power (Due to the nature of this Condenser, it would be unwise to let it touch bare skin; it is, however an excellent aid for all types of banishing spell, courage, willpower and success).

Water

Take your, clean, magical Cup and fill it with fresh water from a natural running stream or river. Add three drops of your Water Condenser and stir in well, whilst reciting a charm. See in the swirling waters the success of your spell. Return to the place where you got the water (or perform the spell there if you can), and cast the liquid into the running water, whilst reciting your charm with full force. Turn and walk away, without looking back, *knowing* that your spell will work.

Anoint any charm pouches that come under the element of Water with your Condenser to give it some extra power.

Add the Condenser to any Potions or Salves that come under Water (This Condenser is excellent for all types of love magic, for anything to do with the emotions, clairvoyance and divination or for communicating with the ancestors).

Remember that in elemental magic, we are not just talking about the four classical elements, but with the raw and truly "elemental" powers of the natural world. At their greatest expression these Powers may take on the form of deities (see chapter seven, Approaching the Powers), or at their least may be little more than subtle breezes in our moods. It is always worth bearing in mind however, that we are also a part of these powers and that, within each individual Crafter, there dwell the raw energies that we may call upon to infuse our work whenever we need them; this is what truly makes our magic work.

Nature Magic

As the name implies, Nature magic is working with simple items taken directly from the natural world. To the Witch, all of Nature is alive and contains Virtue or magical energy, just as we are, and all partake of that divine spark which animates us all. Therefore in Nature magic, we make use of that energy, merge with it and ask it to help us in our spells. We have mainly been looking at plants and herbs so far – all of which is in itself Natural Magic – so here we will look at other ways of working with the powers of Nature all around us.

Stones

As Stones are an integral part of the Earth around us, and hence alive, they can be very useful allies in our spellcrafting. I am not speaking here of the New Age fad for crystals that have been dynamited from the living Earth, but natural Stones that we have found or been called to. Everyone knows the pull of that particular stone or pebble on the beach or riverbank as we go for a walk, and have picked up as a lucky charm. How much more potent the Stone that we have magically sought out as an aid in our magic?

Before going on a walk, consciously and deliberately send out the thought that you wish to find an ally for your magic. Ask that a Stone be shown or offered to you; try to send out friendly thoughts ahead of you. You can compose a chant to this effect if you wish. Whilst on your walk, don't deliberately "look" for a Stone, but be aware when one calls to you. (This may take more than one attempt for the right Stone to be found, so don't be upset if nothing jumps out on the first try).

When you have found it, leave a little offering in its place – some bread, honey, wine, etc. – and take it home with you. If it is dirty, wash off the excess dirt (better still, if you find it near a natural source of water, wash it where you find it), dry it off and wrap it up in a piece of clean cloth or a small bag. *do not* "cleanse", "banish" or "consecrate" it, as you will then get rid of all the natural magic with which it is endowed. This is one of the basic mistakes made by modern "crystal-workers"; if you have "cleansed" your crystal, how will it work properly?

Now, how do you use it once you've got it? As with any form of spellcasting, everyone will have their favourite methods, but here are a few suggestions. Put it under your pillow at night while you sleep and see what dreams you have; the Stone may convey to you directly the way it can help you. When you are making up a charm pouch, writing out a spell or mixing herbs together, place your Stone on or in your materials for a few minutes, to impart its special magic to your spell. When making up any potions, simples, etc. place the Stone in the liquid whilst it is "brewing" to empower it. Always wash your stone with fresh, pure water afterwards – not tap water. Finally here, as I'm sure you will think of many ways of your own, hold the Stone in your receptive hand, to receive its energy, whilst you are casting your spell with your dominant hand, perhaps by holding your dominant hand over your potion, herbs, etc. whilst reciting a charm.

There are many other ways that you may discover yourself, all of which will be perfectly valid for you. Some Crafters have more than one Stone, for differing purposes or types of spell; this is fine but try not to overload yourself with too much "ritual" equipment. The essence of spells is simplicity and too much "stuff" can cloud the focus.

(A note here: Whilst the stone is a natural conduit for raw, elemental energy, some Witches feel that it can become depleted after a while and need re-charging or re-energising. If you, personally, feel that this is the case, take the stone back to where you found it – if this is practicable – or a secluded, natural place otherwise, and leave it on the ground for a period of time to re-charge. The length of time you leave it is up to you, but if you are in tune with your magical ally, you will instinctively know when it is "ready").

Weather

There are numerous traditional spells for *changing* the weather, but here I will look at a couple of ways of getting in touch with the energy *behind* the weather, in an attempt to use it in magical practice.

One way is to experience the energy that forms, shapes and changes clouds. On a day that has a lot of fluffy clouds in the sky, but is not too windy and not raining, take a trip to a safe place outdoors. Sit or lie down and choose a group of clouds that are fairly stationary. Attempt to "feel" them with your mind; the shape, density, energy of them. Reach out with your hands if you like and attempt to "touch" them. When you have examined them for a while, try breaking them apart with your mind. Focus on a particular largish cloud or patch and attempt to push it apart - what does it feel like? Can you feel movement, any resistance and taste or hear anything? Use these feelings to increase the pressure where it is needed and you will find that, with practice, you will be able to affect the clouds in surprising ways. Of course, this should not be done regardless of consequences; it is O.K. to bring rain if it is needed, but if it were unseasonably wet, then it would be wrong to bring more.

Another way to work with the weather is to use its energy in casting your spells. On a particularly windy and stormy day, wrap up well and go outside, having your spellcasting items with you. Using the experience you gained from working with the clouds, "feel" the energy of the storm. Feel it building and take that energy within you, letting it enhance your own energy. You might like to begin a chant or charm, building it into the rhythm of the wind, or the sway of the branches of the trees. Continue your chant as the storm builds, letting the energy increase, then, either at the height of the storm, or when you can't hold the energy any longer, release it into the wind and let it go to do its work. A lot of self-control is needed with this technique, as it is very easy to lose the focus of what you are doing and just "ride the storm", so to speak. Use the weather to help build your own powers, but do not lose sight of what you are trying to do. (Of course "Riding the Storm" is actually a magical technique employed by Traditional Crafters for specific purposes apart from spellcrafting. It is a difficult skill to teach and to learn so I shall not go further with it here; suffice it to say that personal experimentation with this technique, if undertaken with care and seriousness, could literally take one far!).

Finally in this section, something to try on a fine day, for a change! When it is nice and sunny, go outside, taking the appropriate spell items with you and stand in the direct sunlight. *Do not look directly at the Sun,* you will damage your eyes. Close your eyes and experience the warmth and energy of the Sun, feeling the golden light play about you. "See" a golden aura begin to surround you, starting as a light yellow colour, then building and deepening to a rich, dark honey colour, which fills you with a glowing warmth as it grows. Lift your hands to the Sun if you wish - all the better to call on the energy. When you can feel the golden light, strongly, all around you begin to let it soak into you, a little at a time. Continue this until you can feel yourself tingling with a golden warmth, or have taken as much as you can. Don't overdo it, you can get light-headed with this! When you have reached this point, you can do various things with the energy. Pick up your spell items and let the Sun's energy flow into them via your hands, charging them with your intent by reciting a charm, or similar. Take up a bowl of fresh, clear, spring water and charge that, keeping it safe to empower future spells. Infuse a talisman or amulet with the energy. Use it for self rejuvenation or healing. The list is endless.

Birds & Animals

Just as we have seen earlier with herbs and plants, animals and birds also have their magical uses and correspondences. This aspect of spell casting is ancient and derives ultimately from the totemic and worshipful practises of our ancestors, as well as their keen observations of nature. We all know expressions such as "the wise old owl", "cunning as a fox" and "slippery as an eel", and these are just some of the meanings and attributes associated with our natural cousins. In spell casting, these attributes are taken literally and made magical use of, often incorporating parts of the animal or bird into the spell itself, either actual or symbolic. I need to say here that, if using actual body parts of an animal or bird, make sure that the animal they were taken from did not suffer in any way. Often we can use things that we find, like dropped feathers, fur, hairs, wool, old bones or a skull that we have found. There is no magical value in deliberately causing an animal pain or death to obtain some of its body parts – although there is magical value in using them!

The ways of incorporating animals into magical practice are many and varied and, obviously, will differ from Witch to Witch, but one prerequisite is to know the type of animal well before you use its powers. Studying it in the wild is the best way; observe its habits, its feeding practices, its mating habits and you will have a *good* idea of what abilities it has that will help you in your magic. If observation in the wild is impossible, get a good natural history book and study that in depth. (For native British birds and animals, I would recommend "Fauna Britannica"; it is quite comprehensive and includes sections on folklore as well, which is very useful for discovering how our ancestors used and viewed the animal powers).

The best way to illustrate how to use animals and birds in your spellcasting is to give some examples, so here are a few to give you an idea. Obviously you can then go on to compose your own.

Horsehair binding spell

Obtain a long hair from the mane or tail of a horse. Thread it through a fine needle and then thread on some holly berries, to make a sort of rosary. With each berry, utter a charm or chant, detailing the attributes of the person you wish to bind. Tie this into a circle and hang up somewhere to dry. If you've really 'got it in' for the person concerned, make the rosary as above, then hang it up in the middle of a Holly bush. In both cases, leave it to work its magic in its own way.

Another way to use horsehair in this manner is to take nine strands and plait them together, 3 x 3.Use them to bind a poppet of the person concerned, stuffed with appropriate herbs, using a charm of your own composing while performing the spell. Place the bound poppet into a jar, seal the lid and bury somewhere safe where it won't be accidentally dug up. However, do remember where you buried it, in case you wish to dig it up and undo the spell.

Feather protection spell

If you know you are going on a journey that involves flying in a plane, collect together as many smallish feathers from the wild as you can find. (Obviously it would be good practice to use the feathers of a competent flying bird!). On a clear day, outside, in full sight of a flock of birds on the wing, bind these together with red thread, reciting a charm of protection, calling on the powers of safe flight. When they are tied together, hold them up to the birds and recite your charm again, waving them nine times in the direction in which the birds are flying. Keep them about your person during your journey, maybe pinning them on your jacket as a brooch, or suchlike.

Stealth/Cunning spell

This is for those times when you would rather not be noticed at a gathering that you have to attend, for when you may need to make a sneaky getaway without being seen or need to pass unnoticed through a crowd or wood, etc. and relies on the attributes of the Fox or the Mouse. It is possible to find mice that have died of natural causes in the wild, or fox fur caught on a bush or barbed wire. If you cannot find either of these, or are too squeamish to use them (in which case, what are you trying to work traditional magic for?), a small figurine or colour photo will suffice. (If you do find a dead mouse, it is best to put it in a bowl of sea salt and cover it with the salt for about three weeks before using it. This will not only kill any bugs that may be on it, but will dry and preserve it for easier use).

On a night of the waning moon, collect together your spell ingredients – your fox/mouse link, herbs of a "concealing" nature, a black, drawstring bag and some Thieves Vinegar. Place the herbs in an earthenware bowl, naming each one and its powers of concealment as you do so. Place the fox/mouse link on the herbs, reciting a charm calling on their special attributes to keep you unseen and bestow cunning upon you. Mix these together, sprinkling the herbs over the link, reciting your charm again. Place all these into your black bag, draw the string tight and knot it. Place three drops of Thieves Vinegar on the knot, stating that the bearer will henceforth be invisible when they wish. Keep this about you when you are in "tricky" situations.

On Collecting Plant Material for Magical Use

Have clear in your mind what plant you wish to collect and why. Alone, preferably at dawn or dusk, go to a place where the plant grows in profusion. Explain, aloud or silently, to the plant what you are going to do and why, then wait a little for the plant to absorb the information. Then, as swiftly and cleanly as you can, cut the material that you need with a non-iron blade. Take a little from each of a group of plants rather than a lot from one, so as not to do any one plant irreparable harm. Do not let the plant material you have gathered touch the ground once cut, but keep it in a clean cloth. Once you have enough, give your thanks to the plant/s and leave a small offering such as bread, wine, mead, milk or honey. Go straight home. (Always collect your plant material from a place that is at least a hundred yards away from any well-used roadway. The exhaust fumes from cars and other vehicles can be taken up into the plants and render them, at best, useless for healing/magical work or, at worst, toxic to use).

Depending on your use for the plant, you can either use it immediately or dry it for later use. If drying, tie the plant material up in bundles and hang in a warm, dark place until it is dry, then store it in a clean, dry, airtight container, labelling it carefully. Keep out of direct sunlight until you need to use it. Plants thus gathered will usually have a shelf life of about a year, so you will need to renew your supply when the plant is next in season.

If cutting the aerial parts of the plant (leaves, flowers, etc.), cut them on the waxing moon. If cutting the fruits, take them at the time of the full moon, or a day either side of it. If taking the root of a plant, cut at the time of the waning moon, but make sure there are plenty of the same plants in the area; taking the root will obviously kill the whole plant, unlike gathering the leaves or fruits.

As well as the moon tides, the solar cycle should also be taken into account. The best time to cut leaves is in the spring, when they are fresh and full of life. Fruits will obviously be gathered in their own season, but roots are best gathered in autumn/winter, when the plant is dying back and drawing all it's energy down into the root for winter.

A final note in this section: It is now illegal for many plants to be taken from the wild, due to their scarcity. Do check the status of any plant you intend to collect *before* cutting it; if it is on the prohibited list, the alternative is to buy your own plant from a good garden centre, or grow it from seed yourself. This can quickly become an obsession, and you will be looking for spare space in your garden very soon!

CENSING *the* SACRED

In the previous chapter we looked at using various types of herbs and plant material in magical practice. Following on from that, I would now like to look at a more specific use of this material, namely in the preparation and use of incense. This is a substance that every Traditional witch would be wise to learn how to make and use, as it can be an exceedingly useful addition, if not an essential ingredient, in many practical workings and rituals. I would first like to look at some of the history and background to this subject and then move on to the more practical art of incense making.

History and Background

Historically, incense has been used throughout the ages, by nearly every culture around the world. Pretty much every religion or belief system has realised the value of using some form of scent in its rites and rituals and various ways have been devised for their preparation and offering. The reasons for using incense vary from culture to culture and can cover different ground, depending on the desire of the participants.

Originally, it was burnt as a pleasing aroma, to attract the gods and spirits and acquire their favour and goodwill. The reasoning behind this was that if we like the scent and it makes us happy, then the gods and spirits must surely like it as well, so we'll give them some when we worship them. Secondly, in the early days of humanity, it had a more practical use, as it masked the foul smells arising from burnt, blood sacrifices and it was also used to clear the air during funeral rites; some bodies could give off a very strong aroma if they weren't buried or cremated soon enough. Later on, as humanity progressed and human and animal sacrifice waned in popularity, incense itself became the sacrificial offering in its own right, particularly to petition or as a thank-offering to the Powers and Spirits.

The rarity and distance travelled to procure some of the ingredients made some incense blends exceedingly expensive and were therefore considered suitable and fitting offerings to the gods. Lastly, incense was/is offered when spells and prayers are made, because it is believed that the petitions to the Powers and Spirits were carried straight to them in the Otherworld on the spirals of sweet-smelling smoke; the incense itself is seen as the medium by which requests and favours can be asked of the supernatural powers, in a pleasant and thankful way.

In Ancient Egypt, the compounding of herbs, flower extracts, gums and essential oils to manufacture incense of the best quality was a task considered so powerful and important, that it was restricted to only a few specially trained priests. During the process, magical words of power were chanted and after its preparation the incense was sealed in clay jars. This was to protect it from the desert heat and also to prevent it being stolen by those outside the priesthood who wanted it for their own, magical purposes. Anyone who stole the recipes for the temple incense faced the death penalty and his family was ritually cursed by the priests for his crime. So potent were these recipes and formulas that when the 1922 expedition led by Howard Carter and Lord Caernarvon broke into the tomb of the Pharaoh Tutankhamun, they could still smell the subtle aroma of the incense that had been burnt during his funeral rites. Tombs still being uncovered today have the same qualities and many of the resins found inside can still be used for making incense. I can testify from personal experience, that the pyramids and tombs of Egypt do, indeed, still have a subtle and magical aroma when visiting them, because of the incense used in the rites there.

The use of incense acquired an occult mystique, as opposed to a purely functional use as an offering, when Babylonian astrology infiltrated European paganism during the first 400 years after Christ. The Neo-Platonists, groups of pagans who practised a composite religion made up of doctrines and deities drawn from the ancient Egyptians, Greeks, Romans and Babylonians, passed their arcane beliefs on to unorthodox Christian sects known as the Gnostics, who in turn were drawn upon by Arabian occult philosophers. These scholars, who called themselves Sabians, laid special stress on the use of astrological prayers, sacrifices and suffumigations (burning of incense), and the works of the greatest among them were the source books for later mediaeval grimoires and books of magic and necromancy. As the use of incense was seen as inherently pagan and heretical, offered to the Caesars and Classical gods, it wasn't until the early Middle Ages that incense was adopted by the Roman Church for its rites. However, it was already in wide use by witches, magicians and cunning-folk for conjuring up spirits, clearing spaces, making talismans and other forms of magic and had been for centuries beforehand.

In general Western religion these days, it is only the Greek Orthodox, High Anglican and Roman Catholic churches that still tend to use incense. After the Reformation, the

Protestant sects fell back on the old views of considering incense to be pagan and heretical, despite the Biblical references to the contrary. Nevertheless, many still-room books and household recipe books from the 17th. Century onwards, used in the great Manor Houses of Britain and Europe, list incense recipes, as did the popular printed booklets of the Victorian era. Many of these were overly complicated and expensive and unnecessarily so; once the basics are understood, it is a relatively simple art, but one that can be richly rewarding in and for magical work.

Practical Applications of Incense

From the perspective of a Traditional Witch, incense is a very useful and powerful tool in their working equipment. As we have already seen, one of the most important and principle uses of "smokes" (another term for incense), for the Crafter is as offerings to the Powers and Spirits that are habitually worked with. This can be as thank-offerings for favours already received or work performed or as gifts in exchange or hope for future work to be done. This is not done in any sense of, "you do that for me and I'll give you this", as that is not the working mentality of a Crafter. The attitude is one of a reciprocal exchange of gifts and energies; the worker is due his wage and what is received must be paid for, in like kind, on all levels. This is a subject that I will look at further in future chapters ("SpiritWorking" and "Approaching the Powers") but it cannot be overly stressed how important incense is in a magical, working relationship with one's Spirits and Gods. An offering of incense can convey a deep and heartfelt gratitude and appreciation for the bond between working partners – Witch and Spirits/Powers – and should not be overlooked in your working practice. I will include a suggested Rite of Offering at the end of this chapter that you may like to use for your own practice.

In addition to offerings, incense is a powerful aid in the changing of levels of consciousness, something that we will look at further in a future chapter (see "Entering the Twilyte") but a brief mention can be made of it here. As we know from modern, scientific research (and as has been known for centuries by magical workers of all types), smell is a very important aspect of the human senses. For instance, the natural odour of the human body plays an essential role in the chemical reactions in the brain that cause sexual attraction and arousal. Different smells, pleasant or otherwise, can act as mental stimulants and trigger images, memories, feelings and sensations. This is because scent works on the limbic area of the brain, what is often called the "Lizard brain"; this is the most primitive area and the first part of our brains to have developed, millions of years ago. It, therefore, responds at a very deep and basic level and can produce the most surprising results and effects. A lot of the power of an incense lies in its ability to change the thoughts, mood and mind of the witch and transport them to a more conducive attitude, the better to perform the required working. Not all incenses smell nice, however. Not all are designed to but it is the response from the deeper levels of our being that we are interested in, coupled with the magically focussed attention/intention - not just whether it smells "nice" or not.

Along side this, goes the question of the "correspondence" of the ingredients in the mix. I have mentioned this previously, but would like to address this again here. I am not of the opinion that a plant, herb, or anything else for that matter, is "ruled" by a particular planet, planetary sign, deity or element, as is the general comprehension of this concept. Rather, I think it should be seen as a corresponding type of energy or vibration i.e. the items in question vibrate harmoniously or on a similar level to each other. If that sounds too 'New-Agey' for a Traditional Witch, consider that they are of like kind or of a similar spirit. No one thing rules another; they simply walk the same Way. Having said that, we need to consider the correspondences of the ingredients used in the incense mix. They must all be of a like kind for the work in hand. If you wish to honour a specific Power or Spirit, you should use those things associated with that particular Being. Likewise, if you wish to compose a smoke for a specific magical working, you must include those things that are in harmony with that particular operation. In this case, the smell may become secondary or non-applicable to you; if you cannot find corresponding ingredients that you like the smell of, then you will have to use the ones that you have got, whether you like them or not, if they are appropriate to the operation.

Another use for incense is in the charging, hallowing or consecrating of charms, talismans, sigils and runes. Once properly constructed, these various items may be held in or passed through the smoke of an appropriate incense, so that the inherent power of the smoke may add its force to the magical item. This is an ancient and valuable use for incense and a pretty indispensable one in most Crafters' working practice.

Incense Burning

Before we get down to the practical side of incense making, a short word is needed on its actual burning. Incense generally comes in two main forms - loose grains, lumps or powder which is burnt on charcoal (generally termed "grain incense") and joss sticks or cones which are self-burning. The latter are relatively simple and easy to use, requiring little more than a container to hold them while they burn. Cones can simply be placed on a special plate, tile or small tray and joss sticks can be stuck into practically anything, as long as you have some way of collecting the ash that falls. Grain incense (which is what we are mainly concerned with in this chapter), is a bit more tricky and needs a bit more thought and preparation to burn. To use grain incense, you need to place it on burning charcoal, so that the aromas of the ingredients can be released by the heat; it will not burn by itself. It may sound a bit stupid to warn people of this, but from personal experience it is more than worth it. Burning charcoal gets very hot! You therefore need a suitable container for it to be placed in safely. You can buy or make all sorts of fancy incense burners; from cast metal ones with pierced lids, specially designed ceramic ones, to the giant "swinging-handbags" seen in the Cathedral at Santiago de Compostela, but these are not really necessary for successful incense burning. As burning charcoal can be very dangerous if knocked over *(do not ever try to pick it up with bare hands if this happens, as you will seriously hurt yourself – I know!)*, the use of a static incense burner, placed somewhere safe is recommended. You may buy or make yourself one of the traditional forms of incense burner, or thurible, and these are very atmospheric and appropriate. However, a burner can be made very easily by simply filling a fired ceramic or metal bowl 2/3 full with *dried* sand and placing it on another plate or tile and setting this on a heatproof surface. The sand is to absorb some of the heat from the charcoal, as the burner itself can get very hot, and you don't want to put a hot metal or pottery bowl on a wooden or any other flammable surface.

The charcoal block is lit, either in a candle flame or something like a gas hob flame, by holding it *with a pair of tongs or tweezers, not your fingers.* Most incense charcoal is what is called "self-igniting" these days; this means that it is impregnated with saltpetre to make it burn. Holding the block in the flame will make it begin to spark, which is the saltpetre igniting the charcoal. Hold the block in the flame until the sparking has crossed the whole surface of the block then carefully place it in your incense burner. Next, place a *small* pinch or piece of your incense on the block to burn. When it has burnt through, add some more, until you have finished whatever you are doing. The reason for adding a small amount of incense at a time is basically two-fold.

Placing a large amount of incense onto the charcoal will smother it, cut off the oxygen supply and put it out; hence wasting the block and the incense and you will have to start again. Secondly, the incense will take some time to burn through – how much depends on the type of ingredients used; you don't really want to still be enveloped in clouds of incense once you have finished your work, as it is very difficult to get rid of and wasteful if you put on more than you need. If you put on a small pinch at a time, you can gauge how much more you will need for the time you are working. Once you have finished your rites, just leave the charcoal block to burn out completely and then dispose of it safely. You can tell when it's burnt through, as it will turn completely white and powdery.

Of course, the instructions given here above are for using incense indoors. If you are lucky enough to be able to work outdoors, then the situation can be a little different. Some Crafters like to have a small fire burning during their rites, either in the centre of the compass, or at one of the directions. Otherwise, a larger bowl, or even small barbecue burner can be used, in which larger amounts of outdoor charcoal can be placed. In this instance, larger quantities of incense can be cast onto the glowing coals to burn and you do not need to worry so much about amounts. This can provide an excellent atmosphere within the compass and lends itself well to spirit manifestation and contact. Outdoors, the smoke will clear much more quickly than indoors, so you do not need to worry about dispersing excess smoke either.

Incense Materials

Now we come to the interesting subject of the actual ingredients used in the incense itself. Although you can burn just one or two items as an incense, to make a really decent and useful one you will need various types of ingredients. These are very carefully blended together in a certain manner and then "preserved" for future use when you need it. Almost every known material item has been used as an ingredient for incense down through the years, from the sensible, like fragrant Cedar wood and Cinnamon bark, to the ridiculous, like powdered Unicorn horn, Faerie tears and everything in between. Ground and powdered gemstones and pearls were a favourite in the middle ages and even feathers and crushed egg shells have been used at one time or another. Many of these would not have been used by witches or Crafters, but by the more ceremonial or ritual practitioners; witches tended to use what they could find in the wilds, barter for or buy locally (or steal!) but more on that later.

However, most ingredients used these days can be broken down into 3 basic categories; Gums or Resins; Flowers, Leaves or Roots, and Essential Oils. There are one or two added items that can be used, but we'll go into that a bit later.

Gums or Resins

The word "gum" used in this context is actually a little inaccurate. What are known in incense making as incense gums and in varnish making and elsewhere as gum resins are simply the resins exuded by certain trees, mostly of the conifer variety; in other words, solidified sap. A gum is water soluble, a resin is not. Resins and balsams (known as oleo-resins - half essential oil and half resin) burn with a smoky flame and give off their essential oil when heated. Resins are the chief ingredients of the various Church incenses you can buy ready made, the most popular being Frankincense, Myrrh and Benzoin. In general incense making, they form the basis of most formulae.

Flowers, Leaves or Roots

Literally what it says on the label. Pretty much any form of dried flower, leaf, root or bark can and has been used in incense making. All will have their own particular qualities and scents when added to the incense formula. In addition to the flowers etc. the berries, seeds and nuts of certain plants can also be used, some containing a high degree of oils in their make-up, which adds to the overall effect. One example would be the Juniper berry, which gives a spicy note, well known from its inclusion in the distilling of gin. A word of caution here, however; although you CAN use any plant material you like, it is not always wise to do so. Although we are talking about scents here, when burning the incense, you will also be taking in minute quantities of the plant material through your mouth as well as your nose and hence ingesting it. Many plants are toxic when ingested and/or have psychotropic properties; always check your ingredients first before using dangerous plants. Examples of these would be Belladonna, Aconite, and some types of wild Mushrooms.

(This whole area of toxic and psychotropic plants comes under the general heading of Entheogens, which literally means "generating the divine within". It is the magical and/or ritual use of said psychotropic plants to aid the practitioner in getting closer to the Powers and Spirits and has been used around the world for millennia. However, it is a highly skilled area of practice and one I cannot go into here. Best advice is, if you do not have a knowledgeable teacher, leave well alone).

Essential Oils

These are the extracted oils of different plants and are extremely potent; most cannot be put on the skin without diluting, or they will burn. They are basically the concentrated liquid scents (not really oils), of the plants they are taken from and add the higher, initial tones to an incense. Because they are so volatile they burn off quickly and leave the way for the deeper, more long last scents of the plant materials and resins, but do give the initial "tone" to the incense. They can also act as a binding ingredient in some cases.

The additional items that can be added to an incense are the binding agents and some form of chemical to keep it burning. In loose incenses you don't use the latter but cones (and joss) do need it. We will look at this one later, below, when we discuss making cone incense. For now, we will consider the bonding agent. If you have used both an essential oil and a resin in your incense blend, you may find that the oil combines with the resin when dried, to bind the ingredients together. If this is not the case, you may like to add a bonding agent, which is usually a vegetable gum of some sort. The two most commonly employed are Acacia gum (commonly known as Gum Arabic), and gum Tragacanth, the sap of the *Astragalus gummifer* shrub. Both are available from art-supply shops or herbalists. If the gum comes in solid form, add boiling water (two parts water/one part gum) and leave to soak for several hours. When it is well and truly dissolved add just enough of the liquid to bind your loose incense together, but not to soak it. Other "liquids", such as wine, mead and honey can also be used as binding agents, but these tend to burn with a sickly, sugary scent, so need to be well disguised by the other ingredients used. If not dried correctly, they can also make the incense go mouldy, so make sure it is very dry before sealing it in a jar or suchlike.

Incense Blending

Having discussed all the disparate groups of things that go into an incense, we are now ready to look at how they all come together. Considering the complexity of the above, the actual practice is comparatively simple, but the blending of incenses can take years to master successfully. The easiest way to make an incense, is either to use purely one ingredient, either to burn on coals or in a cone. However, there is another method for the single ingredient, which suits the witch or Crafter very well, as it is a very natural method. You need to obtain your plant material in long, leafy stems and partially dry them out. When they are nearly dry but still pliable, simply plait the stems together, into as long and thick a bundle as you like, then leave them to dry out the rest of the way. When ready, simply set fire to one end then when it is fully alight, blow it out so that the end is smouldering. You need to wave this "plait" around to keep it smouldering, by having an air current rush over it, but it can be very effective. This method is used by many indigenous peoples around the globe and does away with the need for more complicated methods of combination and burning. When you have finished, simply let it go out by itself in a dish or bowl – as it will without a constant air flow – and use the rest later when you have a use for it. This can be used for single plants, or you can combine different plants for a more specific effect.

Now onto more complicated methods of incense blending. I will split the following section into two parts, the first dealing with loose incense burnt on charcoal, the second dealing with how to make incense cones that burn by themselves.

Grain Incense

With grain incense, there is a very simple method of preparation. Once you have decided on the ingredients you want to use, place the gums/resins in your mortar first - many of these are the hardest of the ingredients that you will use, so start by grinding these down with your pestle first (you may have to bash some quite hard at first). If you are using any roots or barks, add these at the same time, as these tend to be quite hard too. Don't mash them into a powder as yet as you will be doing further grinding later; just crush them into smaller grains or pieces of root for now. Next you add your lighter ingredients, such as any nuts, seeds or berries and grind them down too; the gums will now help in the process, as they act as a grinding agent in themselves and make the process easier. Next you add the lightest ingredients, namely your leaves and flowers as these are the most delicate of items and take the least grinding.

How finely you grind your mixture down is up to you; some people like a fairly rough mix, others like a fine powder. A finer mix tends to burn quicker with more smoke; a rougher mix with larger pieces takes longer. It also depends on how you're going to finish off your incense too, but see below for that. Next to last, you then add any essential oils that you want to mix into the blend. Don't grind these in with the pestle, but stir the mixture round with a spoon until they are absorbed equally into the ingredients and spread evenly throughout the mix. (The same goes for any "liquid" ingredients, such as wine, honey, etc.).

Throughout the whole of this preparation, you will be keeping your mind fixed wholeheartedly on the operation that you are making the incense for. You may wish to compose a short chant or charm to intone over the incense as you make it, the better to empower it. The incense ingredients are only the physical side of the operation; you need to infuse your work with the force and power of the operation that it is to be used for, or it will lack in efficacy. Some people have a set way of doing the actual grinding of the ingredients together with the pestle; so many turns one way, then so many turns in the opposite direction. Some people will only grind in a sunwise direction for beneficial works and in a widdershins direction for those of maleficia. The choice is yours but remember to keep the focus and concentration going throughout the process, which can take a long time in some cases. The more energy you can infuse into the incense mixture, the more powerful and efficacious in your work it will be. You will know when the energy is building, as you will feel it as a heat or a"thickness" in the atmosphere surrounding you. Focus this within your mortar and fix it there with your charm.

Depending on the ingredients you have used, you may or may not now want to add your binding agent. If so, add it in very small amounts, a few drops at a time, and mix these well in. As I said before, you don't want to soak the mixture, as it will take too long to dry out and you may end up with a solid ball of incense instead of a nice, crumbly mixture.

If it doesn't dry out properly, it may also go mouldy as well, as previously mentioned. Now you can just leave the mix to dry out in a warm, dark place, stirring occasionally to make sure it is thoroughly dried, before storing it in a screw-top jar, or similar, for future use. Keep it covered with a cloth, or similar, whilst drying, to prevent the essential oils you have used from evaporating off prematurely.

Alternatively, some people like to make "pastilles" or small balls of incense that will dry hard; now is the time to do this if you wish (in which case it is better to have a more finely ground mixture than a purely loose incense). Simply scoop up the mix with a spoon or your fingers and form them into the shape required. Set these to dry on a sheet of cooking parchment, and then store them safely somewhere dry. These have the advantage of being able to be placed on the charcoal, one by one, without having to think about quantities, at a time when you may be distracted with other actions during ritual.

If you have a hearth at which you regularly work, it is good practice to leave your incense here over night to "cook", before putting it away. It can absorb the influence of your magic and make it even more potent. Alternatively, if you don't have this space, why not place your incense in your working Cauldron overnight, for the same purpose.

Cone Incense

As mentioned before, if you are making the self-burning cone type of incense, you will need a chemical agent to keep it burning. This is invariably the same chemical used in cigarette papers and firework fuses, namely potassium nitrate, otherwise called nitre or saltpetre. This may be purchased from specialist incense suppliers, or from certain food suppliers, as it is also the same ingredient that is used to cure various types of meat and is sold as "Preserving Salts". Once obtained, the proportion of saltpetre to your other ingredients should not be more than one part in ten; otherwise its smell overpowers the other ingredients.

With this type of incense you cannot use resins alone, but must add at least twice as much aromatic herb material, powdered finely, for the saltpetre to work properly. It doesn't matter how large the proportion of woods and herbs are, as long as the resins do not exceed half their bulk proportionately. The easiest formula that I know of – and there are many – is based on the use of Orris Root powder (Florentine Iris), as the basis for the mixture, and goes as follows. (If you don't use Orris, then you need to add a binding agent, like gum Arabic).

Measure or weigh out Orris Root powder. Weigh out ground resin/herb mix (bearing in mind proportions as above), equal parts resin mix to Orris. Mix resins/herbs with Orris powder; all should be thoroughly powdered and well combined. Weigh out saltpetre. You want 10% saltpetre to dry mix (so if you have ten teaspoons dry mix you need one teaspoon of saltpetre). Dissolve saltpetre in water. (You need one part water to every three parts dry). *Slowly* add wet to dry, mix, add more of the saltpetre solution, mix (like making pastry) until a smooth, soft dough is formed. It shouldn't be 'wet' and there shouldn't be any dry hanging around. Aim for 'play dough' consistency. Add essential oils if desired and knead in, but watch the "wetness". Pinch off small balls (size of a small marble) and shape into cones. Place on sheet of baking parchment to dry and leave at room temperature for a week to 10 days. Store the incense in a cool, dark place and use as required. These may spark a little as they burn but still give off a good aroma - if you've blended the herbs and gums correctly.

(Note: When mixing your ingredients for incenses, it's a good idea to let the mixture stand and "rest" overnight to "take". Be a little sparing with the oils and other wet ingredients until you gain experience, so that you don't make the mixture too soggy. Remember, it is much easier to add to a mixture than to take away. If it ends up being a bit too sticky, add more dry ingredients until the right consistency is attained).

Formulae

Below I have included some basic incense formulae to get you started. There are many thousands available, but you will gradually get to know what you like for what purposes after a time and begin to devise your own. The measures used are multiples of a standard 5ml. teaspoon, but as long as you use the same measuring tool for each ingredient, the proportions will remain the same. Essential oils are a very personal thing, so add to "taste", but be sparing – they are strong, just a few drops will do!

A quick word on ingredients here before we begin with the recipes. For magical purposes, it is always better if you can collect and dry your own ingredients, either from the wild or from your own garden, bearing in mind the guidelines given on collecting herbs in the last chapter. If you have collected them yourself, you are not only assured of pure, natural ingredients, but have the confidence that they were taken in a magically conducive manner, without harm to other wildlife. You may also leave offerings to the spirits of the plants, who may add a little bit of extra power to the materials you are gathering. You will obviously not always be able to gather all the ingredients yourself for any given incense recipe but, after a little experience, you may be able to start substituting locally grown materials for more exotic or shop bought ones. These will have the benefit of being collected by yourself with extra power and may even be better than the original recipe for you. Experiment and have fun!

"Universal" incense can be used for any occasion; hopefully the rest of the titles will be self-explanatory.

Universal.
1 part Frankincense
1 pt. Myrrh
1 pt. Benzoin
1 pt. Vervain
1 pt. Rosemary
1 pt. Lavendar
1 pt. Cinnamon
Cedar wood Ess. Oil
Pine Ess. Oil.

White Goddess.
2 pts. Myrrh
2 pts. Jasmine
2 pts. Rose petals
2 pts. Willow bark
½ pt. Camphor
Clary Sage Ess. Oil
Melissa Ess. Oil.

Horned God.
2 pts. Benzoin
1 pt. Cedar
1 pt. Pine
1 pt. Juniper berries
1 pt. Oak bark
Patchouli Ess. Oil. Red wine.
(A variation on this recipe is given in the last chapter).

Healing.
3 pts. Myrrh
1 pt. Rose petals
1 pt. Eucalyptus leaves
1 pinch Saffron pwdr.
Cedar wood Ess Oil.

House Purification.
3 pts. Frankincense
2 pts. Dragon's blood
1 pt. Myrrh
1 pt. Sandalwood
1 pt. Wood Betony
½ pt. Dill seed
Rose Geranium Ess Oil.

Divination.
2 pts. Sandalwood
1 pt. Acacia
1 pt. Hazel wood
½ pt. Calendula flrs.
½ pt. Bay lvs.
½ pt. Clary Sage
½ pt. Mugwort
1 pinch Nutmeg pwdr.

Spirit Offering.
5 pts. Frankincense
3 pts. Myrrh
2 pts. Rosemary
2 pts. Marjoram
1 pt. Basil
1 pt. Gum Arabic
1 pt. Allspice
1 pt. Gum Tragacanth.

Wrath & Chastisement.
Equal parts of the following;
Dragon's Blood
Rue
Peppercorns
Frankincense
Cayenne pwdr.
Ginger
A pinch of Sulphur
A pinch of Iron filings.

Consecration/Hallowing.
8 pts. Frankincense
6 pts. Ash leaves
5 pts. Myrrh
5 pts. Cinnamon
5 pts. Vervain
2 pts. Orris Root pwdr.
Basil Ess. Oil.
(Can be used for tools or Talismans).

A Rite of Offering

This is a simple rite and is very easy to adapt for many different situations. It may be used on its own, or incorporated into other rites that follow in this book, or any of your own. It is intended mostly as a thank-offering for some task done by the Spirits and Powers that you work with, or as an act of empowerment to those Beings during a working rite. Alternatively, it may "just" be used to create a stronger bond with the Beings that help you in your work and forge a better working relationship. You may use the incense recipe given above for Spirit Offering as it stands, or adapt the ingredients to the specific Spirits and Powers that you work with. If offering to specific Beings, be sure to only offer the things that they like and not anger them with things that displease! In this instance, the incense is to be seen as a source of nourishment and sustenance – food – for the Spirits and is your gift to them.

Within your hallowed space, at the part of the rite that you consider appropriate, have your incense and burner ready on your altar or before your Stang on the ground, if outside. (If you are working with/offering to Spirits/ Powers from a particular direction, have your things placed at that compass point). Do not place the incense on the charcoal yet.

Face the appropriate place and say words to this effect:

"Spirits of the Land, the Sea and the Sky,
Come, Be welcome!
Shades of the Past, the Present and those yet to Be,
Those whom I have aided and who have given aid unto me,
Spirits who Protect, Guide and Teach me,
Come, Be welcome!
All Powers of the Natural World with whom I work,
All those of this place who inform and advise me,
All Beings to whom I look for support, wisdom and enlightenment,
Come, Be welcome!
Come All here to the best of your abilities that I may gift and thank thee with sweet food and smoke!
Come, Be welcome!
Come, Be welcome!
Come, Be welcome!"

Pause a moment to allow the presences to gather, before making the actual offering. Light the charcoal (if you have not already done so), then sprinkle on a generous helping of incense; remember, this is an offering and a gift, so don't be mean. Lift the burner and walk round the compass, letting the thick clouds of incense waft away on the breeze. (If you are working at a particular direction, continually raise and lower the burner, so that the smoke is wafted towards that direction). Say the following words, or similar, or tailor them to your particular situation:

"Smoke of Offering I raise to you,
Sustenance, nourishment and suffumigations!
Come, feed and take your fill!
May this Offering rise to your most special habitation,
May it be of the most pleasant and pleasing kind to you!
Come, feed and take your fill!
Spirits and Powers from the past, the present and the future,
I am grateful for your kindness and guidance.
Come, feed and take your fill!
Spirits of my Work and Teachers of its secrets,
Be free with your counsel and generous in wisdom.
Come, feed and take your fill!
Guides, Protectors and Helpers,
Be thou filled and satisfied with this repast!
Come, feed and take your fill!
For all of you I offer great delights,
Joyful festivity and feasting.
Be welcome at this Giving and see that I am Sincere.
See my Truth and Honour,
And may our Bonds be Strengthened and Secure!
Come, feed and take your fill!
Come, feed and take your fill!
Come, feed and take your fill!"

Continue to pace for a while, then return to your original place. (Alternatively, if you are at a direction, continue to waft for a while and then stop when it feels right). Pause for a while for contemplation and to receive any impressions or "messages" from those you have welcomed. Replenish the incense as required and as you feel appropriate.

When you feel that the time is right, you must formally close the Offering session and shut down the connection. Never omit this, as open doors can be dangerous! Again, use these words or similar:

> *"Respected Spirits and Powers, those who have answered my call,*
> *This Feast of Offering is now to end.*
> *Enjoy your final repast and prepare to return to your realms with peace between us.*
> *Go now to your realms and dwellings as best you are able,*
> *And may you be to me as Guides, Friends and Keepers in all ways.*
> *So Be It as I Will!"*

Pause a few moments to let the Spirits withdraw and then finish in your usual manner.

ENTERING THE TWILYTE

Some Definitions

As mentioned briefly in chapter 1, "Hallowing the Compass", the Traditional Crafter is sometimes referred to in a specialist way as a "Hedge Rider". This is an old, Anglo-Saxon term referring to the fact that the Witch spends much of their magical time and work beyond the boundaries of what we usually refer to as "normality". Much of the Crafters work involves entering worlds and realms that the average person has never dreamt of, let alone visited and the "Hedge" referred to is the symbolic boundary or barrier between this world and those others.

The reasons for journeying to these other worlds are various; it may be that another realm is a better vantage point from which to cast a spell or make a charm (and we have touched upon entering light trance in a previous chapter). It may be that the Crafter wishes to meet with various spirits or deities, native denizens of those Otherworlds, the better to further their knowledge or abilities. It may also be that they can obtain added energy or insight by visiting different realms, or it just might be that a better understanding of this world in which we all live can be achieved, by viewing it from a different angle or vantage point. The reasons are many and will probably vary with the individual, but the fact remains that entering different levels or areas of reality – working in trance or "Entering the Twilyte" as it is sometimes called – is a major part of the Traditional Crafter's work.

Now, before I go on to describe the various techniques whereby trance working may take place, a word about what a "trance" actually is. Contrary to popular opinion, unless it is an exceptionally deep experience, the Crafter does not normally lose awareness of what is going on around them; their focus of attention and awareness is simply placed elsewhere. And this is basically what the kind of trance that I am going to discuss here is; it is placing the immediate awareness of the Witch into a different place or reality to that which we normally inhabit in our everyday, waking world. It is not losing consciousness and thrashing around on the floor, moaning and groaning in "tongues". It is not lying frozen in a catatonic state from which you have to be violently shaken to bring you back, nor is it sitting still and gazing vacantly into space for hours at a time (although this latter could come close).

The type of trance entered into by a Crafter is very different to that utilised by a devotee of Vaudou being "ridden" by one of the Lwa, or a Spiritualist Medium during a séance; these trances serve a completely different purpose and, by common, cultural consent, the Medium and the Vaudou devotee are not expected to remember what happened whilst they were in trance and are positively encouraged to forget what they did, or what was going on around them. The Witch on the other hand, has very different reasons for entering the Twilyte worlds – or wherever – and usually needs to be very aware of what is happening in every level that they inhabit. Indeed, the whole point of trance working in Traditional

Craft is that you do remember what happens all the time. Part of the training of a Traditional practitioner is in awareness of who and what they are and also of *where* they are. This involves practice in focus and attention, coupled by a keen sense of visualisation, before any trance-work proper can begin. The Crafter also needs to be conscious of their own power levels, both during work of this kind and for practical magical purposes, so power accumulating techniques are also developed, again before trance working can start.

However, the most important thing to learn before deeper work of any kind can be entered into is the care and succour of the individual Crafter, their physical, mental and spiritual wellbeing – personal protection in other words – and this is where I propose to start for this work.

N.B. Before I begin to describe any specific practices, it would be well to sound a note of caution. These techniques, although harmless in themselves, are real and valid and are intended to cause changes in consciousness. If you are taking any kind of prescription drug for depression, anxiety or any other kind of mental problem, or are taking any of the so called "recreational" drugs as a pastime, it would be well to leave the practices I am about to describe, alone. Wait until you have no need of medical or chemical support before experimenting with any of these techniques.

Regarding recreational drugs, I make the above comments with no form of moralistic intent in mind; what one does in one's own time is one's own affair. I make them from a purely practical point of view. Vegetable-based, and other drugs do open up the "doors of perception" but there is very little control by the individual over what actually happens thereafter. Historically, I have to say that various forms of fungi have been used for these purposes – and indeed continue to be used by some – but this is a very skilled and specific area of practice and should not be undertaken unguided.

Personal Protection

I have already discussed hallowing the compass in chapter 1 and the forms of security and warding that that conveys, so I do not propose to talk about that subject here. What I am referring to by "personal protection" is a more intimate and individual form of practice, which not only harmonises the forces in the individual, but also gives a measure of individual defence. Now, when I talk about "defence" and "protection" here, I do not mean that you are protecting yourself from a horde of raging demons that are ready to attack you at any second, should you put even the tiniest of steps out of place. Nor do I mean that you will be whisked away to some gods-forsaken realm, there to be incarcerated forever if you stumble over a word in your rite or make the "wrong" move. Leave all that to Hollywood! What I am referring to is achieving a level of equilibrium of the flow of energy within you, such that you are balanced enough and prepared enough to perform the rite or work on which you have planned. This procedure also has the benefit in some of its forms, of calling on outside agencies to give you extra support, should you need or desire it. It should also be borne in mind, however, that not all forms of non-physical being are human-friendly, so a form of personal security when venturing into other realms does not go amiss.

We are all composed of many parts and many levels, not all of which work together at any given time. We are all subject to external – and internal – pressures, that throw us off balance and sometimes put us out of sorts. During ritual, all energies and pressures are heightened and increased and therefore any imbalances in our beings will become more pronounced and obvious, such that – in an extreme situation – we may be unable to continue or complete our work. The practice I am going to describe is a very simple method of equilibrating our internal energies, putting ourselves in touch with the greater forces outside ourselves, connecting to the powers in and of the Land

and hence creating a much better internal and external framework on which to commence working.

The Circle-Cross Method

Stand facing the direction in which you are going to begin your work (usually north), feet about a foot apart, arms by your sides. Close your eyes, take a few, deep breaths and visualise. Raise your dominant hand and touch your brow. Say;

'*From Above*'.

See a source of shining, astral light high above your head, sending down a stream of energy to connect with your brow area. Trace a line of light down from your brow and touch your navel. Say;

'*To Below*'.

See the line of light continuing down and penetrating the earth at your feet.

Touch your left shoulder. Say;

'*From the Left*'.

See a source of light coming from your infinite left and connecting with your left shoulder.

Trace a line of light across to your right shoulder. Say;

'*To the Right*'.

See the line of light continuing off to your infinite right.

You now have an equal armed cross emblazoned on the front of your body, stretching to infinity and linking you to the four quarters of the universe, in whatever direction they may be.

Cross your palms over the centre of your chest where the lines meet. Visualise a circle of light whose circumference touches your left and right shoulders, your brow and navel. Say;

'*I stand whole and contained*'.

Now, breathe in and visualise the cross; breathe out and visualise the circle surrounding it. Repeat twice more (three times in all). Continue with your work and maintain at least a minimal awareness of the circle-cross held before you.

You have now completed the basic Circle-Cross and harmonised the energies within you. This also gives a measure of personal protection going into any work that you don't consider it necessary to erect a formal compass for, but don't feel comfortable performing with nothing. It will charge up your own, personal powers and ward you against any stray interferences or distractions. You may use this technique before erecting your compass as well, if you feel the need, or instead of the centring exercise described in "Compass Hallowing", in chapter 1.

At the end of your ritual or work, after you have cleared away your compass, it is considered good practice to repeat the circle-cross. This time you are not attempting to place any protection around yourself, but "re-calibrating" your personal energies. You have just performed something that has altered your energy flows, to a greater or lesser extent, and this can often be quite disorientating. There is nothing wrong with giving yourself a good harmonising; all the better to come back to this world with!

Having learnt the basic method, there are various slight alternatives that you may like to utilise. If you are dedicated to a particular, named deity or deities (see chapter 7, "Approaching the Powers"), you may like to substitute their names instead of "From Above" (God) and "To Below" (Goddess) in the basic method. If you have personal guardians/spirits, you may like to substitute their names instead of "From the Left" and "To the Right". Try experimenting and see what works best for you. Do not forget to visualise at the same time. You may also find that the colour of the light that you are "seeing" changes with who or what you call on. Crafters are an individual and cantankerous bunch, so what works for one may not work for another; just follow your nose. However, do remember to keep visualising the cross and the circle, as this is what forms the focus and powers the rest of it. Once you have set this firmly in your energy field at the start of your work, you can leave it to work on its own for the rest of the time.

Here is another example of a version you could use whilst working in a wooded or forested area.

Using the same stance and visualisations as in the basic circle-cross, touch your brow and say:

"Viridos, Forest-Father."

Trace the line down to your navel and say;

"Erda, All-Mother."

Touch your left shoulder and say;

"By the Oak."

Trace the line across and touch your right shoulder, say;

"And the Elder."

Cross your hands over your chest and say;

"Around me forms the Woodward."

Allow yourself to experience the energies and see what differences there are. You may find that this simple exercise helps your work immensely.

Focus and Attention

Having looked to our immediate physical and spiritual well-being, it is time to turn the attention to some finer details. Before being able to enter any form of trance or Otherworld, it is necessary to sharpen the focus of the mind and concentrate on where the attention is placed, the better to be able to place it where we will, when we will. This may seem obvious and simple to many people but if you think about it, it's not that simple a matter at all. We are all bombarded every second of every minute of every hour of every day by constant sensations, emotions and distractions. The average person spends no more than a few seconds at any one time focussing on a single thought or object, before the attention is whipped away by the demands of something else. And I'm not even just referring to the demands of modern life; take a relaxing walk in the country and you will still have multiple areas to focus on, even if they are natural. The trees, the plants, the sky, the birdsong, the sound of running water, the wind in the trees; all these things impinge on our conscious minds and distract our attention. To be able to enter trance and/or project our consciousness into different realms of reality, we have to hold the focus of that conscious attention onto a single thing or point, without interruption or distraction. The beginning of this focus is the control of our breathing.

The Breath

As breathing is the single most important factor in keeping us alive, it is amazing how little importance most people attach to it. Breathing oxygenates our blood and eliminates waste like carbon dioxide; it therefore regulates our heartbeat and controls our state of consciousness; ultimately it affects our mental clarity and thought processes and dictates what state of "reality" we exist in. Nearly all cultures throughout history have placed great emphasis on the control of the breath for the production of any kind of mystical state or experience. Breath is considered to be – literally – the stuff of life and sacred in many cultures. Some techniques, such as certain forms of Yoga, elevate breathing to an art form and claim all sorts of things for it, but we need not go that far here. As stated elsewhere, the Craft has essentially a practical and common sense approach, so we need only look at what is practical to our purposes here. We are aiming at stilling and quietening the conscious mind, the better to focus our awareness on the areas we are concerned with.

Breathing should begin from the stomach, by pushing the belly out and pulling the diaphragm down, hence, pulling air in and filling the whole of the lung capacity on the in-breath. Conversely, the out-breath should begin from the top of the lungs, pulling the diaphragm back up, hence ridding the lungs entirely of stale/used air. Both in-breath and out-breath should be through the nose, not the mouth, as that's what it's there for. A full, proper breath is cleansing, inspiring (literally), healing and energising and forms the essential basis on which to begin any form of exploration into other realms. Be careful not to overdo it though, as prolonged "total breathing" for one not used to it can cause hyperventilation and collapse! Here follows an explanation of the basic, total breathing technique.

Loosen all tight clothing (or discard them all together), particularly around the middle. Lie down flat on your back, maybe with a pillow under your head and make sure that you are comfortable. (Don't do this exercise when you are tired, as you may fall asleep in this position!). Place your hands on your belly, lightly. Exhale fully – through your nose – and feel your belly sink in. Keep pushing the air out until your lungs and belly are quite empty.

Now, gradually begin to breathe in – through your nose – and feel your belly begin to rise – don't let your chest rise yet! Continue the in-breath until your belly is fully risen, when you should automatically feel your chest begin to rise, as your lungs fill completely. Continue breathing in until you feel a "push" under your collarbones, then you are full. Do not pause, but commence the out-breath. Breathing out slowly, allow your chest to gradually fall, keeping your belly full. When your chest has fallen, you will automatically feel your belly begin to sink. Continue the out-breath until your belly has sunk to the position where you began. This is one complete breath.

When doing this exercise, never strain or push yourself too far. If it hurts, stop immediately! To begin with, most people like to count through their breathing until they establish their own rhythm. Try breathing in to a slow count of 4, then out to a slow count of four and see how that goes. You can then alter it to what suits you best. To begin with, try doing a cycle of 4 complete breaths, but only if that suits you. Some people will feel comfortable with more, some with less, don't strain yourself! Once you get going, you should feel that your body is making a wave-like pattern, flowing up and down in rhythm with your breathing; this is the reason for placing your hand on your belly. Once you've got the knack you can dispense with this. After some while practising this breathing technique, you should naturally find yourself breathing in this way; pushing your belly out, filling your lungs, then emptying your lungs and pulling your belly in. As well as stilling and quietening the mind, you will also find that this technique allows you to think with greater clarity. Once mastered, it is not necessary to continue consciously breathing in this manner, as your body will find its own rhythm and you will be able to move your attention to other things. See, you didn't even realise that you had begun to focus your attention, did you?

Ready to Hallow the Compass.

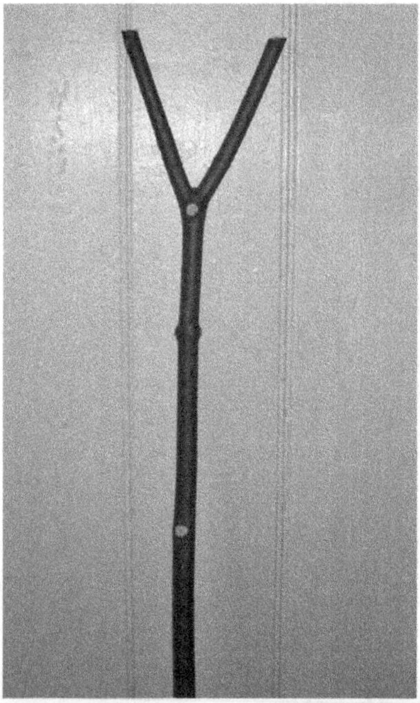

Left: A simple Stang.

Below: A selection of knives in the author's collection.

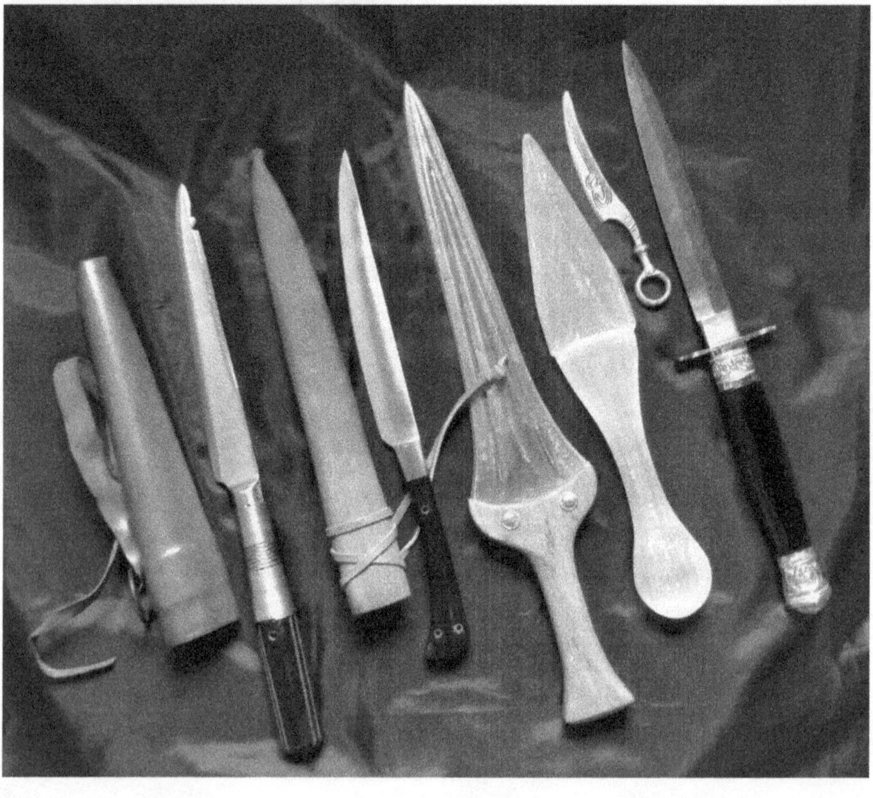

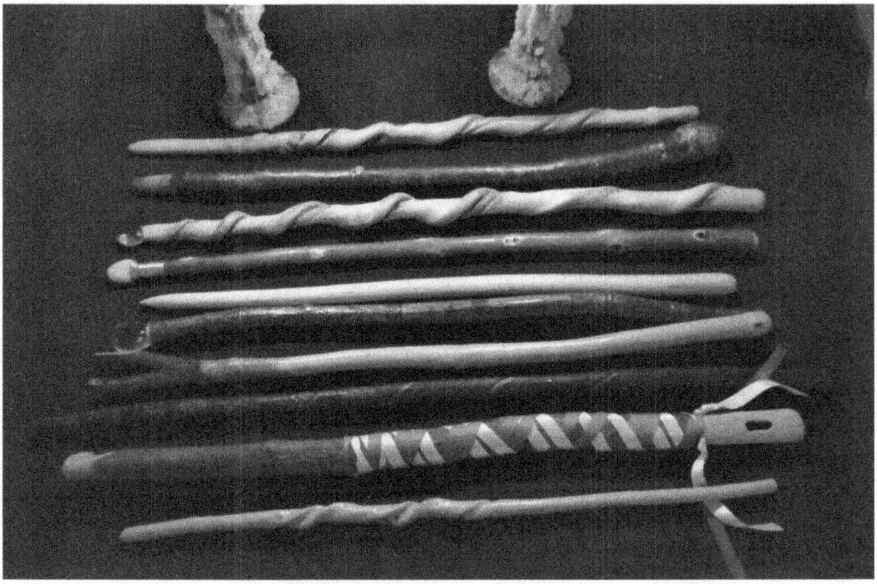

Above: Hand crafted wands owned by the author.

Below: Examples of cups in the author's collection.

Above: Horseshoe, cord and foliage house protection charm.

Left: Composite charm for the blessing and protection of doors and passageways.
Right: Rowan-berry apotropaic charm, alternatively used as a Witch Ladder.

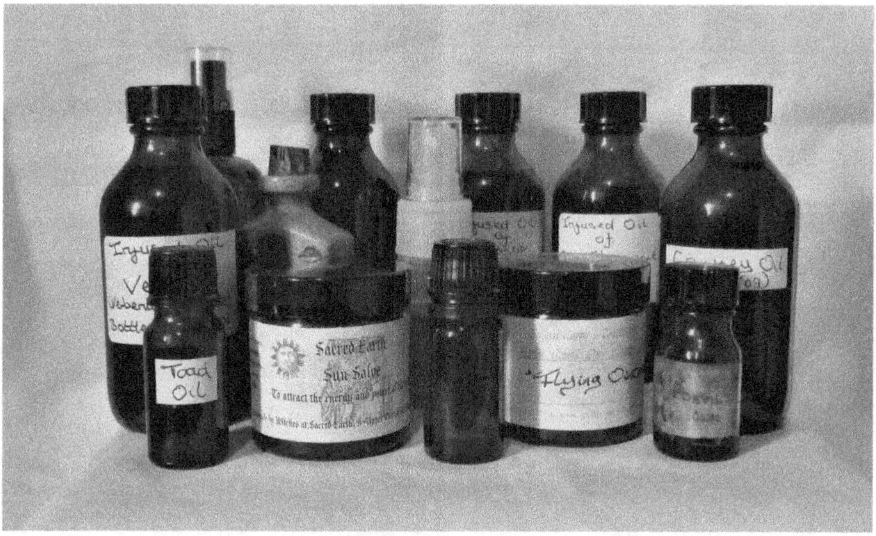

Above: Infused oils, lotions, creams, salves and sprays.

Below: Amatory charms.

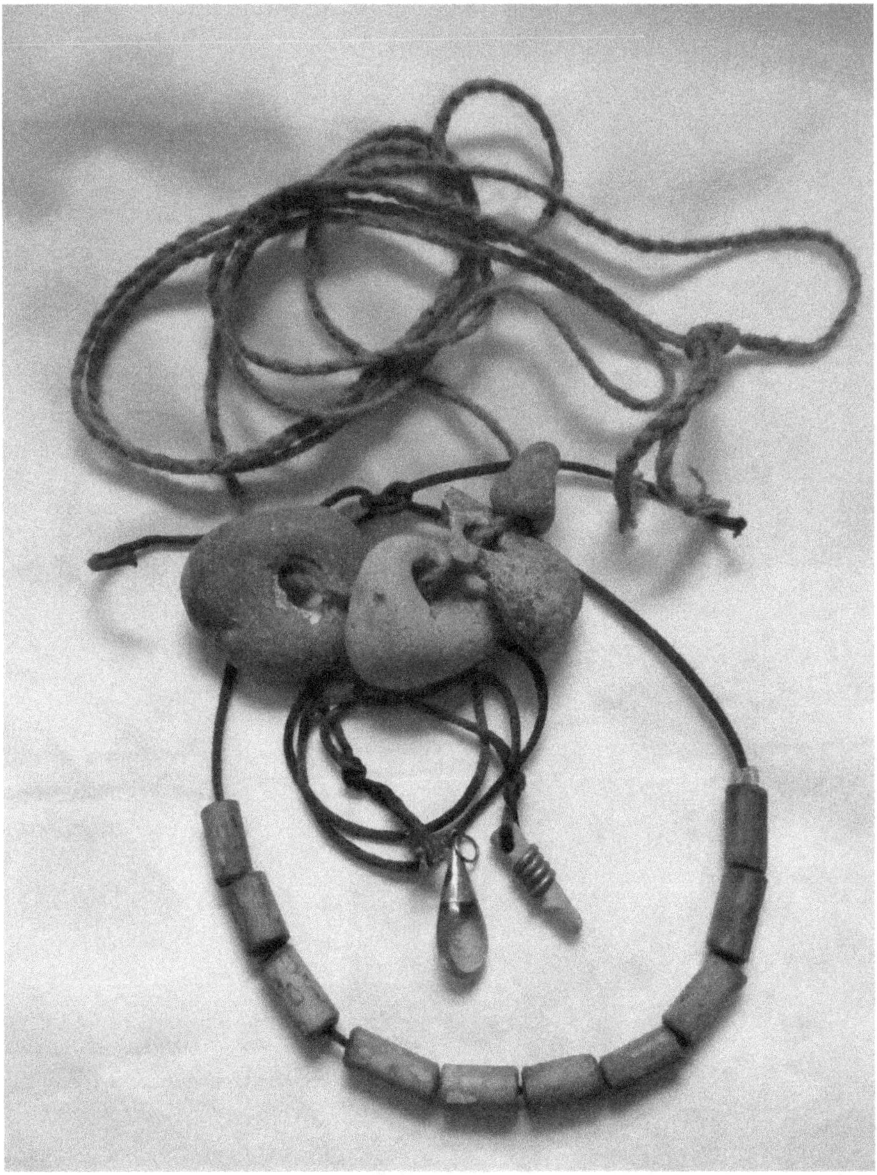

Strung cord charms for personal protection.

Above: Horseshoe and related charms for safeguarding livestock and wild creatures.

Left: Charm for protection on long car journeys.

Facing, top: Stone, shell, flint and bone; natural materials for making magic.

Facing, below: Herbs, gums, resins and oils for the incense-maker's craft.

Facing top: The Path of the Moon.
Facing below: A hearth rite for the Household Spirits.
Above top: The witch-ball.
Above: An example of the Cord Cage.

Hollow tree base; a contact point with the Elvenkind.

Facing top: A hearthside rite to honour the ancestors.

Facing above: Examples of God statues in the author's collection. The carved wooden figure is an example of the work of Bel Bucca.

Facing below: A rite to the Horned God, bringer of Illumination.

Right: Front and reverse of a stoneware "Earth Mother" figure in the author's collection.

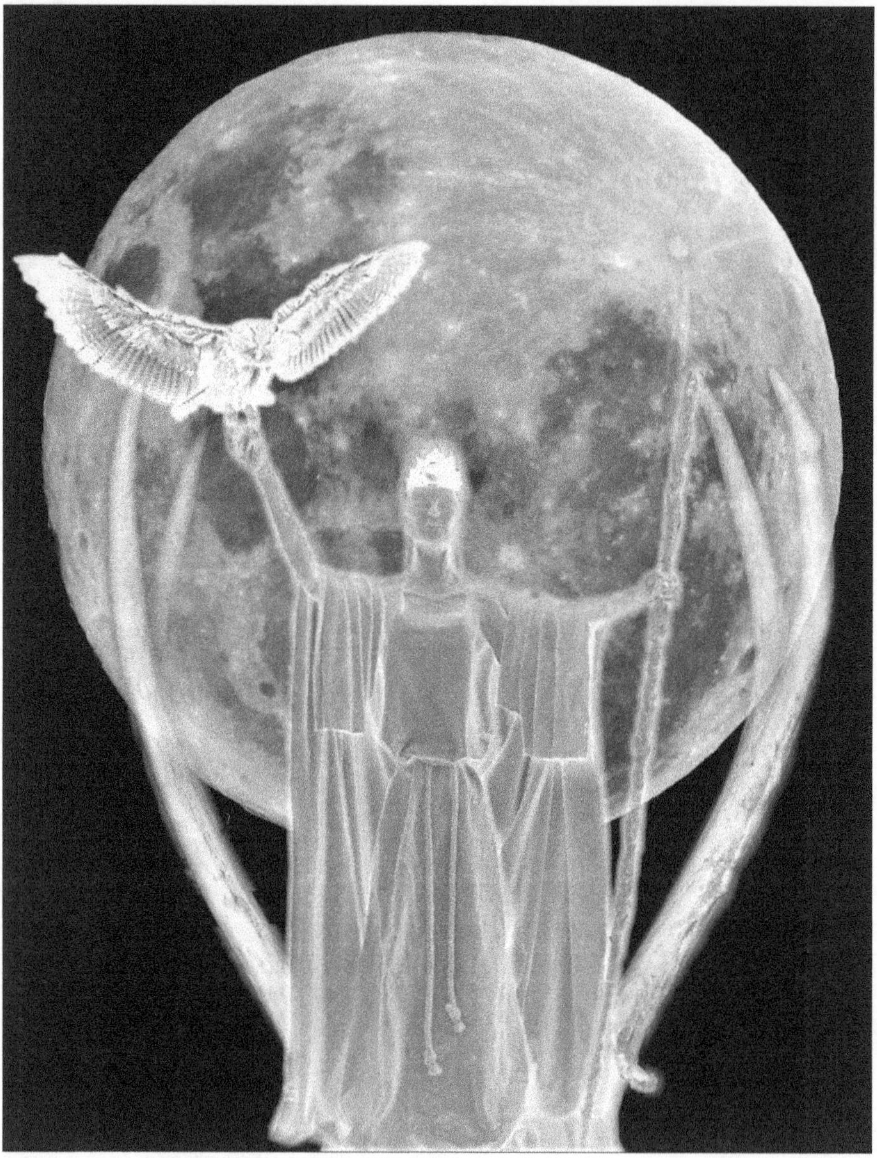

Resolving the Opposites!

Placing the Awareness

Once you are fairly competent at the increased control over your breathing and the greater sharpness of mind it brings, you can begin to practice placing your awareness in different locations. This will be of great benefit later on when you begin trance working proper, or wish to project yourself into other realms of being. To begin with it is best to keep this close to home, i.e. parts of your own body. This is for two reasons; it will teach you how much – or little – you know about your own physical vehicle and will also prevent any involuntary projections to places you may not be familiar with – and from which you may have difficulty returning! Begin this exercise with the basic circle-cross, then a short session of complete breathing, either sitting in a comfortable position, or lying down.

Choose a part of your body; it can be anywhere you like, but best to avoid any major organs. Pick something like a knee, elbow or shoulder. Try to focus your awareness on it; such that you can feel what is actually going on there, not what you think is going on. It is useful to remember here that we are not *thinking* of an area of the body and seeing a picture of it in our mind, but placing our awareness there. The difference will become obvious as you progress. Try to be aware of what is going on; can you really feel the texture of the skin, the flow of the blood, the beat of the pulse, the movement of the joint? Are you really there? Reactions will vary from person to person, obviously, but most people become aware either of a tingling or "buzzing" sensation when they have successfully placed their attention in a particular spot, or else a slight tightening of the muscles in that area. You may not be conscious of it at the time, but will usually become aware of loosening the muscles after the exercise. Both of these are good signs and show that you are making progress. This is one reason that we do not focus on major organs whilst practising, as we may inadvertently affect their function – and you wouldn't want to turn your heart off would you!? Try this practice as often as you can, moving on to doing it in everyday life as well as in quiet moments when you are lying or sitting still. It's fairly easy to do when you are doing nothing else, but much harder when you have the world around you. Once you feel fairly competent at placing your attention at a single location, try moving it around your body to multiple locations and feel the differences in the varying places. What are the differences, what does it feel like when you are actually *moving* your awareness, is there a difference in this feeling as opposed to staying in one place? As you can probably see, all this is preparing you to be able to shift your attention and focus in other realms but, if you can't do it in this one, what hope have you of doing it in a world that you are *not* familiar with? We shall now move on to the next step of the preparation and that is the practice of seeing in a place where you are not physically present.

Visualisation

This is probably one of the two greatest tools in the Witch's armoury, the other being the power of the Will (or, in many cases that I know of in the Craft, sheer, bloody-mindedness! However, the results are the same). If you can visualise something accurately and strongly enough, you are more than half way to achieving it or being there. All the modern techniques of "creative thinking" and "seeing to achieve" or "positive realisation" are all based on this and it is nothing more than good old-fashioned Witch magic! Now, there are a lot of people who say that they cannot visualise, cannot see pictures in their head – piffle! Everyone can! If you couldn't visualise making a cup of tea, you would become very thirsty. If you couldn't see yourself clothed, then it might be rather embarrassing for you or the people around you. To be able to do something, we – all of us – have to be able to visualise it first. When people say that they can't do this, they just mean that they do it so often without thought that it's not a conscious thing and they don't realise it. The point is in bringing it on to a conscious level, directing and focusing it into the areas or places that we wish to visit or things we wish to achieve. And this takes practice!

By now you should be fairly confident at focusing and placing your awareness around your body, having cultivated a clear and sharp mind with the aid of correct breathing. You are now going to learn to place your awareness *outside* of yourself, in locations both near and far, but still in this world. It is better if you begin with a place or an object that you know well; something that you have an emotional attachment to - whether you love it or hate it is up to you, as long as there is a connection there. Choose this object and place it in a location that you cannot see from where you will be practising, or pick a place where you will not be, but that is still fairly close. Make sure that you will not be disturbed for a while and get yourself comfortable, performing the basic circle-cross and an initial few rounds of complete breaths, consciously (because, of course, by now you will be breathing this way all the time sub-consciously).

Relax and see in your mind's eye the place or object that you have chosen. Forget the fact that you cannot "see", just do it. Pick up the object or slowly walk around the location and examine it in as much detail as you can manage. Remember the feelings and sensations that you experienced when you were placing your awareness at different areas around your body and draw on this now. It is not enough to just picture the object or place; you must actually *feel* as if you are really there and experience it in the same way. Try to remember as much detail as you can and file this away for future reference. Don't over-exert yourself to begin with; ten minutes will suffice at the start and you can lengthen this as you become more proficient.

Once you have finished the exercise, do the circle-cross again and have a few deep breaths. Now, go to the place or object you visualised and examine it closely with your physical eyes. Be brutally honest with yourself here, as there is no room for self-deception if you are to be successful in this. Did you see everything correctly? Did you see the marks or dents or colours on the object accurately? Is everything in the location in the same place that you saw it in the visualisation? You need to check all these details as, if you did not see correctly, then all you were doing was remembering the object or place and not focussing your awareness there. This is why you need to draw on the feelings you experienced when placing your attention around your body – you can then tell if you are being successful or not.

This practice can be quite difficult for a lot of people and it is only through hard work and diligent application that you will become any good at it. It must be practised however, as it is one of the vital building blocks of future Craft working and one that will be necessary for more developed work. Take your time and don't rush. Enjoy the experience and look forward to your sessions. Before you know it you will be placing your awareness in all sorts of strange places – and being very accurate with it too.

Once you have mastered the technique for the physical world, you can attempt a non-physical location and I will finish this section with a short visualisation journey to what some call "The Otherworld Garth". This is a place between the worlds, which is yours alone, that you create by the power of your visualisation and will; none may enter, physically or otherwise without your express permission and where you may simply re-charge your batteries, or have encounters with other beings that you may like to call or invite to it. Do not use it, however, as a kind of "spiritual bolt-hole" when times are hard, as it is part of the Craft ethos to face problems and sort them out, not run away and hide from them!

(A note on Visionary Journeys. These are sometime called "pathworkings" or "guided journeys", but essentially amount to the same thing, in that they are scripted, or semi-scripted descriptions of journeys that the individual begins by visualising them, which then take on a life of their own, within their own realm. The key here is that they *do* take on a life of their own; otherwise it is all pure imagination. I am aware that some Traditional Witches find these practices anathema and condemn them, considering them nothing more than New Age platitudes and self-absorbed imaginings. All I can say to this is that these techniques have been a part of my training in the past and I know that they have been and are used by many experienced, powerful and well-respected Crafters in their work today and have been by Old Crafters in the past. There is one important point to be made here though and that is that these techniques *can* be nothing more than self-absorbed imaginings if not performed properly, with discipline and discernment. As we have already seen, focus and attention are *all* in these practices and without them you will get nowhere. A properly performed visionary journey should and will take on a life of its own in the performing of it. At some point as you go along, you will be aware that it is not you visualising in your imagination, but that the journey has become real, in its own world, on its own level. The colours you see will become brighter and more vivid; the smells, sounds, tastes and feels that you experience will all be alive and valid; the Beings that you meet and converse with will be real Beings and you will *know* that it is not your imagination. If this does not happen then you have not achieved your goal and you should try again later with improved focus and attention).

"The Otherworld Garth"

This is a visionary journey to find and create your own place in the Innerworlds. This is the individual's own healing/ritual/meditation/learning space, which is accessible to them alone, unless they chose to call/invite some other being to be there. It exists in its own dimension and is just as real as any other place you may chose to visit. Perform the usual preliminaries, including the circle-cross, settle yourself and begin.

Find yourself standing before a heavy and solid looking, ironbound oaken door. The door, which is taller than you and set into an arched doorway, is placed in the middle of a very tall, old brick wall, which gently curves away from you on either side, until it is lost to your vision. Take note of any symbols you may see carved, etched, painted or drawn on the door. They may have relevance for you, now or later. Now, silently will the door to open for you and see it swing softly and silently inwards, on well-oiled hinges.

At your feet you will see the beginnings of a redbrick pathway, leading off into the distance. In the bright moonlight, it runs across lush green meadows for a way and then disappears under the branches of a welcoming, shady woodland, composed, as far as you can see of Oaks, Ash and Thorn. Step onto the path and begin walking towards the wood. The light of an almost Full Moon shines above you and illuminates the path ahead.

As you walk, take in the sights, smells and sounds of your journey; the scent of the grass and the flowers that are growing in it, the colours of the flowers and herbs that you can see, the scent of the herbs that are crushed underfoot as you walk, the sights and sounds of the night birds that fly overhead and sing their roosting songs as you pass. The Moon is shining high overhead and you are filled with a strange light that is almost physical and reaches down into your innermost being. You feel that you are making a journey that is taking you home; back to a place where you really belong and which you have always known.

Looking up and ahead of you, you can see that you are about to enter the wood. The darker shade under the branches looks most inviting and as you step into it, you feel wrapped in a different kind of light, one that is welcoming and comforting. The light around you now changes to one of a shadowy green, with lighter and darker hues glinting off the trees. As you walk, notice the type of tree you are passing, look at the age of the trees, the colours of the leaves and the texture of the bark. Fix these things in your mind. As you walk further into the wood, listen to the rustling in the leaves, of the creatures scurrying in the undergrowth and, once in a while, you catch a glimpse of a larger animal, as it passes through the shafts of moonlight, shining through the gaps in the branches high overhead. You feel no fear, but only welcome, as all around you is alive and thrilling to your presence.

Look ahead and you will see that the path makes an abrupt turning, either to your left or your right, so that you cannot see where it finishes. A feeling of intense excitement and anticipation fills you as you realise you are approaching the goal of your journey. Follow the path onwards and as you turn the corner you can just see ahead of you an opening in the trunks of the trees, a woodland glade that is waiting for you to arrive. Step up to the edge and look around. This is your place, the Otherworld Garth - no one but you may enter, here you may feel safe and secure, able to rest and heal, to learn and experience those things which you wish to know.

Spend some time here now, getting to learn your special place, seeking out its secrets and discovering its joys, feeling what its energies have to offer you. Be at peace in this place for a while...

It is now time to make your return journey. Finish whatever it is you are doing, thank any beings you may have encountered and for now, bid farewell to your special place. You may return here on your own at any time you wish, in perfect safety. Go to the start of the redbrick pathway and begin your journey back. Walk back through the wood, again taking note of your surroundings, see if anything has changed, how does it feel? When you get to the edge of the woodland, walk back through the meadowland. Has anything changed here at all? The scents, sounds, colours perhaps? Continue walking until you come to the oaken door and once more will it silently to open. It swings outwards from you and lets you exit, swinging gently shut behind you. Now just sit quietly and let yourself gradually return to everyday awareness, then perform the basic circle-cross and take a few complete breaths. You then need to make notes on your experiences, anything you have seen, symbols on the door etc. for future reference.

We will now go on to look at various, personal power accumulating techniques, which can be used in conjunction with the techniques we have already covered and those yet to come.

Accumulating Power

There are two basic reasons for collecting personal power in the sense in which we are talking about it in this book; one is for practical, operative forms of magic and the other is used for altering the Crafter's consciousness. It is the latter with which we are concerned at the moment. It is also here that we will begin to look at that fourth "element" mentioned in the next chapter, "SpiritWorking", that of Fire.

Fire, in this context, is not really seen as an element; indeed, as mentioned elsewhere, many Crafters don't work with "the elements" as such and those that do don't always work with the commonly acknowledged four. The fire we are discussing here is the life-giving, divine spark that was gifted to humankind by the Witch God, the All-Father, at the dawn of time. It is the gift of consciousness and self-awareness and something a bit more than that; it is also the knowledge of the divinity within; the knowledge that where the gods now tread, we also have the ability to tread in time. This is manifested in the human frame – at a physical level – as the sensation of inspired heat. By this I do not mean that you feel hot – although this may happens as a by-product – but that you are aware of an intense, internal warmth, which is at one and the same time almost a physical vibration too. This is akin to the heat felt during sexual arousal and indeed, they both partake of the same source, but are different in kind. It is also similar to, but *not* the same as the Hindu-yogic "kundalini" fire snake, which is said to rise upwards from the base of the spine during certain practices. I need not go further into the question of eastern techniques of mysticism here but suffice it to say that some Traditional

Crafters use techniques similar to some yogis and with the same end in mind. They do not, however, work with the so-called "chakras", so beloved of the modern New Age movement, but it is acknowledged that there are indeed certain points in the human physico-etheric body at which certain types of energy are focused and can be worked with.

However, let us return to our current theme. The internal force of the human body can be aroused, intensified and focused by various practices, a few of which we will look at now. The previously described techniques of focus and concentration must already have been pretty well mastered for the following techniques to work with any great effect. The first practice is deceptively simple, but can bring about quite profound shifts in both power levels and consciousness; another reason for mastering the preceding techniques of both personal protection and focus. (Note: Some people are put off or disturbed by the use of the term "power", seeing it as having connotations of oppression, subversion and dominance. I obviously mean nothing of the sort here, referring purely to the force that is variously known as Virtue, Mana, Od, Vril or simply just energy. It is a fact that, like it or not, Witches have always sought power but it is the sort of power that comes from within and can be used constructively for various magical and spiritual purposes - "borrowed" or "loaned" from the spirits or deities that we work with, it is paid for in some form afterwards. It is not sought as having power "over" someone or thing as Crafters are not interested in that sort of thing. Likewise the terms "energy" and "energy raising" are looked upon askance by some modern Traditionals, as smacking too much of neo-pagan terminology and practice. I would say, what's in a name? The practicalities are the same whatever you call them; some people just prefer different terms. I have attempted here, then, to keep to a traditional terminology, whilst acknowledging that people use different words to mean the same things).

Arousing the Internal Fire

Perform the circle-cross as previously, to your own satisfaction. Light a single candle and place it at about eye level as you seat yourself comfortably. Perform a few complete breaths before you begin. Now, bring your attention to focus on the candle flame, until you are aware of little else. See only the flame and think of nothing but the flame. You will now take nine focused, complete breaths. On the inhalation you will visualise taking the light of the flame into your chest. On the exhalation you will visualise sending this flaming light throughout your entire body. On completion of the nine, complete breaths, close your eyes and visualise a fire, like an old-fashioned blacksmith's forge, at the very centre of your being. Place your focus on this fire and continue the complete breathing, sending the fire around your body. Hold this visualisation for as long as you feel comfortable.

The first few times you try this, you may feel nothing at all, but gradually you will become aware of some effect. The results will be different for each individual, but you may expect one or more of the following; you may feel yourself becoming warmer and warmer, as if you had just eaten a very hot curry, but without the usual sweating; you may begin to feel yourself become sexually aroused, achieving erection if you are male, engorgement if female (this tends to fade as you proceed, however); you may find different parts of your body become very warm or more sensitive and your attention focused there; you may find sudden insights occurring on the nature of the divine fire which were previously unknown to you. These and other effects are perfectly normal. Continue with this exercise for as long as you feel comfortable with it, then, slowly and gently, allow the heat and visualisation of the forge to subside. Never end this type of practice abruptly as it may cause damage, both physically and mentally, if you suddenly change levels of power and awareness. You took time to build up to this level, so you need to wind back down gently. When you are ready, open your eyes and take a few more complete breaths, this time focusing on a cooling effect, just to re-adjust your system (not too cold though!). Blow out the candle, stand up and perform the Circle-Cross to re-equilibrate yourself and go and have something to eat and drink. You will probably feel very energised after this experience, so try to put it to some good, practical use as a counterbalance to the mystical exercise. Dig the garden or help a neighbour with their shopping!

As I have said, it may take some while for you to feel any particular effects with this exercise; be patient and continue to practice until you do. Once you can feel the effects, it is relatively easy to produce them at will, without using the candle, with some concentrated breathing and focused visualisation. This technique may then be used to increase your own power for any magical workings you may wish to do, or as a preparatory to any trance workings that are needed.

Once you are fairly competent at producing the feelings that tell you your own internal force has been increased, it is then time to practice directing it to the desired aim or end. For magical purposes, directing the energy would generally be done using a staff or wand, via the hands.

A simple exercise is as follows:

Raise your internal fire to a level with which you are comfortable and which does not exhaust you. By focused visualisation and will, direct the energy up to your chest, along your arms and into your hands. Bring your hands together with a sharp clap and begin to rub your palms together, as if you were rolling a stick between them (like kindling a fire!). You will soon feel an intense heat begin to build up between your palms and you should keep this up until you can stand the heat no longer. At this point, pick up your wand, staff or stang and channel the energy into the tool, sending it out the other end, in the direction of your intent. This should be done as a quick, shooting out of energy – like a blast – filled with the intent of the working. No long, drawn out invocations or spells, just *see* what you wish to happen and send the power on its way. Again, much practice is required to reach a proficient level, but most people can achieve this with dedicated work. Once a Crafter has reached this stage of course, it should be obvious that the staff or wand is no longer actually needed, a simple gesture sufficing to send the focussed will of the witch on its way.

The point of this present work, however, is in entering the Twilyte realms using the power raised to enable us to do this - to effect a change in consciousness in other words. Before we look at techniques that are designed to do this expressly, there is one main technique that almost all Crafters employ or would recognise which is a sort of halfway stage between gathering force and entering a trance state and we shall look at this now.

Treading the Mill

Also referred to as 'Pacing the Mill', 'Treading the Round' or 'Working the Mill', this is one of the basic techniques of Traditional Craft and the term can also be used to mean CraftWorking in general. As with most things in the Craft, it is apparently very simple in practice, but quite profound in its effects. In essence, the practice involves treading, or pacing, a circle around a fixed point in the centre, all the while keeping your eyes focused on the central point. In other words, you are walking round in a circle, with your chest facing forwards, but your head turned to one side to focus on the centre of your Mill. This focal point may be a natural feature in the landscape, such as a tree stump or standing stone, or may be one that you have placed there yourself, such as your Stang/ Staff or a fire you have lit. The focus will depend on the intent of the rite and what is available. Remember the Craft is always practical, so if you haven't got what you ideally want, use something else. The direction of your treading will also be dependent upon the rite you are working. As mentioned elsewhere, if the rite is purely for celebratory reasons, then the tread would normally be clockwise or sunwise; if for magical or other practical reasons, the tread would normally be widdershins or anti-clockwise. The currents set up by the different directions of pacing may have a direct effect on the purpose and use of the Mill, but have no moral or ethical connotations in themselves. This practice may be performed indoors or out and is equally effective, whether in a fully prepared compass or not. Depending on the reason for the working, it may sometimes be better not to hallow a compass, but to use a naturally occurring circle within the landscape; as ever, it all depends!

Here I would like to note that it has been commented to me that a mill would not normally be trod just to deliberately increase the force in the compass or otherwise to "raise the energies"; it would normally be done to alter the consciousness of the Crafter, whilst focussing it intently upon the work in hand. Whilst agreeing with this comment, it must also be said that, by the mere fact of treading the round, the power in the compass is automatically and naturally increased and, hence, is available for any magico-spiritual purpose that the Crafter wishes to put it to. Again, these things happen independently of our volition, but a canny Crafter makes use of whatever they can, wherever they can!

So, how does one go about "Treading the Mill"? Let us assume that you wish to increase your energy and to create a light trance state, for the purposes of contacting the local Land spirits. You would go to your accustomed working place outdoors and having performed all the usual courtesies, place your Stang upright at the centre of the working area. In this case you would hallow the compass first, purely to create a liminal area for contact with the spirits. Lightly increase your internal force, (although it would automatically become raised by this technique anyway), concentrating on your intent and starting from the north, begin to tread the inside edge of the compass, in a widdershins direction. Turn your head to the left so that you can place your focus on the Stang in the centre, but keep your body facing forward in the direction you are going. You may wish to intone some form of chant to reinforce your purpose – and most people find this helps – but keep it simple and softly voiced; there is no need to shout! Keep your tread at a steady pace to begin with - a slightly slower than usual walking pace is good – and your eyes focused on the Stang as you tread round. As you go, you will gradually find that your internal power begins to increase and you can feel yourself becoming warmer; this will not be due to the physical exercise alone, as this is minimal. You will also find that you will naturally begin to enter a light trance state, where you become more relaxed, your focus becomes more acute, your mind becomes clearer and your purpose sharper.

From this point on, the rite tends to take care of itself and you will find that you have little conscious control over what takes place; just go with the flow. As with most rites in Traditional Craft, once you have reached the actual working stage, where things are beginning to happen, if you can consciously direct what is going on, then you're not doing it right, or it just isn't happening! Practice at letting go is just as important as knowing how to keep control. In this instance, you will come to no harm as you have called on the local Land spirits and they will only come if they are interested in you; if not, they just won't be available for contact. You may experience them in any number of ways; by direct sight, either as recognisable forms or maybe shifting patterns of light or colour at the edge of vision; by "sensing" their presence and communication; by direct apprehension as if of mind to mind, or in various other ways. Your Treading of the Mill may or may not have spontaneously come to an end by now but if not, once you are aware of what you are doing again, cease pacing and sit down. Hallow some food and drink to take and share with the spirits, then clear away and depart.

It is difficult to say how any one individual will experience treading the mill, as all are different, as are the reasons for working the rite. The time it takes to perform the rite is also very flexible; all one can do is start and see where it goes. It will end in its own time, be that half an hour or three. From my own experience I can say that the results and effects vary markedly from occasion to occasion. For example, at one time I was treading the mill, intending no more than a gentle contact with the Land at the time of Michaelmas. The pace became quicker and quicker as time went on, until I found myself practically whirling round the Stang, with the distinct impression of running with a pack of hounds. At another time, I was building up to a concerted attempt at entering a certain realm, with the aim of contacting a specific Being and "all" that happened was a feeling of great languor and I was left with a gentle, fading chuckle in my inner ear. All you can do is start and see where you are led... but that's half the fun!

I shall now go on to look at some techniques specifically designed to induce trance and to enable us to enter the Twilyte Realms.

Trance Working

The Traditional Craft uses many different techniques to induce trance and enter altered states of consciousness, as it is often referred to these days. One could almost say that there are as many techniques as there are practitioners, as entering the twilyte realms is an intensely and deeply personal thing. All people are individuals and, perhaps, Crafters more so because of their calling, so it stands to reason that what works for one individual may not be suitable to another. Also, each individual's reason for entering upon trance work may be radically different to any other's, hence they will use widely differing techniques. There are, however, some techniques that are generally used and widely recognised amongst Crafters and I will describe a few of them here.

Gazing

One of the simplest techniques to learn – but by no means productive of the least results – is the technique of 'Gazing". This is sometimes called "Fascination", but this really refers to mirror-working proper and I will come on to that later. In its basic form, this technique can mean nothing more than looking at an object or action to the exclusion of all else and hence producing an introverted attention, which leads on to contact with other realms – or *the* Other Realms. It is ideally suited to contact with the spirits or denizens of the realms of Nature, what are often called "Elementals". The technique relies on holding the focus of the eyes, whilst allowing the mind free reign to travel elsewhere. I shall describe a simple version of it.

Find a secluded place where you are unlikely to be disturbed for a while, beside a running stream or brook, preferably one that has a pebbly bottom, on a bright, sunny day. Seat yourself comfortably beside the stream, making sure you are unlikely to fall in should you reach a deep state of trance. Focus your attention on the water as it flows by and the sunlight as it plays upon the ripples of the water, running and tumbling over the stones on its way. Do not *stare* at the water, just simply let your sight rest gently on its surface and be entertained by the play of light. Gradually you will find yourself falling into a gentle state of reverie, a sort of half-awake, half-asleep state but still retaining control over your volition (which is basically what a trance is anyway), whereby you may now turn your mind to the subject or realm you wish to investigate. Shift your focus of attention to the area you are interested in and proceed. It may be that you begin by constructing for yourself a simple journey, or what many people would call a daydream, but with the focused will and attention of the trained Crafter, this will certainly take on a greater reality and significance than that. Perform what needs to be done and, once you have found out what you have sought, you may simply retrace your steps and bring yourself around, or, if you feel secure enough, you may allow yourself to fall asleep, there to go further perhaps on your quest. Either way, you will naturally come around at some point and there is no need to fear being "caught" in some other realm.

This technique can just as easily be used by gazing at the branches of trees, gently swaying in a breeze, or clouds slowly floating by in an otherwise clear sky. Experiment with what works best for you and then work to better your technique.

Swinging and Swaying.

Although these are separate techniques, both methods rely on rhythmic body movements to achieve their purpose. Whereas in the previous method, we relied upon the movement of some natural object to hold the focus of attention, it is our own bodies that we move here, whilst keeping the mind still and focussed. The body movement relaxes the mind and allows it to reach the trance state we desire.

The technique of Swinging is exactly what it sounds like - sit on a swing and go backwards and forwards!

However, the swinging is done with intention and with full knowledge of what we intend to achieve. Slightly more difficult than the previous method, in that we have to put more effort in ourselves, it is nonetheless rewarding and quite a bit more fun! Again, find yourself a secluded spot (with a swing – if not make one!), where you are unlikely to be disturbed for some time. Sit on the swing and push off, establishing a gentle rhythm; you want to go at a decent rate, but not so fast that you fly off. At first, focus on the swinging, backwards and forwards, backwards and forwards, up and down, up and down, until you begin to feel that slight detachment that is characteristic of the beginnings of the trance state. Now, here's the tricky part. At one and the same time, you need to carefully decelerate the swinging motion as well as shifting your focus on to what you are entering the trance for. Of course, you could just carry on swinging, but then you risk falling off and ruining everything, not to mention possibly transporting yourself to the Otherworlds permanently via a cracked skull. So, slow down to just a slow swing, which will gradually wind down of its own accord and follow the path that you have laid out for yourself, or let yourself be carried away by whatever contact you have made. As previously, you will be perfectly able to come back when you are ready, because you are in full control.

Using Swaying (sometimes also called Rocking), as a method of trance induction is both easier and more difficult. Easier in that you can do it anywhere and don't have to have a swing, more difficult in that you have to put a bit more effort in, again. Find somewhere comfortable to sit, where you have room to move backwards and forwards (side to side also happens sometimes spontaneously, but is less usual); a chair is fine if you sit on the edge, a stool or the floor/ground is better (there's less far to fall if you get it wrong as well!). Get comfortable and begin a gentle backwards and forwards motion, to a timing and rhythm that suits you. Most people like to chant with this one, or otherwise a gentle humming to oneself can work wonders. In addition to, or as an alternative to this, tapping two stones or bones together to make a rhythmic "ticking" sound, or gently clapping your hands together can also help to deepen the trance experience. (Many Crafters find that by performing the tapping and/or humming/chanting, that swaying occurs naturally with little conscious volition. Alternatively, it may spontaneously begin on its own during any rite). Again, continue until you feel the beginnings of the trance, then shift the focus of your attention to where you want to go/what you want to do. You will find that as you go deeper into your work, the swaying will stop on its own accord and you need not worry about it. If you are on the ground and you feel like lying down at that point, go ahead – it's your trance!

With both of the above methods, you may also find that as the rhythm of the swing or the sway gets going, you also feel your inner force rising or getting warmer and also that you may feel an internal vibration or "buzzing" occurring; both of these are perfectly normal and will continue as long as they need to and then fade away. However, by this stage, if you find them at all disturbing, then you should have developed enough control to stop them if you wish to do so.

Tracing the Line

This method involves a lot more focus and concentration on the part of the Crafter, as there are very little in the way of what one could call "tools" to aid in the trance. This involves the use of a pre-prepared diagram/symbol/glyph, usually carved or drawn onto stone or wood. The piece of stone or wood (tablet) is fairly large, about the diameter of a football, to enable the symbol to be of a decent size. These tablets, often called "Troystones" because of the maze-pattern carved on them, are employed like maps to the inner worlds, guiding the Crafter on an otherworld journey. The technique is to sit quietly with the tablet on the lap, increase the inner force and maybe start a gentle swaying motion. The Crafter then places the forefinger of their dominant hand at the beginning of the glyph on the tablet and, with total focus and concentration, traces the line of the symbol to its conclusion, by which time the trance state should have been entered. Repeat this until the desired level of trance is achieved.

Tracing the line can also be accompanied by a short, repetitive chant or charm, as well as the aforementioned humming or droning. The symbols involved are usually maze-like or spiral in nature, hence leading the mind of the Crafter into an ever decreasing focus, the result of which is the entry into the Otherworlds, or wherever it is that the Crafter desires to go. This technique must be performed very slowly, as to trace the symbol quickly would produce no result at all, with total attention to what is being done. It involves quite a few of the techniques and abilities already mentioned in this chapter, bringing them all together in a working praxis.

The Witch's Ladder

The Ladder is a piece of string, ribbon or cord, often the Crafter's own Cord or Girdle, into which have been tied a certain number of knots, beads, stones or other countable objects. It is used like a rosary, passing it through the fingers and counting off the number of times a repetitive chant or verse, determining the nature of the trance, is sung or intoned. If accompanied by a swaying motion to increase the rhythmic feel of the method, a better trance state may be achieved. The number of times that the chant is to be repeated may be decided beforehand, but it is unlikely that this will be adhered to once the trance begins to take hold. It is better to use the counting itself as a rhythmic repetition and let the mind go where it will.

Fascination

We now come to a description of mirror working as previously mentioned. Sometimes called "Scrying", the basics of this technique can be used with a crystal ball or bowl of inky water as well, but this particular method is best used with a mirror. The mirror itself (sometimes called a "Speculum") has often been prepared in a certain way beforehand but this is not strictly necessary and can involve long and complicated procedures. It is a whole area of study in itself and, whilst eminently valid and worth pursuit, does not fit well in a book of this type. I shall therefore not expand on those techniques here, considering that a plain, clear and cleansed mirror, either black-backed or with normal reflective surface, being sufficient in this case, or for the beginner. It is mostly the mind of the Crafter themselves that achieves the work, the mirror and its preparation being a tool that aids the operation.

The following is a description of a technique that was communicated to one of my mentors in the early 1980s by his Otherworld teacher via automatic writing, in my presence, so I am able to personally vouch for its authenticity. This particular instruction has never been published before but, as similar-seeming techniques have in recent years been made public, I feel it right that this version should now see the light of day. I give it here in its original wording, with alterations made only for the sake of grammar and comprehension.

> "Instruction for making an etheric journey for the purpose of enlightenment upon a matter, or for communion with your Master, Goddess or God.
>
> Sit before your astral doorway, or a mirror sufficiently large to reflect your face. Darken the room and place a single, lighted candle beside you in such a manner that it does not reflect in the mirror, or be seen from the corner of your eye.
>
> You now sit relaxed and consider the purpose of the journey whilst looking at your reflection. Focus your attention to your eyes. Do not stare, rather contemplate them and as you watch you will notice a change in your features. This denotes the first change in consciousness, i.e. the mind is dropping to the deeper level. As your mind is allowed to lower still further, it is probable that your features will become grotesque and you will imagine a demon or such is peering at you from the mirror.
>
> Do not waver, for as you progress further the mirror will turn black and no reflection will be visible.
>
> Hold your gaze steadily at this stage because shortly, commencing as a point of light at the centre of your vision, the mirror will become completely illuminated. There will be no reflection of yourself. You will become aware of an open door before you and a pathway ahead. Turn your mind now to the knowledge that you seek, or the entity that you wish to contact and wait for manifestation; or mentally step through the door and proceed along the path.
>
> Although the exercise is in no way dangerous, it is nevertheless best performed in the presence of another who will act as invigilator, should the trancelike state become too deep and the exercise last too long.
>
> If a time is fixed then the invigilator, using a soft voice, will call you back from the Other, the mirror will

cloud over and your reflection will return. Do not move until this has occurred.

This exercise may be conducted by anyone, but it is given for those who are training or who are competent in the Arts and is best performed in Temple or Compass."

I think that explains it all pretty well, without need of further comment from me. You will notice however, that not only does this technique enable the Crafter to achieve a deep level of trance, but also offers the opportunity of projecting the consciousness through the mirror totally. This leads us on to the final section that I would like to discuss in this present chapter.

Soul Flight or Transvection

Sometimes also called "Astral Projection", Transvection is a method of entering the Otherworld that Witches have used for centuries and is one of the true derivations and reasons for the term "Hedge Rider". We have all heard the old tales of Witches flying on broomsticks to the Sabbat, aided by their familiars and demons, cavorting with the Devil all night then returning exhausted in the morning. Alternatively there is the tale of Witches "borrowing" local farmers' horses and "Hag Riding" them through the night, leaving them dripping with sweat and near comatose the next morning. Although fantastical, these tales do have their origin in factual techniques, although far less dramatic than is usually portrayed.

It is a debatable point as to whether the soul of the Crafter actually takes flight or not during transvection, or whether the attention or consciousness is so focused on the flight and arrival at another place that it seems in reality to be so. It matters not, either way, as it is the experience that counts and the knowledge and learning that can be derived from that experience. The whole point of the exercise is to "rise above" yourself and travel to a different realm, there to consort with others, either of your own kind or different, with the aim of advancing your abilities, skill and knowledge. Most of the "higher" knowledge of the Craft is imparted in such a way and it is only those who are capable of developing such advanced skills that are deemed worthy of having that knowledge imparted to them. Not, I might add, by human agencies but by those Beings who keep and guard that knowledge from those who are unworthy of it.

I shall now give two methods of achieving Soul Flight and leave the reader to go as far as they are able with them.

Riding the Stang

Although this technique is called Riding the Stang, the Broom may equally be used and so the comments I shall make may be considered to apply to both.

At the Dark of the Moon, go to your outdoor working site and make the usual courtesies. Hallow your compass, making sure you call upon your guardians. Make the circle-cross before any other actions. Place your Stang (Broom) upright in the centre of the hallowed space and light a small fire or large candle before it. Bearing in mind the prohibition on metal in creating sacred fire, light it with matches, not a lighter, if you are unable to make need-fire. Starting at the north, begin to tread the mill, widdershins, to the following chant:

"Throughout and about, around and around,
Between the worlds my path is found.
Around and around, throughout and about,
I'll traverse the hedge astride my grey mount.

Throughout and about, around and around,
Betwixt and between my true path is wound.
Around and around throughout and about,
I lift myself up and soon shall take flight."

Once you have built up a good feeling of power, take up the Stang and continue to pace, placing the Stang between your legs as you do so. (This may feel somewhat silly or foolish at first, but if you can get over your ingrained self-consciousness, you will realise that it is perfectly practical and traditional. A "gambolling" step is appropriate here). Focus now on the fire in your treading, continuing your chant until you feel the trance state come upon you strongly. When this happens, at the last possible moment, turn back upon yourself and leap over the fire saying with full conviction:

"Across the bridge I now take flight,
Over the hedge and into the night!"

As you land on the other side of the fire, let your mind fly free…

When you have returned to normal consciousness, hallow some food and drink to take and remember to share this with your guardians and the local spirits. Ensure that you are fully back to normal consciousness before clearing away your compass and finally performing the circle-cross.

Night-Journeying

The other main method of Soul Flight is through dreaming. Most people are aware of their dreams, but usually awaken with only vague, scrappy memories, which can often be muddled scenes of two or three separate dreams. The Witch trains him or herself to not only remember in detail each dream, but to dictate the direction and destination of the dream. One of the places where traditionally much lore is to be found and where Otherworld teachers may be met with is within the Hollow Hills, the realm of the Faerie Folk. Many Crafters have sought and received knowledge and inspiration in the realm of the Elven kind and I shall now describe a method whereby their realms may be entered through "the door that hath no key", i.e. through focussed and aware dreaming. (More can be read about the Faerie Folk in the next chapter, "SpiritWorking").

This technique requires a strong control over both the Crafter's powers of attention and also of will. The method entails beginning a journey as you lay down to sleep and in continuing it, with full awareness, once you pass over into sleep. It is at the liminal point between sleep and waking that full attention must be focussed on the journey and where the Soul Flight takes place. Much practice will be necessary with this technique, but the rewards more than justify the effort put in and many Crafters find this to be an excellent way of enriching their knowledge, once learned and mastered.

Do not eat heavily or for several hours before retiring for the night. Many people find that a small pillow full of dried hops and lavender, with a little Mugwort and Wormwood added, helps with this. Just place it under your usual pillow and inhale the aroma as you prepare for your journey. Lie on your back with arms comfortably by your side to start with, take a few complete breaths deliberately and begin the visionary journey. Focus your attention and awareness on the traditional imagery closely and follow the path as it unfolds, through the doors of sleep.

> *"You find yourself seated on a green, mossy bank, beside a gently flowing stream. The sunlight glitters on the ripples as the water flows smoothly by. A large elder tree that grows from the bank nearby, under whose shady branches you are seated, catches your attention. The heady scent of elder blossom drifts by and you inhale deeply. From behind the tree there appears a fine white horse, slowly walking towards you. She is the most beautiful mare you have ever seen and her coat shines and glistens with every step as she approaches. From her gleaming white mane hang tiny silver bells that tinkle softly as they are rocked by her rolling gait. The sound soothes and seems to call you, as, rising from the ground, you walk towards the horse and quietly greet her. You instinctively know that she has come for you and, looking deep into her liquid brown eyes,*

you become aware of a vast intelligence that appears to be beckoning you. The mare tosses her head and snorts, seemingly impatiently and, getting the message, you climb onto her back with little effort. Your milk-white steed dances slightly as you settle yourself, gripping her mane and then she is off. She leaps forward as if shot like an arrow and soars up and over the stream by which you were seated, crossing the further bank in no more than a couple of strides. Once on the further bank, she settles into her stride and begins to eat up the distance with seemingly little effort.

Your steed flies swifter than the wind, over fields and meadows, her hooves barely touching the ground, directly towards the setting sun. The giant orb hangs just above the horizon, emitting an eerie, ruddy glow, bathing the landscape in an eldritch light, as if you were riding through a sea of blood. On and on you ride, crossing seemingly endless tracts of land, your steed never tiring, her breath coming in effortless sighs. You feel no discomfort during this journey and are lulled into a gentle reverie as you rock rhythmically upon the broad back of your wondrous steed, steadily galloping towards the lowering sun. As you travel, the land beneath you gradually changes and, as the sun finally sets, still showering you with its ruddy glow, you see that instead of lush, green pastures, you are now crossing bare, stony earth, which itself gives onto rocky barren ground. Looking up and ahead of you, you can just make out in the distance a divergence in the path that you are following. Your ride is taking you rapidly to a three-way fork in the road.

To the right, the road turns into a narrow track that twists and turns back upon itself, stony and broken, beset with bramble bushes and thorny shrubs. Ahead the road continues as a broad, broad way, with renewed greenery along its sides, dotted with fair flowers and blossoming shrubs. To your left the road narrows slightly, but seems to become smoother and fairer to your eyes, with a soft verdant shimmer, almost as if it were sprinkled with dewdrops on clover. It undulates gently into the distance, where it disappears behind a line of rolling hills. Your magnificent steed does not slow her pace one jot and as she approaches the split in the road, continues galloping on along the left path, without a second's hesitation.

From this point on, your journey seems to take on a remarkable clarity; the air seems fresher and brighter, the light seems clearer and objects appear more defined with sharper edges, not harsh, but you seem able to pick things out with a keener and clearer sight. As your mount continues on its single-minded task, bearing you towards some fateful destination, your thoughts become more defined and well formed, your emotions broader and more all encompassing than they have ever been.

Your milk-white steed begins to slow its headlong rush and you find yourself now passing through the middle of a fair and green garden, set amidst rolling countryside that bursts with a hidden and barely suppressed life of its own. Your path now leads you towards what appears to be a large, regular turf mound, surrounded by gnarled but beautiful old apple trees, both in blossom and in fruit. The mare slows further still and as she finally comes to a stop before the verdant mound, the wind gusts briefly and you hear a sound like a thousand minute, silver bells all pealing at once. The mare shakes her mane and, as if in accompaniment, the tiny bells in her mane ring out, lending a slightly deeper tone to the miniature peal. You slide off your solid mount, apparently unwinded by the seemingly endless journey she has just borne you on and approach the apple trees before the mound. You see that the fruit is ripe and rosy and reach up to pluck one, inadvertently disturbing a row of silver-white bells that were obviously ringing to welcome your arrival previously. They chime again, with an exquisitely beautiful note that echoes right through you, awakening elusive memories that you can't quite grasp.

As the sound begins to die away a crack appears in the mound before you and begins, slowly to widen. As you watch, intrigued and excited rather than apprehensive, the crack grows larger and larger until it opens upon a narrow but high passageway, stretching into the interior of the mound. You step forward unhesitatingly; still grasping the apple you have plucked and peer into the semi-gloom ahead.

In the distance you can make out a vague light, as if at the end of a tunnel and a faint noise, as if of merry-making and feasting. The sound is hugely enticing and you find yourself stepping confidently along the passage to the far end, both the light and the sounds becoming stronger as you progress. Further you go and a strange eagerness to reach the end of the passage almost overwhelms you when suddenly, a large shape steps forward and blocks most of the light, appearing as a silhouette at the very end of the tunnel. You stop suddenly and stare ahead. The shape seems to be that of a tall, statuesque woman, standing with her back to the light, so that she is little more than an outline to your eyes. Slowly she raises her left hand and beckons, once, slowly, then lays her palm flat, as if inviting you to give something to her. You remember the apple that you plucked at the entrance to the passage, still in your hand and step willingly forward, towards the waiting figure..........."

From this point on you are on your own journey and what happens will be unique to you alone. You must use all the abilities you have learned so far to remember what happens when you awake in the morning, as you will surely have learned more than mortal words can convey.

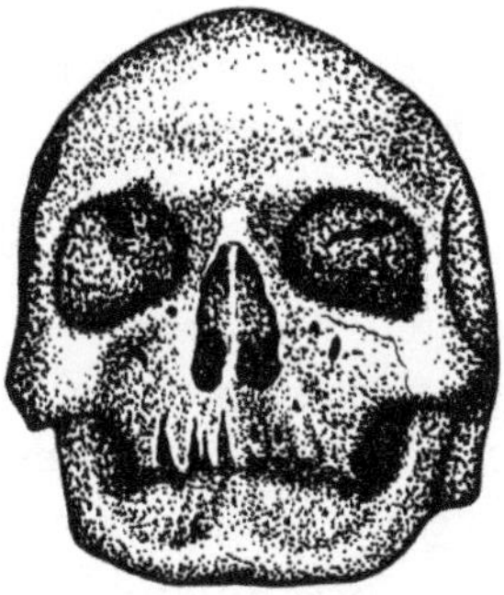

SPIRITWORKING

The world of Traditional Craft is a world that is filled with spirits on all levels. SpiritWorking is an everyday occurrence – some would say practicality – for the traditional Crafter and one that is often taken in one's stride, but never overlooked. To the Witch, spirits are encountered everywhere; everything that exists has a spirit, a form of individual life and intelligence and is to be treated as such with respect and honour. This is a legacy of part of the Craft's origins in the days of animism, when everything was not only considered to have its own spirit, but also needed placating in case it caused harm. Those days are no longer with us, but echoes of the old days can still be heard in some Craft working.

When I talk about "SpiritWorking" in this context, I am not just talking about communicating with beings from other realms as well as ours, although this is a large part of it, I am also talking about working with the spirit that inhabits the Crafter and this will be one of the subjects covered, however briefly, in this chapter. One of the first rules of the Craft, indeed of all serious magical working, is "Know Thyself" and nowhere is this more important than when encountering beings from other realms. One must know oneself inside out and be able to react in a manner of full awareness, as not all encounters with the Otherworlds will be straightforward and knowledge of one's abilities, strengths and weaknesses in dealing with the situation could be essential. This is not to say that every encounter with a spirit will be life threatening, but the potential is always there for some life-changing experiences and this is worth acknowledging.

It is also worth remembering that the morals, values, attitudes and rules of our world are highly unlikely to hold sway in the realms that non-human spirits inhabit; indeed, why should they? Just as there are natural laws, common and agreed rules of communication and interaction within our cultures and lifestyles, so will there be in other realms. Our rules of engagement seem natural and second-nature to us, as will theirs to them; they will not necessarily be the same, however. Denizens of other worlds will not necessarily react in the same way that we do, but this does not mean that they are threatening or malignant, just that different rules apply in their world and they are reacting according to their own rules and natures. This must be remembered and borne in mind in any contact with the Otherworlds and our responses must be appropriate for the situation.

I have divided this chapter into separate sections, dealing with different types of spirit in each. However, please do not think that these divisions are hard and fast, as they are not and are somewhat arbitrary on my part. The world of spirits is not locked into strict compartments and it is often quite difficult to determine where any type of spirit belongs. For example, is a nature spirit a type of Faerie, or is a Faerie an Ancestor? Is a Familiar a type of separate spirit, or is it part of the individual that calls it? Depending on the spirit and the individual, all of these categorisations can be right, so don't go getting fixed ideas about what belongs where, as something is liable to come up behind you and bite you on the rear! However, for all intents and practical purposes the following categorisations will suffice; you can decide for yourself otherwise as your experience and knowledge grows.

Spirits of the Natural World

Most people who have any magical learning will be used to the idea of the division of magical areas into the four elements of classical thinking - namely Earth, Air, Fire and Water. A lot of practitioners of Traditional Craft use this approach, but a lot also do not and use what I like to think of as an earlier system, that was current in North and Western European Lands prior to the classical one. This system uses Land, Sea and Sky as its divisions and can be seen in the oath purportedly used by some of the European Iron-Age peoples and tribes, namely; "I will keep faith until the Sky falls upon me and crushes me, until the Land opens up and swallows me, until the Seas arise and overwhelm me." A totally natural approach to the world in which they were living and one which still holds true today if you are working your magic with a natural attitude in mind. Many people will now say, "Well, where has the element of Fire gone to?" In this system of classification, Fire is seen to be of divine origin, not an element, as mentioned previously and so is looked upon in a different way. This area will be discussed further in the last chapter.

Land Spirits

As well as the problem of categorisation of spirits, there is also the problem of what they are called. The Traditional Craft is not a homogeneous entity and has many regional variations; hence, the names used in one part of the country will be unknown in another, even if the spirit is the same. In the case of Land spirits they are variously called Dobbies, Boggarts, Spriggans, Knockers, Gnomes, Dwarves, Wights, Pucks and many others far too numerous to mention. I am reminded here of another name that comes from my own childhood. Growing up in rural Suffolk, my family knew an old gentleman by the name of Albert Hammond – Bert to us. Now, although I was born not 20 miles from where he lived, Bert had such a strong local accent that I could barely understand a word he said and he loved to play on this. One of the names he would often call me was a "little Woozle" and I just assumed that it was his pet name for me. It wasn't until many years later that I discovered that it was a very local name for a small, hairy fellow, reputed to haunt the woods and heaths thereabouts; a local Land sprite in fact. Due to my short stature and shock of wild and unruly hair (now alas much reduced!), Bert had equated me with the local sprite and named me for him – Woozle. I'm still quite proud of that even after all these years. However, I digress. For the purposes of this chapter I shall use the term Wight, then we will all know where we are.

Whatever its ultimate origin, a Wight is a manifestation of the energies of any given place, in individualised form. You can have Wights of the Land, of individual trees and plants, of mountains, woods and valleys. They are generally protective and guardian spirits who tend to and minister to the needs of the area/plant/tree/piece of land that they are attached to; indeed, they are often the actual spirit *of* the land/tree etc. They can appear in many different guises, and are prone to all kinds of shapeshifting, but are more often than not seen or perceived as male or neuter in gender. However, there is a definite exception to this rule and that is the appearance of the beings known as "White Lady's". These may, or may not, be classed as Land Wights, as many people see them as the direct expression of the Land Herself, Mother Earth if you like, in a localised form. Be that as it may, if you encounter one of these beings, be especially polite.

It will be rare to see or experience a Wight without a lot of patience and effort on the part of the Witch, unless it is an accidental meeting. They are generally very wary of humankind and are not quick in coming forward to forge relationships. As their roles generally involve guardianship of a piece of land or plant, the destruction wreaked by humans on the natural world does not generally endear us to them. However, there are ways of making contact with them and from this contact, the Crafter can gain valuable knowledge and information about the deeper workings of the natural world.

Wight Tracking

The idea of this practice is to introduce the individual into the environment of the Land Wights, in a way that may endear him or her to them and encourage the Wights to appear or acknowledge the individual's presence or existence in some way. this is best performed at dawn or dusk.

Dress according to the season in some natural fabrics and colours, so that you do not stand out in your environment, be that woodland, heathland, moor or mountainside. Take your stang or staff with you and go to the area that you have chosen to make contact with the Wights. The attitude that you must bear in mind is that of a hunter; you will be stalking your "prey" in the wild, just as our ancestors did, not too long ago, but with a different intent. You wish to *encounter* not capture and kill your "prey". This will be more difficult than killing, as your "prey" is wily, skilled and at one with its environment, so you must be likewise.

Begin your tracking by taking a path into your chosen landscape. Step lightly on the earth, but do not tiptoe or crouch down; a gentle walk will do. It is the attitude that counts here. You must be as aware as you possibly can of everything that is happening around you, use all your senses to experience your journey. Smell the wind, taste the breeze, hear all the sounds around you, touch the earth/trees/bushes as you walk and take everything in with your eyes. You must be totally aware. At the same time, you must still all "dialogue" in your head; cease to think of anything at all (as far as possible), and just experience. You may begin by inducing a light trance as described in the previous chapter, if you so wish, but this "wide open" approach will encourage one anyway. Walk at a slow but steady pace, making as little impact on your surroundings as you can. As you progress – and this may take some time, so be prepared – your senses may gradually become overloaded and "shut down", until only one or two are left. You may feel that your hearing is tuning out and that you can no longer smell anything, but that your sight is becoming more and more acute in your surroundings. Or perhaps your sight and hearing are beginning to fade and your sense of smell is sharpened to extraordinary levels. Just go with whatever happens and "follow your nose" so to speak.

If you are lucky, it is at this point that you may become aware of one, or more, of the Land Wights of your location. They may present themselves to you in many different ways, but do not be alarmed, they are not generally actively hostile to humans and can often be just as curious as we are. When you are aware of a presence, stop your tracking and either sit down or stand still. Let whatever happens happen, but do not try to analyse it. You should by this point be in a mild trance state and not wholly in the everyday world, so normal rules may not apply. Do not approach the Wight; let it approach you if it chooses to.

Communication may occur, but is unusual on a first encounter, which is normally quite brief. Experience it for as long as it lasts, until the Wight draws away or disappears. Then rise, if you are sitting, or turn if you are standing and silently walk back the way you have come, without looking back. As soon as you arrive back at your starting point, or back home, have something to eat and drink (not alcohol), as this will help to "earth" you and bring you entirely back to the realm of everyday life. (If you drove to your location, make sure you are in a suitable state to drive back. It may be wise to pause and have something to eat and drink first before driving).

You may repeat this exercise over and again, to build up a rapport both with your local Land Wights and with the Land itself in your locality. Don't be disappointed if nothing happens the first time – it rarely does – but you will all the time be developing a link that will eventually pay high dividends.

Sea Spirits

Although Land Wights are also concerned with growth, sustenance and preservation are their main concerns. In the case of Sea Spirits, their main area of concern is motion and change or transformation. They are variously known as Selkies, Nykerts, Nixes, Merrows and Kelpies. Like all natural spirits, they have immense power and in the case of Sea Spirits it is nigh on unstoppable. Consider the energy of the Oceans, those huge bodies of water from which all Life, including the Land, has come - the surge of tide and wave that can just as easily destroy as create. Then consider the Beings who embody that power and imagine their strength. Sea Spirits can be gentle or harsh, creative or destructive, but like the Sea itself, implacable once roused. Their energies are intimately connected with the phases of the moon and hence to the tides and the seasons. They move to their own agenda – not ours – and are not easily swayed by the concerns of humankind, though not innately hostile to us. In the true sense of the word, they are "elemental" in nature, ancient as befitting their natural domain and preserve a wealth of memory and knowledge in their beings.

Unlike the Land Wights, they are not so difficult to contact as they share a subtle bond with us that makes it easier. We are creatures of emotion; we too have tides that ebb and flow within us and it is here that we have a connection. It is through our emotions and the subtle flow of the tides that we can come to a common ground and communicate. However, be wary. Just as our emotions can be changeable and unpredictable, how much more so can Beings who have the energetic power of the Sea behind them. Do not anger them, as their ire can be devastating.

The majority of what I have written here can also apply to inland water-systems, such as lakes, ponds, rivers and streams also. Whilst not having as much sheer force behind them as the Oceans and their tides, they still partake of the essential nature of "Water", although after another manner. Working with the fresh-water spirits, sometimes known as Meremayds, can also prove beneficial to the Witch and is obviously easier and more appropriate for people who do not live near a coast, or have easy access to one. However, the same precautions still apply when contacting them and care should still be taken, at least initially).

The Path of the Moon

Make a journey to some fairly isolated seashore, (lake or river), but not so isolated that you may not reach help if you need it. Spend some time walking along the shore and getting to know the "feel" of this particular stretch of coast. A few hours should be sufficient initially, but to gain an intimate knowledge can take a lifetime. Plan to stay for at least a few hours after the Sun sets, so make sure you have what you need for bodily comfort and health. As the Sun sets, make a small camp for yourself on the beach, *above the high water line* and ensure you are comfortable; you are waiting for the Moon to rise and this could take some time, depending on where you are and the time of year. Sit and contemplate the water; see how the waves lap the shore. How far out do they originate? Is there any difference between them? Are some bigger than others, if so, are there a set number of waves in between? Gently let yourself be lulled into a light trance state as you watch the waves and wait for the Moon to rise. (Some people find that a herbal infusion taken at this time can aid them in their work; try Vervain, Mugwort or Wormwood for good effect).

When it does, watch its slow progress, see how graceful it is, see how beautifully it shines and how the light glitters on the surface of the water. See how the light makes a pathway across the water into the far distance, right to the very horizon. Let yourself feel a longing to walk along that pathway, to tread the shimmering, watery road that leads to the horizon. Let yourself be seized with the desire to know what lies at the end of the pathway. *In your inner vision,* rise from your position on the beach and begin a slow tread down to the water's edge. Take your time, there is no hurry. When you reach the shoreline, with the waves gently lapping at your feet, see the silver Path of the Moon stretching away ahead of you. It stretches straight ahead and shimmers beckoningly to you, the argent radiance quickening your desire to see where it goes. You step lightly onto the pathway and begin your journey into the realm of the Spirits of the Sea. As you walk you begin to hear a soft wind sighing around you, which, as it gets stronger, begins to sound like faint voices coming from great depths, all around you…

This exercise can take some time, so allow yourself that time and come back as and when you are ready. It is well to have a little food and drink nearby to ground yourself when you return. What happens when you walk the Path of the Moon, only you and the Spirits of the Sea can know, but by repeated practice, you will begin to build up a bond with these Beings and begin to access their store of knowledge and memory. Try to perform this exercise at different moon phases and different times of year as both you and the Spirits will show different aspects of yourselves and grow there from.

Sky Spirits

If Land Wights are primarily concerned with sustenance and preservation and the Spirits of the Sea are concerned with motion and change, then it can be said that the Sky Spirits are involved with matters of expansion and evolution. These Beings can figuratively be said to be the closest to heaven and the realms of the Sky Gods; therefore, to our ancestors they appeared the most spiritual and transcendent of all the spirits. Their natures are very tenuous for a mortal mind to apprehend and are closely linked with the stars; those heavenly, powerful and magical bodies that are only apparent at night, when all else is dark. Possessing very ethereal bodies – if, indeed, any at all perceptible to mankind – these spirits, known by such names as Sylphs, Wraiths, Watchers, Belweathers or simply Sprites, act as go-betweens twixt humanity and the gods. They are frequently to be experienced in the train of the Wild Hunt (should any person wish to experience such a thing in its entirety) and accompany the passage of the Old Ones as they pass over the Land at the times of the Great Feasts. They may be approached by only the most balanced of minds and characters, as contact with them is both extremely powerful and unsettling; minds have been known to be shattered or at least altered out of all previous recognition. This is one of the reasons that the Witch must strive to know themselves on all levels, as well as possible, to prepare for encounters of this kind.

However, attempted with caution and foresight, contact with these Beings can be most illuminating. They are capable of imparting knowledge that both illuminates and expands the mind and aids the Crafter in deciding the direction of their whole working practice.

Scrying the Wraith

Choose a night of middling to high winds, but with a clear sky; the moon phase doesn't matter, but you may like to try it at different times to see if you get different results. Stand out in the open somewhere but near to a stand of mature trees or some solid rocks. Stand facing into the wind, take a deep breath and draw the raw air deep into your lungs. Do this a few times, but take care not to hyperventilate. Now, look up at the night sky and fix your eyes on a single star that immediately takes your attention. (A star will be twinkling; if it doesn't then it's a planet and you should choose again). Many people choose the Pole Star as a focus but it doesn't matter which, as long as you can keep your eyes on it for some time without strain. You may blink, but do not lose sight of the star. Blank all other thoughts from your mind and make your chosen star the focus and whole of your attention. As you do this, feel the winds around you at the same time, caressing and buffeting your body, pulling you this way and that. Feel the tension in the air gradually build up and up as your focus becomes more and more one-centred on your star and the winds continue to whirl and whip around you. As the tension builds, you may begin to see vague wisps and tatters at the edge of your vision. *Do not* be tempted to shift your focus to them, but just let them pass as they will. These will become more and more apparent to you, wafting backwards and forwards, around and side to side, pushed and pulled by the wind and the energy feels more and more intense. If at some point you feel like "letting go" and drifting off with these Wraiths, consider carefully, as many do not return, or return in a very different form. The choice is yours, but they can impart much important information concerning your path. If you decide not to go, but the tension builds too high for you and you become afraid – and there is no shame in this, only common sense – break the contact with the star and go to one of the trees or rocks nearby and take a tight hold. Remain like this until the tension has passed and you feel able to let go again.

This is a strange exercise and one that can take many forms for the individual, so it is difficult to describe fully; it must be experienced. Essentially, it is up to you to "ride the wind" whilst remaining fixed to the ground, hence the focus point of the star. Many people achieve excellent results with this exercise, but do be cautious, as it can have a strange and startling effect on the human mind.

Spirits of Home and Hearth

It is said that, "An Englishman's Home is his Castle", and how much more true is this for the practitioner of the traditional arts? Although many Witches choose to work outdoors most of the time, this is not possible for many and not possible all the time for most, therefore the home is a very special place for the Crafter, being both secure refuge, comfort and living space and magical working place all in one. Some people will be lucky enough to have a room set aside purely for magical purposes and this is definitely to be desired, but most people will not have this luxury and so the whole of the house becomes their working space. Traditionally, the focus and centre of magical practices is the fireplace or hearth, as this is where in times past the whole family would have gathered together. The reasons for this are simple, practical and arcane.

In days gone by, before cookers and microwaves, ranges and Agas even, the only place to prepare and cook food – or to keep warm even – would have been the (central) fire in the hearth. For long ages the fire has been, rightly, treated with awe and reverence, worship and praise. It keeps the body and home warm; it wards off dangerous animals and spirits in the night; it represents the household deities and guardian spirits and, of course, cooks the food. In times gone by, members of the family who had passed over to the Otherworld and become part of the venerable race of Ancestors, were buried under or near the hearth and hence this place also became a focus of continuity and symbol of unity and communication for the whole family, both living and dead members. The hearth became so important, in fact, that much lore and mystery grew up around it, far more than I can deal with here. However, there is one aspect of hearth lore that every Witch knows and works with and that is the Hearth Spirit.

Hearth Spirits

Exactly what the Hearth Spirit is, is difficult to say. It may be a form of Land Wight that has taken up residence in the home; it may be the accumulated energy of all past residents of the house, having taken on independent form and manifestation; it may be the spirits of the family ancestors that keep guard over the present generation or it may be a combination of all of these and more – no-one is quite sure. However, the fact remains that they exist, are well attested to in traditional lore under many different names – Brownies, Boggarts, Hobs, Lobs – and have a definite and material effect on the occupants of the house.

The Hearth Spirit is both a loyal and temperamental spirit. It is loyal in that it serves the family; traditionally doing all those little tasks that have been forgotten or left undone during the day, protecting the home from negative influences and warning family members of impending danger or disaster. It is temperamental in that there are various taboos that must be observed if it is to remain loyal. Traditionally, it should never be given clothes or thanked; when food offerings are left out for it they must not be spoken of and it must always be informed of any changes in the family, for example a birth, death or wedding. To ignore any of these prohibitions is to risk losing the help and presence of the Hearth Spirit permanently. They just up and leave. Follow these few simple rules however, and you have a willing, helpful and obedient guest in your house, one who will be of assistance on many levels.

To aid in the manifestation and hence help of your Hearth Spirit, there is a simple little ritual that can be performed. You are not so much creating the Spirit, as it already exists as part of your home, but giving it a focus, which it can use to interact with you and vice versa. Obtain a natural stone, roughly about fist-sized, that you have found yourself from some natural place and that feels comfortable to you. (If you like you may also get a little "gnome", "pixie" or "goblin" figurine and attach it to the stone, to further aid your visualisation and focus, but this is by no means necessary). On the stone you should inscribe a symbol that represents to you the essence of security, domesticity, the home and guardianship. This can be one of the many traditional symbols, or one you have devised yourself. Colour this on to the stone in red.

In the evening, after dark, and best done on one of the High Holy Days, take your stone, set it in the hearth and place a red candle in a holder beside it. Have a small bowl of bread and milk ready. Place it near you but not in the hearth as yet. Sit down on the ground in front of the stone; compose yourself as for a rite. Light the candle, knock or tap gently three times on the hearth to gain the spirits' attention, then slowly, seriously and from the heart, say these words or similar:

> *"Honoured Spirit of this hearth of mine, I bid you welcome. Please to find joy and satisfaction in this home of mine. I pledge my support to your stay in this place and would ask your help and protection in return. Honoured Spirit of this hearth of mine, I bid you welcome."*

Now, place the bowl of bread and milk before the stone and sit in quiet meditation for as long as you feel necessary - you may wish to create a light trance state as this will make the easier to create contact. You may get a glimpse of your Hearth Spirit, or hear its voice or just receive a general impression or feeling. If you receive a name, count yourself very lucky and *never* tell it to another as you have been trusted with a great gift. Only use it when speaking directly to the Hearth Spirit in times of dire need. When you feel ready, put out the candle and quietly leave that area. Leave the offering bowl there overnight for the Spirit to absorb the essence of the bread and milk. Pour the remains out on bare earth in the morning. You should now have made contact with a very beneficial and helpful Spirit, which, if kept happy, will serve you well for many years. The offering of bread and milk is ideally – silently - made on occasions of family get-togethers, to share with all present or, if you live alone, make an offering every time you have a celebration in the house. You should also light the candle each time as well. (If you do not have an actual hearth in your home, use the place where there would ordinarily be one, or where the prime focus of the household is, be that kitchen cooker or dining room – *not* the television!).

Although called a "Hearth Spirit", this Being is generally found throughout the house and creates a beneficial atmosphere there. However, there may be times when the home, for whatever reason, attracts the attentions of unwanted or malignant energies or beings, which the Hearth Spirit alone is not able to completely negate. As in all magical work, there should be a give and take between the seen and unseen, and this is where the Crafter can add their energy and expertise to that of the Hearth Spirit in keeping the home free of unwanted energies, or, on rare occasions, direct attacks. As the place of your most intimate workings, the home should be thoroughly protected and not subject to any stray entity that comes by, or a more deliberate attack, possibly, from a rival worker. Whilst there are very many traditional solutions and remedies to these situations, there are two solutions that I would like to discuss here; one is the traditional Witch Ball and the other is the magical use of cords or threads for protection.

The Witch Ball

Most people are familiar with the sight and/or concept of this. The witch ball is a large, polished glass or metal ball that is hung in the window, or sometimes doorway, with the intention of reflecting back on the sender any negativity sent to the householder. Old, original glass fishing floats are ideal for this if you can find them, or large Christmas tree baubles if not. Reproduction glass fishing floats are common these days, but do not have the same "feel" to them, so, although these will work, always try for the originals. Once you have obtained your ball, it must be thoroughly cleansed of all previous associations and the best way to do this is to use the time-honoured Witch's standby, Thieves' Vinegar (see chapter 4, "SpellCrafting"). Pour a teaspoon or so into a bowl of warm, soapy water and give the ball a thorough cleanse, drying it after on a clean towel. Now your ball must be charmed to make it truly effective.

Two nights before Full Moon, set your working place with candles, incense, a bowl of fresh (spring) water and one of fresh earth on the *central* altar. Place your Witch ball on the altar also. Hallow your compass as is your normal practice and call in the power in your accustomed manner. (You may wish to tread the mill, using the Witch ball on the altar as a focus, or other methods).

When the power is called to your satisfaction, hold your hands above the Witch ball, about a foot apart, palms facing each other. Concentrate your energy and focus it into a ball, slightly smaller than your Witch ball, suspended between your palms.

See a ball of blue/white light, pulsing with energy, floating between your hands and send all your force into this. When you have achieved this to your satisfaction and can "see" the ball of energy, tell it exactly what you want it to do. Be very specific about it and as brief as possible, no long, wordy incantations. Say this strongly, with intent, in your own words.

Now, lower your hands, until your ball of power is resting inside your Witch ball, take your hands away and leave the energy residing in its physical shell.

In turn, sprinkle the Witch ball with some earth, pass it through the incense smoke, pass it through the candle flame and sprinkle it with water, saying each time:

> *"By (Earth, Air, Fire, Water) be charged and sealed to my will that no malignity may enter where you are placed."*

Wrap the Witch ball in a black cloth and finish the rite in your accustomed manner.

Place the Witch ball in a secure, dark place to "gestate" until the next New Moon, then take it out, unwrap it and "give birth to it", then hang it in your window, repeating the command that you gave it when you charged it.

The Witch ball should be cleaned and washed anew each month (in the thieves' vinegar solution). This will keep it shiny and reflect back or remove any negative impressions it may have received.

The Cord Cage

This method I would like to explain is something called the "Cord Cage" technique. It is a variation on the "God's Eye" formulation, familiar to many, which uses the cage-like structure created to entrap and hold malignant energies or spirits, until they can be safely disposed of. This method uses three sticks, instead of two, all at ninety degrees to each other, which creates a 3D effect, rather than a 2D one. This technique is quite mesmeric, creating a light trance in the worker, if performed with proper concentration, thereby enhancing the power of the cage. When finished, it can be hung anywhere it is needed and left to do its work in peace.

To explain now in more detail: Take three small sticks or twigs of equal length, about nine or ten inches long (you may wish to choose one of the traditional protective and guardian woods, such as Rowan or Holly) and a ball of red wool or natural twine. Take two of the sticks and tie them together in an equal-armed cross with the red cord, then join the third stick to them across the junction, again with the red thread. You should then have a three-dimensional equal-armed cross. With the thread still attached, begin to wind it round each stick, going from arm to arm, changing the angle after every few turns, and working from the centre out. As you go, mutter a charm to the effect that any negative or malignant energy or spirit of ill intent will be attracted to this "cage" and trapped inside until released by you. As you continue to wind and turn, you will enter a light trance state, which will enhance your muttered charm and give it extra energy. You are entering that otherworld where the energies originate and are using that to fashion the "inner" workings of the cage, the actual magical trap that the outward cord and twigs represent. Work slowly and intently, without rush or hurry, until you reach the end of the last arm. Tie off the thread with a muttered "So be it" and snap the thread off, after tying a loop to hang it by. Bring yourself back to this world with a little food and drink.

You may now hang this cage up somewhere about the house where you feel it is needed. At the end of every quarter (solstices and equinoxes), take it down and outside to somewhere wild and unfrequented. Start to unwind the thread from the arms and as you do so, mutter a little reverse charm, to the effect that all negative force or spirits are now released into the wild, no more to trouble your home or family. This time, DO NOT enter a trance state, as you may be tempted to be drawn to the power released and follow them back to their own realm. Keep your focus of attention firmly in this world and banish the forces with the power of your Will. If you feel that there is a continuing problem in your home, on your return create a new cage and hang that back up in place of the one just gone. However, do not use the same materials as they are now tainted. Bury them in some lonely place and use fresh for each cage you make.

That is a very short overview of some of the ways you may work with the spirits of home and hearth, although one type of spirit has been left out which may aid you in your home, or indeed elsewhere and I would now like to look at this in more detail.

Concerning Familiars

There are various types of Familiar but traditionally these tend to fall into four different – but related – categories;

a) A household pet whom the Witch has raised and trained to do their bidding, through a shared link,

b) A natural spirit or being that has been constrained by the Witch to perform a certain task or tasks (although this is little used nowadays as it is seen as a kind of "psychic" slavery),

c) An artificially created thought-form, designed to exist for a certain period and perform magical tasks given by the Witch

d) The extrusion of the "Fetch" body of the Witch.

I will deal with the last category in more detail in the next section, but I would like to describe two others here.

The Household Pet as Familiar

The practice of the traditional Witch keeping and using a household pet or pets as magical servitors is time honoured and well known. The type of pet can range from the usual cat or dog, to the more unusual frog, toad, mouse or rat, to the truly bizarre, such as a fly, worm or moth. Most of the more bizarre types of animal may be products of deluded or misled minds, such as during the persecutions, but the type of animal matters not if the practitioner is able to establish a link with it. Obviously the 'higher' orders of creatures, i.e. the mammals, are much easier to achieve this with than, say, a fly or moth. The actual technique is simple, but requires a very close bond and understanding between the Witch and his/her fellow-worker.

The Crafter obtains an animal at a very young age; ideally they should be there at the animal's birth. The creature should be constantly in the Witch's company, or as much as possible, so that an indissoluble bond grows up between them. There is no great mystery about this, purely the application of natural science; the closer the attachment and more intimate the company, the closer the bond will be and the more nearly the meeting of minds. The animal may share the Witch's bed and accompany them on all outings and holidays, preferably being constantly in their company if at all possible. The animal should be fed small amounts of the Witch's blood in its food, (just a few drops each time), the better to increase the magical bond between them; this is the origin of the story of Witches suckling their familiars. Sleeping and dreaming together is just as intimate a bond between Witch and familiar as it is between human partners and is only to be encouraged in this situation.

When the time comes for the Witch to ask the familiar to do something, this is the technique to be employed. Hold the animal's face gently in your two hands and gaze deeply into its eyes, holding the look for as long as is possible. If the animal breaks contact after a second or two you must begin again. Croon a soft charm under your breath, gently, so that the animal is both soothed and you enter a light trance state. It is here that the test of your link to your familiar occurs (although this should have been practised beforehand). You must impress upon the mind of the animal directly what it is that you wish it to do and retain the mind-to-mind link while it is doing it. This needs much practice, as with any work of magic and success is not to be expected at the first attempt.

Once the link is established and the animal understands what it is to do, the Witch releases it and sends it off to do his/her bidding. The practitioner now follows the animal by the mind contact and sees and senses through those of the animal. If a strong enough link has been established this will occur naturally, however, it is more usual at this point for the Witch to go deeper into trance or to fall asleep and to follow the animal by dream or clairvoyance. (This is one explanation for the phenomenon known as 'repercussion' in the old tales; that of the Witch appearing to have the same wounds as the animal if it had been shot or attacked by frightened cowans. The Witch had actually been *with* the animal all the time). Once the task is performed, the animal either naturally returns or is recalled by the Witch, who then wakes or returns from trance and rewards the familiar with their favourite food (and a few drops of their own blood).

Although very efficient in its own way, the limitations of this type of familiar are self-evident; basically all that can be achieved is a type of "covert surveillance" of a person or place or a method of remote viewing. Even these activities are surrounded by difficulties in that, unlike in previous centuries, animals roaming on their own tend to be reported and picked up by the authorities, unless sent out at night. The sending of spells by this means is naturally possible, but very difficult to achieve. An easier method all round and one much more flexible than an animal familiar is a non-physical or spirit familiar.

The Created Thought-Form as Familiar

Also known as the Puckeril or a Bid, this type of familiar is a deliberate construct from the Crafters own mind/vital force and, as such, can take on any form the practitioner wishes. Before any practical work can be undertaken, the type of familiar to be created must be decided upon. The nature, shape (if any), task(s), name and characteristics must all be worked out in detail – there is no room for error here. Once created, the familiar will be true to its own nature and cannot be altered later; hence, it is no use blaming it if it does not do what you want it to do correctly. Its intelligence will also be limited, so do not ask the world of it. You will need a (natural) object to act as a physical "anchor" or "home" for the familiar once created. This should be of a material that is compatible with the nature of the familiar as you have conceived it. For example, if you conceive of your familiar in the shape of a Gnome or Goblin, then a large pebble or small rock might be suitable. However, many Crafters use jewellery such as rings or necklaces, the better to keep the familiar object about their person and some even use small statues or framed pictures; the choice is entirely individual. You must also consider how you are to energise and sustain your familiar; the old tales of a Witch suckling her familiar, as mentioned before, has a basis in fact. To create your familiar you must empower it, giving energy from your own body in the form of blood is a time-honoured and traditional method. In this case, the finger can be pricked and a drop or two (no more!) can be smeared on the familiar object. This carries with it certain risks however, in that the familiar may become *too* energised and become uncontrollable, not answering to your commands. This needs careful consideration. Fresh milk, bread, honey or a new-laid egg can also be used, poured into a small bowl, which is then left next to the familiar object overnight, for the familiar to draw energy from. Once your familiar is created, this should be done at regular intervals, stated in the original creation ritual, such as once a week or once a month.

The actual rite for the creation of the familiar may go as follows:

Create and fully empower your compass in your accustomed manner. (Make sure you are wearing your cord for this).

Invoke the Old Ones for their aid and power in your work.

Take the familiar object to each compass direction in turn, beginning at the North and say

> *"Spirits of the North (E, S, W), my will do hear,*
> *Let this creature now appear.*
> *My word it shall always obey,*
> *To keep it on the Witching Way."*

Now go to the middle of your compass and lay the familiar object on the ground (or a bowl of fresh earth if indoors), and say

"Upon the Land I place thee,
Creature of my Will,
New Life I now give to thee,
And of power take thy fill."

Leave the object there for a few moments for it to absorb the force from the Land.

Next place, or dip if it is too large, the object into a bowl of fresh sea or salt water and say

"Within the Waters you now lay,
Creature of my heart,
Feel and sense all that you need,
For the practice of my art."

Let the object remain there for a few moments to absorb the powers of emotion.

Next, lift it from the bowl and hold it high in the air above your head. Wave it around gently and say;

"Currents of Air around you flow,
Creature of my mind,
Live and breathe in full measure now,
Your true purpose to find."

Keep the object aloft for a while, to absorb the energy of intelligence from the Sky spirits that it will need to understand your commands.

Now, replace the object on the earth and sit down before it. Raise and focus your inner force and in a firm voice, succinctly declare the attributes and nature of your familiar, the span of its existence and lastly, but most importantly its name. Using the first two fingers of your dominant hand, send a blast of power into the object, at the same time as strongly visualising how you wish the familiar to be. Keep this up for as long as possible but not to the point of exhaustion. Now, pick up the object and wrap the long, free end of your cord around it and say

"Bound to me you now shall be,
X (name of familiar) creature of magic and loyalty.
My will you shall always obey,
And aid me on the Witching Way."

Keep your now fully alive familiar object with you as you thank the Old Ones and dismiss your compass in your usual manner.

That night, place some 'food' in a special little bowl and place it and your new familiar in a quiet corner until the morning. After that, you need to keep your familiar object with you as much as possible and feed it at regular intervals. To give it commands, hold the object to your forehead and visualise strongly what it is you wish to be done. You may also verbalise the command as well. Keep it simple to start with and only use your familiar for magical purposes. Over a period of time, the bond between you will become stronger and you will become very fond of each other, your familiar even sometimes anticipating your requests. At the end of the familiar's set life span, return the object to its natural element of origin – for example, take a pebble back to the beach where you got it – with some whispered words of thanks for its service. A small libation would also be a nice thing to offer, in memory of your time together. If you have created your familiar to last your lifetime, you must command it to pass over with you at the end of your life in the original ritual and arrange for the object to be buried/cremated with you. Without you, your familiar would be lost and bereft and liable to cause magical havoc without direction or command.

I wish now to turn to the last category of "Familiar" mentioned earlier, that of the "Fetch".

The Fetch Body

In brief, the Fetch can be seen generally as the manifestation of the (usually) contra-sexual, spiritual nature of the individual, often also appearing in an animal form, which can be worked with as a familiar. Now, I realise that can sound confusing, so I will try to clarify it a bit. In Traditional Craft, as, in general, in North Western European traditional lore and mythology, the individual is often seen as having three, not two 'bodies' or 'natures'. There is the physical one we are all aware of; there is the 'soul' or 'spirit' which is the immortal part of us that survives physical death, and there is the Fetch. The Fetch acts as a companion, guide, tutor, helpmate and guardian, during our time on earth. In some cases, it is seen as a female guardian spirit and these are often passed on in the bloodline of certain families, similar to the tales of Banshees (Bean Sidhes), in Scots and Irish lore. If the Crafter is of Scots or Irish descent themselves, or practises a form of Craft deriving from this lore, then the Fetch may also be known as the "Co-Walker" and seen as a type of 'shadow' or 'doppelganger' of the individual Witch. This form of Fetch is seen as accompanying the Crafter in their work and during their life, appearing more and more frequently towards the time of the person's death. Once the individual had passed over, this spirit may then become a guardian, tutor or adviser to others in the family or magical path.

The Fetch is often spoken of as the 'spouse' or 'mate' of the Witch and this reflects the intensely close bond that exists between them, on both a spiritual and a physical level. Traditionally, it is quite possible for the Witch to have a sexual relationship with their Fetch-self, which exceeds that of any 'normal' physical relationship. There are tales of Crafters actually "marrying" their Fetch-Self and this portrays the alchemical wedding which unites the two halves of an individual into one, spiritual whole; this is the goal of all true, magical practice. Through continual practice and study, the individual Crafter reaches a stage whereby they have resolved the apparent contradictions of physicality and spirituality within themselves, their so-called "positive" and "negative" natures and have realised the entirety of their whole being. This is, of course, exceedingly advanced and lengthy work and beyond the scope of this book, but hopefully a goal towards which all true Crafters will aspire.

The Fetch is usually worked with in a much less lofty manner in most Craft practice and often has a much more practical application, very similar to the way in which the Crafter would work with their animal familiar and using similar techniques. The Fetch self often exhibits an animal form, which is where it is often "confused" with a separate animal familiar. This represents the pre-sentient, "animal" nature of the individual, which in itself contains valuable knowledge and abilities. In traditional lore, it was common for the Witch to be given their familiar by the "Devil" at one of the Grand Sabbats. In truth this represents the Horned Master of the coven, teaching the Crafter how to contact their own Fetch-self, as represented in a totemic animal form. That the Fetch can exhibit an animal form is indicative of the deep, unconscious nature of the individual; the Crafter gains access to these deeper levels and they are then able to work with them, gradually bringing these powers and attributes to conscious levels.

I will give here two suggestions for initial contact with your Fetch self, thereafter you will learn to work together. Contact cannot be expected easily and quickly, so much hard work and persistence must be put in, sometimes amounting to years of work, before contact can be made. Believe that it is possible and this will take you far.

Housle Rite for Communion with the Fetch Self

A Housle is a kind of shared feast, used in Traditional rites for a variety of purposes, not purely celebratory. In this case it will be used to petition the Horned Lord of the Craft for His aid in calling forth your Fetch self, as a prelude to full communication. This is a magical development on the "feast" given in the first chapter "Hallowing the Compass" and will take many performances to be effective, so determination and application are essential.

Fully empower a compass, created in your habitual manner, but dedicated to your Fetch spirit.

Go to stand before the stang in the north, before which you have placed a cup of red wine and a plate of bread. Invoke the God and your Fetch self in the following, or similar words:

"Horned One, Master of the Wild, Lord of Beasts both seen and unseen,
I call to you with words of welcome.
From near and far I call to you in supplication.
Hear my words and answer to my call.
Grant communion with my other self, my soul -spouse, my Fetch-self.
Fetch spirit, I welcome you as Guardian, Guide, Teacher, Helpmate and Spouse,
I call to you to honour our bond and acknowledge our union.
Come now that we may work and live as one,
Fetch Spirit,
I call to you with words of welcome."

Take your stang and stand it upright in the centre of your compass and place the bread and wine at its foot.

Focussing your attention on your fetch, now tread the mill widdershins to the following chant:

"Come forth, come forth thou fetch-mate,
Come forth, come forth thou soul-beast."

Pace until you feel a strong sense of powerful "otherness" being built up, focused on the stang and the "feast". (After many repetitions you may begin to see a form of manifestation take place, but this is rare). When you feel ready, cease pacing and sit before the stang. Stay quietly in meditation for a while and see what occurs, or alternatively, perform the visionary journey that is given next.

When you have finished, take up the plate of bread and place your dominant hand over it. With full focus, state these words:

"Fetch Spirit,
Here I bring bread, the staff of life,
Sustaining body and spirit.
I bless this bread to the cause of our union.
With all my heart I bless it,
With all desire I bless it."

Put down the plate and take up the cup. Place your dominant hand over it. With full focus, state these words:

"Fetch Spouse,
Here I bring wine, fire in the blood,
Enlivening body and spirit.
I bless this wine to the cause of our union.
With all my heart I bless it,
With all desire I bless it."

Bring the cup to your lips and say:

"I drink this wine to the union of my body and my Fetch.
Let us not be parted."

Drink some of the wine.

Put down the cup and take up a piece of the bread. Say:

*"I eat this bread to the sustenance of my body and my Fetch.
Let us not be parted."*

Eat the piece of bread.

Mix the remains of the bread and wine together in the cup and anoint your forehead, concentrating on the union of yourself and your Fetch spirit. Now take some time to contemplate what you are doing and what you hope to gain from these acts.

When you are ready, pour the remains of the food and drink out on the ground at the base of the stang, saying:

*"As I take, so do I give,
As a true Son/Daughter of the Old Faith.
I make this offering to my Fetch self.
I give this offering to my Fetch spirit,
That S/He and I may know each other.
As above and so below,
As within and so without,
I make this gift."*

Close down your compass as you customarily do, but do not forget to thank and honour your Fetch also.

Visionary Journey for Contact with the Fetch Spirit

This journey may be performed in the compass, once you have done the housle to your Fetch – which would make it particularly effective – or separately, at any other time. Again, as with the housle, this will take many repetitions before actual contact is made, so perseverance and determination are once again essentials.

Compose yourself comfortably and mentally prepare for the journey.

You find yourself seated before a fire, in a well-padded chair, in the sitting room of a country cottage. It is night-time and the curtains are drawn against the darkness outside. All is warm and welcoming and the light from the flames dances over the roof beams and polished pots and pans of the well-appointed room. You rise from your chair and go to stand before the fire, warming your hands above it. You become aware of a soft moaning sound, like the wind through tree branches on a stormy night, but outside all is calm. The sound increases in intensity, if not volume, and you feel compelled to look outside to discover the source. Wrapping yourself in a long, warm, woollen cloak, you take up your trusty staff and open the door, stepping outside. You are met with no gale or gust of stinging rain, but the moaning sound again increases in intensity, now manifesting as an intense keening, as if of loss or regret. You turn slightly, attempting to discover the source of this despair and then notice at some distance from you, beyond the boundaries of your immediate property, a ball of eldritch light floating in mid-air. It is from this direction that the keening wail seems to be coming and so you step towards it. As you do so, the tone once again changes and rather than a sound of loss, becomes more one of crooning and encouragement, of drawing and beckoning. You continue towards this floating spark, yellow-blue, red-green and white, all at one and the same time, which moves steadily away the more you approach.

By now you are fascinated by both the light and the sound and willingly follow where it leads you. Past the boundaries to your lands you go, crossing the borders of the fields as the light floats gently before you, leading you ever on with its gentle crooning and murmuring. You traverse the cultivated lands around you, seemingly light as a feather as your feet hardly touch the ground and your body seems to make little effort or expend much energy. The wastelands where cultivation ends appear in the distance, narrowing into a small valley that stands ahead. Before you now runs a large stream, directly barring your way and the crooning, cooing, fascinating light comes to a stop on the far side of a humpbacked, wooden bridge, floating at head height, beckoning with its entrancing sound. You set foot upon the bridge and at once a tremor runs through you, a shiver runs down your spine, as if at some level you know that crossing this bridge is an irrevocable step, with no going back. The light now emits a subtle challenging tone in its song, as if daring you to move on. There is no choice, you are bound to this light and enchanted by its song and so you step boldly onto the bridge and walk unhesitatingly to the other side, drawn on all the time by the scintillating light. As your foot touches the ground on the other side of the bridge, you immediately feel a surge of excitement and hope, an anticipation of great things to come. You hurry on now, eager to discover what is ahead of you, as the light moves on, leading you further and further into the wild lands and into the ever narrowing valley on the other side of the bridge.

As the walls of the valley gradually narrow and come closer together, the light increases its speed and seems eager to lead you to a point that you can just see at the head of the valley, where the rock sides come together. You can just make out the shape of a tree in the gloom and what appears to be a symmetrical pile of stones beside it, where now the light stops and begins to increase in brilliance. As you approach, you realise that in the increasing brightness of your guiding light you can make out the shape of a small well beside a green and glowing tree. The type of tree is unknown to you but is also strangely familiar and you draw comfort from this. You finally come to a stop before the well, beside which the phantom glow is hovering and emitting a welcoming and comforting tone. The light glitters upon the surface of the waters in the well and attracts your attention. You move forward and, on impulse, scoop some of the water up in your hands and send it splashing over your face and head, as in a lustration. The effect is almost electrifying and seems to sharpen your senses in uncanny ways. You turn once more to your glowing companion and for the first time notice vague whisps and shapes inside the light. As you watch, the ball of light begins to swell and grow, its shape lengthening and broadening until it is human sized, its song reaching almost a ringing tone of triumph and success. Looking deep into the

> *shining light, which now begins to physically wash over and absorb you, you see coalescing shapes, part human, and part animal. An overwhelming desire comes over you; joy and a profound sense of peace wash through you and you step forward and embrace that which has manifested before you...*

What happens now and what you experience now no one can tell. Go with whatever happens, knowing that no harm can come to you, but that your life may be changed forever from that moment on. Spend as much time as you need to and, when you are ready, return to the world from which you originally came.

Remember; this exercise will need to be performed many times before you come to the full realisation of your Fetch self, but each time you perform it, you will be that much closer.

(A note on gender and orientation here: Whilst it is traditional for the Witch to encounter/work with a fetch-mate of the opposite physical gender, most of the records that we have derive from heterosexual encounters. However, in traditional, magical societies, both in Old Europe and elsewhere, before the coming of Christianity, sexuality was not such a hard and fast subject. There are known records and instances of trans-sexual shamanic practitioners, same-sex magical partnerships and instances of sexual encounters with same-sex spirit visitors. Who or what a modern LGBT practitioner would encounter when practising the above workings should be entirely left open to the individual and their circumstances; no one can say in advance what will happen or who they will meet. However, one thing should be pointed out; who or whatever they encounter *will be valid for them*).

The Ancestors and the Mighty Dead

Traditional practitioners have always been associated with the dead in one way or another in popular imagination, whether that be in barbaric necromantic rites at All Hallows, or in using dead body parts in spells and rituals for nefarious purposes. Obviously, the majority of these tales are pure fantasy but they do contain a core of truth. True Crafters have always retained a link with their departed kin – be that of their actual bloodline or that of their particular tradition or Land. Indeed, most consider that they are not departed at all, but here with us all the time. By that I do not mean that they float around us, invisibly, waiting to be summoned in spiritualist rites but that in a sense they never left us at all. It is part of Craft lore that the dead do not necessarily depart to some fixed Otherworld, there to await rebirth or whatever but may become part and parcel of the Land around us. They may merge with the spirit/body of the Land and become almost indistinguishable from nature spirits or other beings that inhabit the, generally, unseen realm "inside" the world around us. Here they perform their allotted tasks, be that as guardian of place, intermediary between the worlds, advisor to an individual person or family, overseer of a particular area, or what have you, until it is time for them to move on to follow whatever destiny has been laid down for them.

In times gone by the ancestors were venerated for their abilities and use to the living. Many of the so-called burial mounds that are to be found in the British Isles and elsewhere are misnamed, as they were actually places where the living could come and visit – and interact with – the dead; asking them advice on various matters, asking their help with problems and to renew ties with old and new family members. Indeed, in many cases, the new members were (and are in family traditions), considered to be the ancestors returning to their own clan or family and were welcomed as such. In certain very specific instances, people chose, or were chosen, to give up this physical life – to deliberately die – to merge with the Land at a specific place or site, to act as intermediaries between this world and the Otherworld, for the tribe or people in that area and to act as guardians, mediating the energies of the two worlds, usually for a fixed period of time. However, once merged with the Land or a specific site, our sense of time has no meaning to them and many are still active, if you know how to approach them. Such individuals are sometimes known as Burial Chiefs or Burial Kings, who may be interacted with at their specific burial mounds or "tombs". This is a difficult and potentially dangerous operation, so I will not go into it here, but will discuss other possibilities for contacting the ancestors later.

Another aspect of ancestral lore is that pertaining to the Master Men and Women, those who have gone on to become part of what is sometimes known as the "Hidden Company". These are Witches who have achieved great knowledge, experience and power whilst in physical life, who have afterwards remained "available" for others of their group, lineage, family or tradition to call upon. They act as guides, teachers, guardians and observers for those of their line and can sometimes be seen as vague (or more solid!), shapes around the edge of the compass during ritual. They may be called upon in times of need to aid the individual Crafter or whole group and often take action on their own initiative to safeguard the knowledge, lore and secrets things of their own tradition. If you have been given admission into a particular Craft lineage or Tradition, these are beings that you may be introduced to as part of your induction or working rites and can expect to work with. If you are a solitary worker, you may meet the spirits of those of the Hidden Company who take an interest in the Craft in general, and work with those not of a specific lineage. For, make no mistake, once you embark on this path, you *will* attract attention, if only to make sure that you're not doing any lasting damage to anyone else!

Contact with the ancestors and particularly beings like the Mighty Dead or Master Crafters, is not undertaken lightly or for frivolous reasons; it is not done because we *can.* It is done to further our own knowledge, wisdom, understanding and experience, because as serious practitioners we can do no other than call on those who have gone before for their aid. Contact is also kept up to keep open the doors of communication between the worlds, the better to further the exchange of knowledge and regain some of what has been lost, both for ourselves and for those that come after us. Once "merged" with the Land, time, as previously stated, takes on a completely different meaning and all things are open for them to see. The rites and rituals of yore, the knowledge of what went before and the wisdom of our forebears is all merged with them too. This knowledge may be tapped for our own advancement if we know how. However, make no mistake, questions such as, "Where did Aunt Lily put her best silver cutlery?" will not only be treated with disdain if genuine contact is made but may also produce serious repercussions; the dead are not to be trifled with!

Before I go on to give a couple of practical suggestions for making contact with the ancestors, I must address the question here of exactly what, or whose, ancestors? By talking of ancestors, I do not necessarily mean your direct, lineal blood ancestors. I once asked one of my teachers whether a particularly Baptist Christian ancestor would answer the call of a Crafter if asked and got told that the best person for the job would probably answer. Unless we belong to a family Craft tradition – and maybe not even then – we are unlikely to get an answer from a "Witch Ancestor" if we as Crafters make some call for help. It will be the person, most likely but not necessarily, in our lineage that has the most appropriate knowledge to help that will reply – if it even happens to come from an individual. It may come from a group. Just because your great-great uncle Fred was a witch, you wouldn't ask him to help you with a gardening question if he was a plumber, now would you? It may be that granny Ruth, a devout Baptist, was a master gardener and could help better. Religion means little to ancestors and they will come as they will. A general call for help is better than calling on a specific individual, as they may be no help at all. Following on from this, who are our individual ancestors anyway? If you go far enough back, we're all related in some fashion, so don't be surprised at who answers your call. The important thing to remember is that, if contact is made, the individual answering will be of the Land you are in – literally – whether or not they are a lineal blood relative, traceable as such. Be open to all possibilities and do not hold a blinkered view of the afterlife; you may be surprised at just who, or what, answers your call.

I shall now describe a couple of techniques that you may use to gain contact with the ancestors, if used correctly. The first is a visionary journey that will put you – metaphorically – in the Land of the Ancestors, where they may answer you as they wish. The second is an actual rite to call upon the ancestors in a physical setting; again, they will answer as they wish.

Visionary Journey to the realm of the Ancestors

Compose yourself and perform your preliminary preparations as normal. (I suggest at least a circle-cross, if not a full compass).

> *You find yourself in the middle of a field at midnight. The field has been harvested and the short stubble casts long shadows by the light of the full moon above. It is late autumn and a chill wind blows around you, flapping the cloak you are wearing. An owl hoots above you and glides past on silent wings. In the distance you can see a long, low, grass-topped mound and you feel drawn to walk towards it. As you come closer you can see that the mound appears man made, as it is far too regular for a natural mound and the smooth top has obviously been shaped by hand.*

Approaching closer, you begin to appreciate just how large the mound is and begin to veer towards your right so that you can take an anti-clockwise walk around it. Reaching the mound, you see that there is a well worn path circling the base, as if many feet have passed this way before you, and you step onto this, with the hill on your left and begin your way round. As you go, the light of the moon, which until now has lit your way, becomes blocked by the bulk of the mound and you are plunged into deep shadow as you make your way round. Eventually, it becomes so dark that you must trail your hand along the side of the mound to make sure you do not lose your way, as even the path beneath your feet has become invisible.

Out of the darkness looms a deeper blackness and you slow down so as not to walk into it. As your eyes adjust, you realise that this is a type of porch, jutting out from the side of the mound and you must take a few steps out to get round it. Stepping round the edge of the porch way, you can just make out two massive upright stones, with a third as a lintel across the top. The gap of the doorway between the stones is uncovered and pitch black, yet you know this is the way that you must go.

As you stand undecided, wondering whether to continue your journey or not, you become aware of a faint scuffling. It gradually becomes louder, although never strong, and you realise it is coming from the doorway in front of you. It is the sound of footsteps approaching up a steep incline; steady, strong and regular footsteps that are coming closer and closer. The doorway is in deep shadow and it is not until the being coming closer is almost at the portal that you just perceive the outline of a large, male figure - a very large male figure. You take a few steps backwards in apprehension and the figure continues to approach, more slowly now. You have stepped back, out of the shadow of the mound and are now in full moonlight. As you back away, the figure advances towards you, although he never comes out into the full light, staying just inside the shadows as befits his role and duty. He is the Lord of the Mound, God of the Underworld Mysteries and Leader of Souls. You both stand where you are, looking directly at each other, absorbing the details of each other's being. (Pause for contemplation).

At length the Lord of the Mound seems to come to a decision and, nodding briefly at you, stands to one side and ushers you towards the doorway with a wave of His hand. You hesitate momentarily but, after another glance towards Him, walk steadily towards the doorway in the hill, pass beneath the stone lintel and begin your descent of the passageway into the hill.

At first you are still chilled by the cool, night air but as you continue, you notice that not only does the rough, stone passageway become gradually lighter; it also becomes warmer the further you go. As you descend, you begin to detect a slight pulsation in the warmer air, almost as if the wind were the warm breath of someone ahead of you. You continue for what seems a very long time, all the while the air becoming warmer but never hot; the light becoming stronger but never bright. Finally, you come to another doorway, this one of highly carved stone; all kinds of bird, animal and plant life seem to be entwined together in such a manner as to make the stone almost seem alive, writhing and contorting with an inner force of its own. It is through this doorway that the breaths of warm air are coming, along with a soft whispering sound, as if many voices were talking quietly together. Taking your courage in both hands, you step through the doorway and into the space beyond.

You are surprised to find yourself in a fairly small, rock cut chamber. The walls are roughly hewn and dripping with moisture, that gives off a warmth rather than coldness, and moss and lichen grow on the walls in patches, giving it almost a cosy feeling. The plant material glows with a soft light, which reflects off the water on the walls and magnifies itself and it is by this light that you can see. Out of the far wall, opposite you, a small stream of water issues from a hole and falls into a rock cut basin on the floor. The collected water also gives off a shimmering light, which adds its strength to the ambience of the chamber.

(Pause for contemplation on your reasons for coming here and what you hope to achieve).

As you watch, the shimmering light above the water begins to coalesce and form a shape, taking on characteristics of a human body but blurred as if unfinished. The form becomes more and more solid, shining with an inner light of its own, although never becoming quite tangible. The sound of whispering voices that you heard on arriving in this place gradually increases, until it becomes a deafening cacophony, as if all the dead in the world were speaking to you at once. The sound increases until it is almost unbearable, vibrating through your skull and then suddenly ceases, leaving you in a silent void, facing the now fully formed image before you. Out of the silence a whispering voice speaks…

"Who are you and what do you desire in the Land of the Dead?"

(Answer in as honest, open and respectful a voice as you can and wait for a reply, if any is forthcoming. You may be asked to give something in return for aid, or to do something instead. Answer as seems best to you but remember, promises given to the dead are binding and must be kept. Do not double-deal with the ancestors, as they will surely balance the books in their own way.)

When you have concluded your meeting, bow respectfully and back away. The form will begin to fade and vanish, resolving itself back into the glow from the water in the pool. Turn and walk back through the doorway you entered by and do not look back! Continue your journey back up the passage to the great trilithon lintel and step out the doorway. Take a few deeps breaths and breathe in what you now perceive to be fresh, morning air. The Sun is beginning to rise above the horizon and flood the Land with golden light. You realise you have spent the whole night with the ancestors and have come back enriched and more knowledgeable than before. Embrace the rising light, hold that newfound knowledge within you and return, gently, to your normal realm.

Calling to the Mighty Dead

This rite must be performed outside, in a place that you have a strong connection to, preferably in an area that your family have lived in for some generations. Apart from the tools that you would normally use for setting up your compass and provisions for a small feast or housle, you will need two further items - you will need two bones. Ideally these would be ancestral bones, but that is pretty impractical and I do not advocate digging up your, or anybody else's relatives to get them. Try to find some that have naturally come to light or been unearthed by ploughing or suchlike. Failing that, any bones will do, but do try not to use those from the Sunday roast – it doesn't have quite the same impact. Animal bones are acceptable if they are from the Land you are in. Do not use imported animal bones as they will have no resonance for you. It is a good idea to perform the previous visionary journey and ask for bones to be made available to you; the ancestors can then put them in your way when the time is right. Keep them safe and use them for nothing else.

You will also need to do one other extra thing for this rite. In the area where you will hallow your compass, determine the Western direction and dig a hole. It needn't be large – about 6"- 8" in diameter – but make it as deep as you can, at least the length of your arm. Have this pit at the West when you create your compass.

Perform this rite at the dark of the moon, preferably around the time of All Hallows, but any other time of the year is acceptable.

Hallow your compass in your usual manner, but create it widdershins i.e. anti-clockwise from the North.

Call all your protective spirits and helpers at each direction, as well as the usual Powers you call.

Place your stang upright in the ground in the West, inside the edge of your compass but behind the pit you have dug, so that the pit is between you. Place your cup of wine and plate of bread to either side of the pit, not the stang.

Now stand before the pit and the stang and make an invocation to the Horned God, as Lord of the Dead, to let the ancestors return to you. Use your own words, speaking from the heart, saying exactly what it is that you desire. Wait some moments for any response that you may feel.

Tread a widdershins Mill, until such time as you feel that the veil has thinned and you have a foot in both worlds, so to speak. As you tread this Mill, envisage yourself as spiralling down and down, deeper into the Land and the Underworld realm of the Ancestors. Slightly unfocus your eyes as you tread, slowly spiralling further and further in, to the centre of the compass. The unfocussing of the eyes makes you turn inwards, within yourself, at the same time as descending into the Underworld, bringing the two together, until such time as you have reached your "destination". Once you have reached the/your centre, pause a moment to adjust to your new position, then go to stand in the West, before the pit and the stang.

You must now perform a housle to and with the Dead, to honour and join with them. In slow and measured tones, with full focus and conviction say the following:

"Honoured and Mighty Dead,
I call to you with words of welcome,
From near and far I call to you in supplication.
Hear my words and answer to my call.
I welcome you as Guardians, Guides and Teachers,
I call to you, blood to blood and flesh to flesh.
Come now that I may do you honour,
Blessed and Mighty Dead,
I call to you with words of welcome."

Take up the plate of bread and place your dominant hand over it. With full conviction, state these words:

"Honoured Ancestors,
Here I bring bread, Life of the Land,
Sustaining both body and spirit.
I bless this bread in the name of the Ancestors.
With all my heart I bless it,
With all desire I bless it."

Put down the plate and take up the cup. Place your dominant hand over it. With full conviction, state these words:

"Mighty Dead,
Here I bring wine, fire in the blood,
Enlivening both body and spirit.
I bless this wine in the name of the Ancestors.
With all my heart I bless it,
With all desire I bless it."

Bring the cup to your lips and say:

"I drink this wine in the Ancestors name.
May I not be found wanting in their eyes."

Drink some of the wine.

Put down the cup and take up a piece of the bread. Say:

"I eat this bread in the name of the Mighty Dead.
With fear and dread and untold awe."

Eat the piece of bread.

Now mix the remains of the bread and wine together in the cup and anoint your forehead with the mixture.

Pour the remains of the food and drink out into the pit at the base of the stang, saying:

"As I take, so do I give,
As a true Son/Daughter of the Old Faith.
I give this to the Honoured Ancestors,
I give it to the Mighty Dead,
That the veil may be parted.
The day and night are wed,
As are the living and the dead.
Thus do I make this gift."

Now, replace the cup and plate, sit down before the stang and pit and take up the bones, one in each hand. Begin to tap these together, gently, to the timing of your heartbeat (try to keep this steady). As you do, softly chant the following:

"To the depths I send my words,
Honoured Dead, that I be heard.
Come to me with insight rare,
I sit before you, naked, bare."

Keep in mind what it is that you desire from the ancestors and continue to tap the bones together, chanting all the time, over and over again. Keep this up for as long as you can, until you fall into a trance state, then let come what will. You may drift off into some ancestor inspired reverie; one of the dead may come to you, or any number of things may happen. Just go with whatever occurs.

When you are finished, make heartfelt thanks to both the ancestors and the Lord of the Dead for their help and insight. Open your compass in your usual manner and clear away. Leave the pit as it is and walk away without looking back. It is advisable to eat and drink something nourishing as soon as you can (not alcohol), to earth yourself and bring you back fully from your experiences. Make short notes for future reference as memories of this type of rite can fade quite quickly.

The Elvenkind or Faerie Folk

As with the ancestors, the association of the Fair Folk or Elvenkind with traditional practitioners is long and enduring. Many a witch has learnt their craft from an encounter with the hidden folk. However, let me make it clear here and now what I am *not* referring to when I speak of the Faerie or Elvenkind. I do *not* refer to the modern, new age diminutive spirit with gossamer wings that flits from flower to flower. I do *not* refer to "Devas", the so-called "plant-oversouls"; and I most certainly do N*ot* refer to the spirits that are supposedly called up in crystal workshops to bless the energies of the stones. *these are not faeries!* They are the product of a literary tradition, beginning around the time of Shakespeare and coming to full fruition with the Victorian Theosophist movement. They are a combination of sexist wish-fulfilment, a misunderstanding of traditional lore and practice and a desire to control that which we do not understand.

Now, having got that out of the way, let us go on to discover what the Fair Folk actually are. Although there are many tribes of Faerie folk, they can basically be divided into the Light and Dark kinds. These were originally called the "Liosalfar" (Light Elves) and the "Svartalfar" (Dark Elves) respectively, by our Germanic ancestors, the term Fee, Fae or Faerie deriving from the language of the Norman-French invaders of later centuries and coming from the Latin term *Fata* meaning "Fates". In Scottish lore, the Fair Folk are divided into two types, the Seelie and Unseelie Courts, meaning respectively, the Blessed and Unblessed folk. In Irish lore, the two types of Folk are known as the Aes or Daoine Sidhe and the Dubh Sidhe, the Light and Dark respectively. Both kinds are closely associated with the Land, the inner life of the outer reality and are seen as living either underground or inhabiting the "hollow hills", the so-called burial mounds of our forebears. It can, therefore, be seen that there is a very strong link between the lore of the Ancestors and the lore of the Faerie – particularly the "dark" variety – and it is considered by many practitioners that the Fay are indeed the spirits of our departed kin, metamorphosed by their merging with the Land in their post-mortem state. They can be seen as very close in kind to human beings, but one step removed from them in type and consciousness. Their awareness of life and energies is much sharper than ours and they appear to exist on the energy within the body of the Land itself. Although legend gives many examples of their feasting on what appears to be the same food as us, examined in a different light, the food turns out to be no more than dust and leaves under a glamour. Their bodies also, although similar to ours in appearance, are not as dense being composed more of a shining type of energy than a gross material nature, particularly the "light" variety of Faerie. This can be seen from one of the names they are known as in the land of Eire, namely Leprechaun. This word comes from the Gaelic "lugh corpan", meaning Light Body and shows the difference in type between them and us. Although generally thought of as smaller creatures than ourselves, this is not borne out by tradition and lore. These state that they are at least as tall as humans and frequently taller, giving rise to some of their other names; the Lordly Ones, the Gentry and the Mighty Ones. However, there are many different "tribes" within these Folk and there are certainly instances of variations in height, ranging from the shorter, more dwarven kind, to the taller Shining Ones.

Another strand of traditional lore gives the Fay a different origin. It is stated that when Lucifer fell from heaven, he took many shining spirits with him. These were neither evil nor good but somewhere in-between and are condemned to wander the Earth forever. They are of a different kind from mortal folk, too good for hell, but not good enough for heaven and became what we now call the Faerie Folk. This is the remains of very ancient lore, relating to knowledge of the stars and stellar energies, the emergence of man as a separate species and the rise of consciousness, which pre-dates Christianity by millennia. After the conversions from paganism, the name of Lucifer, meaning "Light Bearer", and an acknowledged title of the Witch god, was grafted onto an older myth and the whole thing was turned into a story to frighten lowly mortals with. The true essence behind the story is of the "descent" of knowledge and wisdom into matter from "higher" realms, the gifting of consciousness to Mankind by the enlightened Spirits and the working use of it. Similar themes can be seen in the Greek myth of Prometheus the Titan, who gives the gift of Fire (Light/Knowledge/Wisdom/Consciousness), to Mankind and who is then cast down and punished for it by a jealous Zeus. This tradition may also lie behind the myth of the arrival of the Tuatha de Danaan (Ireland's main Faerie Folk), who, in one version of the story, arrived from four celestial cities, bringing with them magical artefacts which later benefited Mankind.

Whereas the essential point of working with the ancestors is to gain knowledge, working with the Fair Folk helps to acquire both a change in consciousness and an alteration in awareness, as well as acquiring arcane knowledge, not otherwise easily accessible in our realm. Although overlaying ours and being both "within" and "behind" it, their world is not quite the same. It can sometimes appear as if a glamour had been put upon people and their senses can become confused, when experiencing the energies of the Fay, not having adjusted to a different awareness. A small story may help illustrate this.

Some twenty years ago, my husband, a friend and I were on holiday in County Donegal, Eire. Co. Donegal is one of the Gaeltacht, the Irish speaking regions of the country and well known for its surviving Faery lore and traditional beliefs. We had driven on to one of the more remote peninsulas for the day, called Fannad Head, to do a bit of sightseeing and exploring. It had been a very pleasant day, with a very good "feel" to it, but at last it was time to leave. We climbed back in the car and began to drive back along the road we had come by, idly watching the landscape slide by. After having seen the same piece of landscape slide by for the third time and still not having driven off the peninsula, we became concerned. Consulting the local maps, we decided that, yes, we had been following the right road, had made no wrong turnings, but had been going round in circles. There was no one to ask at that point how to get off the Head, so we decided to follow a Post van that had just gone past, concluding that the van had to leave the Head at some point as well. After following the van for about an hour and having passed the same church cross twice more, we finally found some people in a little village to ask the way. We told them what had been happening and some slow smiles spread across quite a few faces. We were given completely different directions to the ones we had been following and within ten minutes of being back on the road, we had found the main junction on to the Head and were away back to the hotel. It should have occurred to all of us at the time, but didn't; we had been Faerie-led and the locals knew it. By giving us completely different directions, our confused awareness had been "set straight", so to speak, and we were able to find our way back. Be warned, the Fair Folk love a joke, no matter what you consider them to be!

Set above all of the various tribes of the Fair folk are the King and Queen of Elphame (Elvenhome), who will have interaction with humans when it suits them. The Queen is variously depicted as living in the Hollow Hills, or in an underground cavern, or in a cave in the mountains. It is from Her that many practitioners have been given their magical and herbal lore, their abilities of transformation and knowledge of the past and future. She is known to some as Dame Venus and is the Lady of the hidden Sabbat that some fly to in dreams. She is seen as the Sovereign Power within the Land and confers Kingship and Authority on whom she pleases, the power being Hers to command and dispose of. The King is often depicted as being the same as Gwynn ap Nudd, Lord of the Underworld in old British and Welsh tales. He has also been known as Auberon or Oberon (as in Shakespeare's Midsummer Night's Dream), deriving from the Alberich of Teutonic lore. This being was said to be the king of the Underworld Folk and could be invoked to give knowledge of hidden and buried treasures. He is the leader of the Wild Hunt and takes the souls of those who are forsworn or oath-breakers. Both these beings lead forth the Faerie hosts at the turning times of the year, the four great festivals of the Craft, Candlemass, Roodmass, Lammas and Hallowmass, when they preside over the transition of the power in the earth lines and go from one of their domains to another. To many Witches they are identical with the WitchMother and WitchFather of the Traditional Craft and I shall go into their lore in more depth in the last chapter. For now I will finish by giving a method whereby the practitioner may come into contact with the Faerie folk and possibly have communion with them.

Contacting the Faerie Folk

The traditional places for contacting the Fay are at the roots of great and ancient trees (particularly Oak, Ash and/or Thorn, especially when growing together in a grove or triangle), at ancient burial mounds and in caves in lonely mountains. I shall deal with the first of these here, the last two requiring more knowledge and experience than I can give to the reader in these pages.

At a place in the wild where you are known by the spirits and have worked before, seek out one of the above trees, or an ancient Elder, much beloved of the Faerie race. It is best if you can work at the time of one of the old holy days, i.e. Candlemass, Roodmass, Lammas or All Hallows, but if not, any time will suffice. At sunset, take a bowl of bread and milk to your chosen tree. Perform only a circle-cross, calling upon the powers of the local Land Spirits to aid you. Try to find a hollow or cleft at the base (where roots and trunk meet) and pour your offering into the hole (if you cannot find a hole, pour the offering over the roots, so that it trickles down into the ground). As you do this, say this or similar:

'Fair Folk within the Land,
See here I have brought this offering to thee.
Lordly People deep within,
I bring a gift for thee.
Come, come, come to me."

This must be whispered into the hollow or cleft, or over the roots as you pour. Now, you must prepare to spend the night at the base of the tree, in silent, waking watchfulness. Mark well all that happens and do not leave your place. You may see visions, or hears sounds or receive sensations. You may just fall asleep; in which case take especial note of your dreams as it is likely you will be visited in them. In the morning, thank the People for their communication and walk away from that place, without looking back.

At first glance this may appear to be an exceedingly simple rite, hardly a rite at all. The secret lies in your willingness to wait up all night for a sign or communication. The Good Folk will not come to one who is not worthy of them, so by performing this vigil, you are showing that you are at least worthy of their attention, if not interaction. If you receive nothing, then try again with increased determination another night – they may just be testing you!

APPROACHING *the* POWERS

Traditional witchcraft is not a nature-based, fertility religion; that is modern, pagan Wicca and a different thing entirely. Traditional witchcraft, whilst it contains many different facets in its various manifestations and has its roots in the pagan religions of antiquity, is essentially the approach to and apprehension of – even the union with – the divine Powers of the universe, imaged as gods. This is achieved by the practice and comprehension of the Mysteries, as understood by our ancestors as being the mysteries that surround life and death and all in between. Within the Craft, most things begin with the natural things of the Land, on which we stand and from which we all, ultimately come. The gods, however, transcend this origination; whilst they can be seen as having a very intimate and immanent presence within the energetic matrix of the Land, they essentially have their being in the realms of the stars and the dark spaces beyond and between them.

The Craft is concerned with knowledge, power, wisdom and understanding and the mastery of these, within the individual. As such, Witches acknowledge higher sources of knowledge, power, etc. than themselves and look to them for guidance, inspiration and tuition. In practice, this is achieved by various trance techniques or devotional exercises, that put them "in the way" of these Powers and, hence, enable them to partake of the same energy, if only for a short while. The Powers are generally conceived of in the forms of the gods of the different cultures that have inhabited the British Isles and Europe, as individual Beings and not as aspects or emanations of some, vague transcendent Being. (This does not hold true for all paths of Traditional Craft however, as some eschew the notion of gods altogether and work entirely with disembodied spirits, be that ancestral or of the natural world).

Unlike other, modern traditions however, these Powers are not *generally* given individual names when discussed, being referred to just as Him and Her, the Old Lad and Lass, the Old Horned God and the Pale Faced Goddess, or the Witchmother and the Witchfather; indeed these titles are used in group practice also. (As ever, there are always exceptions and some Traditions do consider themselves dedicated to historical, named deities, such as Woden, Atho, Lilith or Hecate). Where these deities take on a personal form, they are usually not the gods that were worshipped by the general pagan populations of the past, but the lesser known and acknowledged gods, those of the Underworld and the Outer realms. Witches have always been on the fringes of society – whatever that society was and is – and, hence, their deities reflect this, either being those that are sought in the dark, or those that are generally shunned by the rest of society.

On an individual level, however, it is not unusual for a Crafter to be dedicated to, or take as their tutelary patron, an individual, named deity, with whom to work and develop a deep and lasting relationship. They may choose the Power themselves, the Power may choose them in some way, or they may be inducted into a tradition that works with a specific deity only. Thus, as in the case of the late Magister Robert Cochrane, one can be "Od's man" i.e. dedicated to Odin, whilst working in the Clan of Tubal Cain. The Power becomes the guide and tutor of the Crafter, receiving honour and acknowledgement in return. This may be a lifelong partnership, or the patron Power may change at certain times; it is a very individual and private thing. No Crafter would generally speak the name of their tutelary Power to another, unless that other were also similarly dedicated. Hence, the use of titles such as Witchfather and Witchmother used in group work to get over the seeming disparity in the Powers worked with. I say "seeming" as, although the Powers are *not* seen to be part of each other (unlike the oft quoted precept from Dion Fortune that "All gods are one god...."), they *are* perceived of as partaking of a transcendent "unity" at a level where all is One, including ourselves. Indeed, one of the prime focuses in witch practice is to realise the divinity within and to partake of it whist still in the mortal state. (By this I do not mean to say that one "becomes" a god, but that one realises at a very deep level that both human and divine partake of exactly the same essence and that whatever the Powers are, we too may also one day become).

So how does this work in actual practice? To demonstrate this I will look at the two forms of Powers in turn – the "God" and the "Goddess" – and attempt to give some idea of how a Traditional Crafter would view and work with their particular deity. I shall not describe individual, named Powers, but will give an overview of types, "archetypes" if you like, of the Powers and leave the individual to make contact where they will. Finally, I will attempt to give a resolution to two seemingly disparate Powers and show how they can be conjoined within the body and soul of the Witch themselves.

The God

The Guises of the God

I approach from the East, rising in Glory.
The shining Child crowned in Fire and Light,
Yet also the Man who bears the Flame and bestows the Spark,
Cunning in Craft and Artifice, the Smith who shoes the fiery Mare.

I come from the South, powerful in Majesty.
The Horned Man of the Wild and Untamed places,
Who will expose your darkest secrets to the light of day
And howl with delight as I take my pleasure in your flesh.

I appear in the West, wise in Knowledge.
Cloaked and hooded I stand at the Crossroads,
Beckoning those that dare to cross the Threshold
And descend into the Hollow Hills to meet with the Dead.

I am the Ancient of Days and reside in the North.
Devil, Master and Father of All, First created from Night,
I am the Initiator and the Reaver, the Clutcher of Souls and the Guide.
I give and I take, for Her sake.

Historically, the Traditional Craft has been mainly God-orientated and has had the Horned God at the forefront of the majority of its workings, as opposed to the particularly Goddess and matriarchal path of most modern, pagan working. This has not always been the case and the female Powers are coming more to the fore in modern workings. However, be that as it may, the Goddess is always approached through the God, hence, I am dealing with this Power first.

In Traditional Craft there is no concept, unlike in modern paths, of a "balance" of energies between the male and female Powers. In modern practice it is seen as paramount that there is a balance in all things, particularly in the relationship between the God and Goddess. This is not the case in Traditional Craft, where the relationship is seen more as an "equilibrating flow", if I can put it like that. To explain - a balance in all things is considered a very stagnant state of affairs. If you have balance you have no movement, no growth or learning. If there is no growth, then you have decay and dissolution - a very bad state of affairs in a magical relationship, I think you would agree! However, where there is a flow of energy, "balance" being only achieved as a point on a sliding scale of movement, then there is no stagnation and, hence, continuing growth. At some periods the energy of the God is dominant, at others, that of the Goddess. Only rarely are They in perfect balance and that lasts no longer than the blink of an eye. They tend to have separate areas of function, just as in other areas of Life and relationships. When speaking of the Horned God energy, Adam Thorne of the HagStone tradition put it like this to me; "I appreciate that it's all raving, ripping, raping and rending but this is what the Male Mysteries are all about and the poor old Goddess is on the receiving end! Students of Old Craft realise that Goddess energy is passive energy... well, most of the time!" Whilst acknowledging that not all Traditional paths would agree with this statement (and some would violently disagree), it is indicative nonetheless of the way things are generally viewed. Although acknowledged as not being Traditional Craft, Aleister Crowley's "Hymn to Pan" is suggested as a good *starting* point in familiarising oneself with God energies, as viewed in the Old Way.

The Traditional witch does not view the God in the sense of "the God of X (Sun, Sea, Thunder, etc.)" as in the revivalist and neo-pagan paths. Apart from the individual deity dedication, the Crafter views the god as a sum total of these things and more, the individual deity being aspects maybe of two or three classical attributions, depending on how it affects the practitioner. It will probably be of more help now, if I go on to examine a few different "archetypes" and leave the reader to take it from there.

The King of the Wildwood

This is probably the aspect of the God that will be familiar to most people, that of the traditional horned or antlered god of nature. However, in Traditional Craft he is looked upon in a very different way to modern pagan practice. He is no gentle, loving, father-figure; he is not the comforting protector of his wild family nor is he the mild defender of the rights of "New Man". This is the aspect of the God that is most feared, and rightly so. As mentioned above, he may be seen as the render, the destroyer, the ripper and raper. He may send mortal terror into those that come in his way and can bestow madness and chaos upon those that are not careful in their dealings with him. This is the aspect of the God that the inquisitors of the past loved to scare their flocks with - the very Devil of the Sabbat himself. I do not mean to imply here that there is anything negative or even "evil" about this aspect, purely that he embodies the pure, unrefined driving force of the masculine side of Nature, which is truly "red in tooth and claw" and elicits a comparative response in us when we encounter Him. This is an aspect that we have mostly forgotten in our modern, comfortable, sanitised world. Life *can* be harsh and cruel; it does *not* conform to our concepts of what should and shouldn't be; it IS raw and painful sometimes, which is perfectly natural, even if we don't accept it. If all was sweetness and light, what would we learn from that? Where would be the challenge, the impetus and urge to go forward and achieve against all odds? So, essentially, what I am saying here is that the King of the Wildwood is the Challenging side of Nature; that force that impels us to become more than we currently are and enables us to overcome barriers that we thought were insurmountable, both within ourselves and the outside world.

As an aspect of the Natural world, the Wildwood King can be seen as having, himself, different aspects and these are often described as the Summer and Winter Kings, or the Oak and Holly Kings (whilst still acknowledging that they are one and the same being at the same time). Modern, neo-pagan practice tends to place the "reigns" of these two kings as occurring from winter solstice to summer solstice (Oak King), and from summer solstice to winter solstice (Holly King). This is missing the point and confusing terms entirely. Traditional Craft takes its inspiration from what actually happens in the natural world, rather than what some people write in books (sic). If you look around you in the wild, when do these two trees/aspects come into and go out of season? The Holly is admittedly an evergreen plant, so would fit any time of year, so we must look to the Oak for the answer. If you look at this tree, you will find that it is totally bare and devoid of leaves and life at the winter solstice, and will be for months to come, so how can it naturally – by observing the natural world – take over at this time? The Oak comes into new leaf and life around the end of April/beginning of May; around the time of the festival of Roodmass or Beltane. At the opposite end of the year, it drops its leaves and starts its winter dormancy around the end of October/beginning of November; around the time of the festival of Hallowmass or Samhain. So, the actual reigns of the Oak and Holly Kings are from Roodmass to All Hallows (Oak) and from All Hallows to Roodmass (Holly). This also correlates with their alternate names of Summer and Winter Kings. The attribution of their reigns to the winter and summer solstices actually refers to the solar aspect of the God, which is a very different thing altogether and not an aspect of the King of the Wildwood. The equinoxes and solstices are the times of great change on the inner levels; new tides of energy are released at this time and the inner currents change. This is not immediately reflected on the outer levels and, hence, refers to different aspects of deity, be that male or female.

During the summer months the Oak King holds sway. This is the male Power concerned with impregnation, growth and ripening, and not just on the physical level. During this period we look to the god for the energies of expansion and learning. It is an active period when Crafters would be out and about in the wild, studying the workings of life in their own environment. It is a time to feel the energies of life in the natural drive to procreate, to reproduce and to give birth at the harvest. During this period, those that are lucky enough to have a vision of or encounter the god, may experience him thus; a tall, muscular, "virile" and naked man, wild haired and bearded, horned as a bull or antlered as a stag, his skin tinted green or light brown, with tendrils of plant life wrapped and growing round him, perhaps shaggy of thigh and cloven footed. His eyes are feral, like those of a cat or wolf and are uncomfortable to meet; he inspires a feeling of great energy and power, but wild and uncontrolled, almost overwhelming in its intensity. His presence cannot be endured for long but his passing leaves an ache and sorrow as of great loss or bereavement and a feeling of enervation or depletion.

During the winter months the Holly King reigns. This is the Power concerned with dissolution, death and decay, clearing away the detritus of the past year. He is the male leader of the famous Wild Hunt that searches throughout the dark months for the souls of those unlucky enough to be lost and alone in the dark. He inspires terror and chaos; madness awaits those who meet him face to face on a lonely, windswept night and cannot control their inner turmoil. He is the Great Initiator that forces us to look into the dark and fearsome corners of our souls where we hide our most coveted secrets. He is the one that rips our homely security blankets from us and reveals us as we truly are, left bare to both face the challenge and continue, or to cower and retreat screaming back into the realms of so-called "normality". He is terrifying, awesome, soul-scarring and those granted a vision of him may see him thus; a tall manlike-shape in tattered black cloak, flying in the gale surrounding him, the rest of his body clad in dark trousers and tunic. A hood is drawn up over his head and his face is invisible, but ghostly white horns can be seen above him and an eldritch glow emanates from beneath the hood. There is a musty, decaying smell about him and it is impossible to look directly at his face. He inspires a sense of immense panic and fright, that freezing clutch in the bowels that portends utter terror and flight. If this can be overcome, great insights and revelations may be had.

Walking the Way

You may wonder, after the descriptions above, why anyone would want to put oneself in the way of such a terrifying entity as the King of the Wildwood. Traditional Craft is not cosy, it is not safe, and it is not "nice". The Witch is a certain type of person that deliberately seeks out experiences that will push them to their limits and beyond – hence, becoming more than they currently are. An encounter with this Power will certainly do this and this is why this particular Power is sought out. This exercise is essentially a development of the Wight-Tracking practice, given in chapter 6, SpiritWorking, but with a much deeper and more profound purpose. It is best if the Wight-Tracking exercise has been done with some success quite a few times before; this will enable the practitioner to be familiar with the actual territory to be used on a deeper level and also add some support from the local spirits if extra strength is needed. I shall repeat the basic instructions to refresh the readers memory, but with some essential differences and, hopefully, outcome. (Please refresh your memory of the entire procedure proper, before undertaking this working).

Best performed at dusk, in an area of woodland that you are familiar with (or, for the really adventurous, an area that you are totally unfamiliar with!). Dress according to the season in some natural fabrics and colours, so that you do not stand out in your environment. Take your stang or staff with you and go to the area that you have chosen to Walk the Way. The attitude that you must bear in mind is that of a hunter, only you are more likely to be the prey; be well aware of this. You wish to encounter, not capture and kill. This will be more difficult as your "prey" is wily, skilled and at one with His environment, so you must be likewise. Before you start, make a declaration – aloud or silently, it matters not – that your intention is to Walk the Way to encounter the King of the Wildwood in whatever form He chooses to manifest himself. State this firmly, with conviction and be sure you mean it.

Begin your tracking by taking a path into your chosen woodland. Step lightly on the earth, but do not tiptoe or crouch down; a gentle walk will do. It is the attitude that counts here. You must be as aware as you possibly can of everything that is happening around you, use all your senses to experience your journey. Smell the wind, taste the breeze, hear all the sounds around you, touch the earth/trees/bushes as you walk and take everything in with your eyes. You must be totally aware and also fixed on your intention. At the same time, you must still all "dialogue" in your head; cease to think of anything at all (as far as possible), and just experience. Walk at a slow but steady pace, making as little impact on your surroundings as you can. As you progress – and this may take some time, so be prepared – your senses may gradually become overloaded and "shut down", until only one or two are left. Just go with whatever happens and "follow your nose" so to speak. You should plan to end your Walk at a place of significance to you and of Power in the Land. This may be a standing stone, an ancient tree, a glade, a woodland spring or pool, any place that has power for you and is natural. When you arrive at this place, begin to Tread the Mill as previously described (if there is no natural, central point, place your stang upright in the ground and use this as your focus). Continue to pace until your sense of the Otherworld around you becomes almost overpowering and you are unable to continue. (You may wish to use a short chant embodying your intention here. Just keep it short and clear). At this point you should just stop, be still and await what will happen. Offer yourself up as a sacrifice to the Hunter in the Woods and be prepared for anything. Accept what happens and go with it. No-one can say what will occur; you are on your own. However much or little occurs, do not ever be fooled into thinking that nothing has; if you have performed the Walk with intent, sincerity and conviction, something always will and you will be changed in strange and subtle ways. When it is over, simply turn your back and walk away, retracing your steps without looking back. As soon as you arrive back at your starting point, or back home, have something to eat and drink (not alcohol), as this will help to "earth" you and bring you entirely back to the realm of everyday life. (If you have driven to your location, make sure you are O.K. to drive back. It may be wise to pause and have something to eat and drink first before driving). Take careful note of your dreams on that night, as they may be useful and revelatory to you.

It is unlikely that anything overly dramatic will happen on a first Walk but then again, it just might. Perform the Walk at different times of year and in different weathers to gain further experience.

(After the publication of the first edition of this book, a reviewer criticised the above working for being too simple and said that it would not produce the results suggested in the form given. I beg to differ. I can only suggest that the reviewer had not tried the working, or had performed it with insufficient focus or sincerity. I shall here give you the results of my first working of the rite, over 30 years ago. The effect of the rite may be judged in that I still remember it in perfect clarity.

After performing the rite and, whilst not receiving a visitation from the King of the Wildwood, being thoroughly shaken-up by the process, I returned home and went to bed. That night I dreamed of once more being in the woods where I had performed the Walk and this time I was not walking at a steady pace, I was fleeing through the trees in utter terror. I was being chased by I knew not what, only that it *wanted* me and I was petrified of it. I ran on and on through the woods, until I came to a clearing, in the middle of which was a small caravan. I rushed into it and slammed the door, locking it behind me. I stood there panting for a moment, before the van was hit a mighty blow and rocked back and forwards on its chassis. Then one of the windows smashed and a huge arm reached in; it was long, hairy and muscular, ending in very long and sharp nails. I was utterly terrified and am not ashamed to say that I screamed my head off, while the arm began to grope for me inside.

At that point, the dream image changed and I found myself lying on my back in some straw in an old, wood-timbered barn. I seemed to be a bit dazed and took a moment to get my bearings but almost immediately I became aware of the Being in front of me. Many, many times my size, this Being was looming over me and, I thought, about to lunge forward. It was in the shape of a huge, naked man, with a hairy skin, wild shaggy hair and beard and antlers sprouting from his head. He had an enormous erection and was coming towards me with an absolutely wild and manic gleam in his slanted eyes. At this point I woke up, sweating profusely and thoroughly disturbed. It took me a great while to get back to sleep that night, I assure you.

So, to say that the above rite will produce no discernible effect is completely wrong. As you can see, I still have the memory of that night with me over 30 years later and, whilst I initially misinterpreted the meaning of the dream, it certainly had a profound and life-changing effect on me, nonetheless.

For that reviewer to discourage people from even attempting an experience that could be of great benefit to them I consider to be wrong and, at the least, short-sighted. Hence, my very personal comments in this instance).

The Lord of the Mound

This aspect of the male Power is very elusive and difficult to grasp – that is His nature. He represents all that has gone before and is the sum and accumulation of ancient knowledge and practice. He is that which is Beneath and Within, Beyond and Underneath. He is the substratum of existence and the energy thereof. His realm is through the doors of the Hollow Hills and across the waters of knowledge and memory. He dwells in the Halls of Elphame and is Lord over the Faerie Folk in their Underworld realm, those possibly metamorphosed, ancestral beings. The Lord of the Mound is the representative, in a very special way, of the Ancestors, as it is through him that all their experiences are channelled. Some call him the Elven or Faerie King, as mentioned in the previous chapter, SpiritWorking and it is difficult to determine whether they are the same or separate beings. For all practical purposes it matters not, and you should react to him in whatever manner it is that he chooses to present himself to you. Many physical locations are associated with him, such as burial mounds and barrows and particularly places like Glastonbury Tor, Newgrange in Ireland and Sutton Hoo in East Anglia. He embodies the archetypal wizard or "shaman", learned in all things of the past and wise beyond measure. It is to him that we come in any form of divination or augury, as the knowledge of the past informs the future and directs it also. It is from these origins that we have the stories of mortals entering the Hollow Hills and seeing piles of gold, jewels and other riches just lying around. However, when they try to bring them back, all they find on their return is dross, leaves and twigs. The knowledge of how to recognise, understand and use the

Underworldly knowledge is not lightly given and the Lord of the Mound guards his secrets well.

Paradoxically, for one so intimately connected with the Dead, he is also the source of all future life – fertility if you like – as well. Our ancestors considered that all good things in life, all benefits, came from the Underworld gods. Julius Caesar writes of this in his book "De Bello Gallico", when describing the gods of the Gauls, declaring that they believe themselves descended from the god Dis, Lord of the Underworld. Because all folk when they die go to the Otherworld/Underworld realms, it is necessarily from here that all emerging new life comes. There are echoes of this theme in the tradition that the Faerie hills fling open their doors and the Otherworld Host rides out at Roodmass/ Beltane, one of the prime Old Sabbats of the Craft. This is not merely reflective of some simple, peasant fertility festival but an ancient truth indicative of the fact that new life emerges from the place it went when it died i.e. the Underworld. The Lord of the Mound is the guardian, protector, preserver and dispenser of this knowledge/ wisdom/life/fecundity and, as such can be seen as a dual-faced god, as many of the old gods were and are. The Light and the Dark, two sides of the same coin; one cannot have one without the other.

One of His prime images and the way in which he is most often seen or encountered, is as the White Stag; the mysterious being who bounds from the Underworld and will lead us back there, as part of our initiation into the Mysteries, if we are willing and able to follow Him. As when dealing with the King of the Wildwood, this can be a terrifying ordeal, as the Lord of the Mound allows us no hiding place, no veil to cover our innermost and darkest fears. He *knows* who and what we are and there is no point in approaching Him if you are not prepared to admit to all your faults and divulge your deepest secrets. The White Stag may lead us on a merry chase, but at the end you will come face to face with yourself.

Entering the Maze

To encounter the Lord of the Mound you may follow the path of the White Stag and enter the Hollow Hills. One way of attempting this is to enter and walk the path of the Maze, either in actuality or symbolically. If you wish to do this in actuality, you need to mark out the maze on the ground, in some lonely place where you will not be disturbed for some hours at least. You can mark it out either by scraping it into the ground with a stick or your staff, or you may wish to mark it with stones, sand or coloured soil, which can all be scuffed over later to leave no trace. A deserted beach at low tide is an ideal place; the maze can be traced into the sand, which will then be washed away later at high tide (keep an eye on the incoming tide though!). If you wish to hold or take a power-object or charm with you into the Mound, place this at the centre of the maze first and create the pattern around it.

If you are going to attempt this practice symbolically, the traditional way is to employ a Troystone. This is a large, flat pebble or piece of slate, on to which you have painted or inscribed the maze pattern. The maze pattern is then traced over very slowly with the forefinger, repeatedly, whilst reciting your chant and concentrating on your journey into the Hollow Hills. (See chapter 5, Entering the Twilyte). Below is the pattern you should use, either on the ground or on the stone.

(Some people may wonder why the term "Maze" is used, when the actual pattern utilised is that of the ancient Labyrinth. The reason is that the intention is to become "mazed" or "mazey", i.e. entranced. The term is taken from both Cornish and East Anglian dialect and means the same in both – to become giddy or tranced).

When you have prepared your maze, hallow your compass around the pattern using your knife to lightly cut a groove around it, considering it to be a perimeter around your entrance to the Hollow Hills – the Maze – a boundary ditch in fact. Call your guardian spirits at the directions to watch over you as you make your journey and continue with an appeal to the Lord of the Mound. Use these words or similar:

"Lord under the Mound, White Stag of the Hollow Hills
Give ear to my request and grant me entrance to your realm.
I have created a place hallowed in your name, Wise Lord,
Grant this boon of mine and usher me into the Hallowed Halls,
The Halls of the Fay, where dwell the Ancestors and the roots of all knowledge."

Commence a widdershins Mill and continue this until such time as you begin to feel the veil begin to thin. Now, either slowly begin to walk the maze to the centre, or slowly trace the design on the stone, with full concentration and attention to what you are attempting. As you do so, repeat this chant as many times as you feel necessary:

"I take the path that leads under the Mound.
Going around and around and beneath and within.
The path into the deep and the world forsake.
I take the path that leads to the Hollow Hills."

When you finally arrive at the centre of the maze, sit comfortably and close your eyes (take up your charm if you so wish). You should by now be in an entranced state with your mind receptive to receiving those impressions you seek. Conjure before your mind's eye a great, carven doorway, set into the side of a hill or mound. Push the door forwards and step over the threshold into what lies beyond…

At this point you are on your own; no one can say what you will encounter. However, remember that the rules in the Otherworld are not the same as in ours and beware of giving offence to any you may meet. Act with politeness but challenge anything you feel to be definitely wrong or purely illusory.

When you have finished your journey, come back through the door, closing it shut behind you. Open your eyes, then stand and retrace your steps through the maze, again going slowly and steadily. (Alternatively, trace the reverse pattern with your finger on your Troystone, starting in the centre and working your way out). When you reach the beginning, give thanks to all that have aided you, by including them in a housle feast. After this, dismiss your compass as normal and clear away all the things that you have used and simply walk out of the area, leaving offerings for the spirits you have encountered. Never neglect to thank and respect the People of the Hollow Hills! Do not look back.

The Master of Light

On one level, this aspect of the male Power *may* be seen as the Sun, the force that enlivens, illuminates and gives life to this world; the All-Father. He is the source of all the sun gods in human history – their waxings, wanings, risings and settings – and encompasses and subsumes them all. In actuality he is the divine power behind the sun, which originates and sustains it. He is the original point of Light from which all else proceeds and is so much more than "just" the god of the waxing and waning sun tides of the year. It will now be seen why the "Sun King" is not the Oak or Holly King and how very different they really are.

Yet, just as the Sun still shines at night, even though we cannot see it, so too does the Master. In the Darkness, the source of all things, and from within which our ancestors believed, all things had their beginning, He is the Light. He is that divine knowledge, wisdom, understanding and inspiration that shines out in the Dark but at the same time is also a part of it; He is the Lightbearer and the Teacher of all Humankind. He is the Witchfather, also known as Lucifer. For this reason He is depicted as the Horned/Antlered Lord of All, bearing a flaming torch upon his brow between the horns. In the ancient days He was the original friend of mankind; it was He that gifted humans with the spark of divine fire that lifted them above all other animals, that divine spark that burns in all but is ignored by the vast majority of mankind – the spark of divine life that is called by some the "Cunning Fire".

This fire, called "Teine" by the "Celts" and "Logi" by the Norse, is the source of all inspiration, magic, power and craft within the human body. It is the final fourth "element" as discussed in the previous chapters, Entering the Twilyte and SpiritWorking and is the gift of the Master of Light. This fire is present also in the Land on which we live and is that which enlivens the "spirit paths" and "ghost roads" that criss-cross and snake around our country. Indeed the power is akin to and likened to the serpent or the dragon, for it normally lies coiled and dormant within the human frame until, awakened and uncoiled, it arises like a flaming torch and takes its seat between the eyes, giving vision of the divine light and illuminating the whole physical frame. This is one aspect of the famous "Mark of Cain", said to be stamped upon all true Crafters and by which they may be known. This mark sets them apart from the rest of humankind and shows them to be spiritually descended from the Watchers, those angelic beings that aided the Master of Light in the ancient days in the tuition and education of the infant mankind, lifting it above the level of the ignorant savage. According to lore, all arts were then taught, particularly those of smithing, forging and crafting metals and precious stones. For this reason, one of the alternative names for the Master is the "Coal Black Smith" and He is, hence, also the Master of Horses and all the lore that is associated with them. Indeed, under this title He is honoured greatly in the Old Craft and this can be seen as a bridge between the Underworld powers of the God – the fires in the forges of the Hollow Hills – and the bright, celestial, transcendent powers of the Upper or Over world. In His guise of the Coal Black Smith He is also linked with the mysteries of the ancient Society of the Horseman's Word and the Toad and Bonesmen. All of these societies are known for their skill and craft in the old mysteries and their adherence to and devotion for the old Master of Light. There may also be a connection here between the "Black Face" Morris Dancers of British tradition and the lore of the Coal Black Smith. Many rural workers belonged to tradesmen's guilds that had a very dubious allegiance to the Church and preserved many of the old, pre-Christian aspects of knowledge. The fact that the dancers blacked-up their faces may not all have been due to the desire for anonymity, but also to show their true allegiance to their real Master.

The effect He has on the individual when called upon effectively is to open up the Crafter to the higher possibilities of the spiritual life. He can teach and show the development of the higher faculties of the soul, rather than the material interests of other aspects and will help in guiding and encouraging the Crafters' personal spiritual evolution. He is the highest manifestation of divine power within our sphere of mortal comprehension but is not transcendent for all that. He is vitally alive and permanently immanent, with us perpetually because of the divine spark He donated to us from His own being. It is said that He has actually physically incarnated many times in the history of our world and traces of His teachings and guidance can be found in many mythologies and legends throughout the world. It is suggested that for our own cultures, the seeker re-examine native Arthurian and Faerie lore to find traces. Amongst Traditional Witches, the historical Jesus – not the political creation of the Christian Establishment – has always been honoured for His teachings and it is not for nothing that he is known as the "Good Shepherd" and the "Divine Light".

The ritual given here is intended to have the effect of contacting the Master but also at the same time of fanning and raising the divine Fire within the individual. It appears to be quite simple in content and execution but do not underestimate it! It is far reaching in its effects and actions and is not necessarily gentle when first experienced. The first time I performed it, had I not been sitting down at the critical time, I would have been shaken off my feet!

Calling the Master

This rite needs to be performed outside at the Dark of the Moon, graphically embodying the Light in the Darkness. It employs a slightly different version of hallowing the compass, which can be seen as a development of the techniques discussed in chapter one. Start to mark out your area when there is still enough light to see, as no flame must be lit before the beginning of the rite. Alternatively, if it is already dark, wait a while for your eyes to adjust to the dark, well enough to see, before beginning. When the area is cleared, place an unlit lantern at the centre of your ritual space and one at each of the four direction points, at the edge of the compass. Place the Stang in the ground at the North, with the thurible and things for the housle feast before it. You will also need a fresh, beeswax candle/taper.

Physically mark out the edge of your compass using your knife and words of your choosing, or as suggested here. Lightly score the ground as you go and see the depression filling with living fire, the fire in the Land that is the same fire within you that you seek to raise in this working. You may say something like the following:

"Fire in the Land, Flame of Night,
Awaken the Master's inner Light.
Scribe this compass moat around,
Ward all in this hallowed ground."

Go round three times with this.

Return the knife to the foot of the stang and take up the taper. Go to light the central lantern and envisage the flame so created as the first Light in the Darkness, first created from Chaos. Light the taper from the lantern and go to light the candle in the north. Stand before it and envisage yourself as before a great chasm in a rock face, looking up towards the starry night sky. Say:

"I stand at the North and take the first step upon the Way.
Powers and Guardians of the Northern portal, I call thy attention!
Rise here at this threshold through which I pass,
And may thy strength sustain me upon my journey."

Turn and walk sunwise around the compass edge. With your inner vision, see yourself passing through the chasm and onto a curving path that leads out of the darkness, towards the dawning light. The path leads to your right and slightly uphill, as you are travelling a spiral path, not a circular one. Continue round the compass, back to the North and on until you stop before the East. Light the candle and say:

"I have come to stand at the East.
Powers and Guardians of the Eastern portal, I call thy attention!
Rise here at this threshold through which I pass,
And may thy strength sustain me upon my journey."

Continue on round the compass. With your inner vision, pass under a rustic archway at the bottom of a hill. The dawning sun lights up fertile farmland and in the distance you can see and hear a working forge. It rises slightly above you and waves of heat emerge from it as you approach. The sound of a hammer on an anvil is loud and skilful, yet you cannot see the smith. Continue round the compass, back to the East and on until you stop before the forge at the the South. Light the candle and say:

"I have come to stand at the South.
Powers and Guardians of the Southern portal, I call thy attention!
Rise here at this threshold through which I pass,
And may thy strength sustain me upon my journey."

Continue round the compass and in your inner vision, pass through the doorway into the forge. The heat is intense and the sense of power immense yet, although the sound of hammering is deafening, you still cannot see the smith. Follow the path round and through the forge, still heading upwards and out the back of the forge, where there sits a large tub of water on a slight rise. You pass round the compass, back to the South and come to stop before the tub of water at the West. As you light the candle, you hear the loud hiss and bubbling of the water as a red hot piece of iron is quenched in its depths. Say:

"I have come to stand at the West.
Powers and Guardians of the Western portal, I call thy attention!
Rise here at this threshold through which I pass,
And may thy strength sustain me on my journey."

Continue round the compass, passing the water tub and along the path as it curves upwards to your right. The sound of the smith working behind you begins to fade, as you climb towards the entrance of a dark cave at the head of the path. Pass on round the compass, back to the West and on to the entrance of the cave before the Northern candle. Blow out your taper and say:

"I have come to stand at the threshold of the Master of Light,
hidden in the Darkness.
I call the attention of all the Powers and Guardians,
As I step through this portal and continue my journey.
May all your strength sustain me."

Remain standing before the candle at the North and in your inner vision, step forward into the cave.

Once you are ready, go to re-light your taper at the central lantern. Pace the edge of the Compass, widdershins, gently chanting:

"Kindle the Flame and fan the Light,
Call the Master in the Night."

Make as many circuits as you feel necessary.

Return to the Stang at the North and fix the candle – still lit - between the horns. Say;

"Horned Master of Cunning Craft,
Behold the Light between the Horns.
Come forth Master, All-Father and Ancient One,
O Son of Morning, hear my prayer."

Light the charcoal and sprinkle on the incense*. Raise the thurible before the Stang and make an offering of the incense, before placing it at the foot. As you raise it, breathe deeply of the smoke and say:

"All hail, Great Shining One,
Here is my offering, here is my breath.
Fill me with Thy subtle wisdom,
Grow forth at the sound of my call."

Now sit/kneel in the centre of the Compass, facing the Stang in the North, with the lantern at your back.

Begin the following chant, slowly and continue for as long as is felt necessary:

"Fire within, Fire without,
Master within, Master without."

Go with whatever happens.

When finished, hallow some bread and wine and make the usual offerings at the base of the Stang.

Give thanks and put out the candle between the Horns.

Beginning once more in the North, make your return journey out of the cave. Say:

"I have passed over the threshold of the Master of Light, hidden in the Darkness.
I thank all the Powers and Guardians,
As I return through this portal.
Your strength has sustained me."

Go to the West and thank the Powers and the Guardians at each direction, re-tracing your steps widdershins as you wind back down the hill and out through the chasm in the rocks. Blow out the candle at each direction as you go. Say:

"I return through the West (S/E/N).
Powers and Guardians of the Western (S/E/N) portal, I thank thee for thy attention!
Withdraw now from this threshold,
Your strength has sustained me."

Dismiss compass in your normal fashion.

Clear all away as if you had never been and walk away without looking back.

It is imperative that you ground yourself properly after this rite and make sure that you give yourself time to recover fully; it can be some time before you return to normal consciousness if the rite has been effective.

*Incense
1 measure Pine needles
1 measure Holly wood
1 measure Basil
1 measure Wormwood
1 measure Pine resin
1/2 measure Blackthorn flowers
2 drops Pine oil
2 drops Clove oil
Small amount of Honey
Few drops of Sloe Gin.

Combine the ingredients as previously explained in an earlier chapter, with enough of the honey and gin to bind all together. Place in a stoppered, dark glass jar and allow to mature for a few days on a warm, bright windowsill. Keep in a dark cupboard after. Use sparingly.

The Goddess

The Threads of the Goddess

Consider the Initial Thread.
I am Virgin, I am the Beginning,
The Seed from which all else will follow.
I am the Blood-Daughter,
The Cleft One who emerges from the Earth.
I am the Sacred Dancer, the Seductive Spirit, the Vital Force.
From my Body flow the Waters of Life.

Consider the Second Thread.
I am Mother, the Fruitful One,

She who enlivens the Land.
I am the eternal Dam,
Mother of the Soul, Wellspring of Comfort.
I am the Weaver, the Artist, the Fountain of Repose,
The Divine source of Feminine Fecundity.

Consider the Third Thread.
I am Age, the Midwife of Wisdom,
She who tends to the birth of Knowledge.
I am the Divine Ancestress,
The Sorceress with the Cup of Inspiration.
I attend the Sowing and the Reaping and hold the Land in my Care.
I determine the span of Life and Death.

Consider the Fourth Thread.
I am Ancient, the Crone in the Darkness,
She who rots the corpse at the end of Lives.
You may not see me, for I am as the Dark Moon,
Shrouded in secrecy, midst the far Stars.
I bear the Soul in that passage between Life and Life,
The Dissipater, beyond all Limits.

Combine the Four Threads.
Consider the Fifth?
The Great & Terrible Queen who is Within and Beyond All.
I am the Luminous Moon and the Fertile Earth, the Blood-Mother,
The Controller of Time and Tides and Destiny, the Space between the Stars,
Creator and Destroyer, who Is, who Has Been and who Will Be.
I am the Continual Vital Force, I am Fate.

The Goddess, as perceived in Traditional Witchcraft, is not the "Triple Moon Goddess" of Robert Graves' "White Goddess", so beloved of modern pagans and Wiccans. Neither is she solely the fertile Earth Mother of so-called

"Neolithic" belief. She does indeed encompass both of these elements but She is so much more. Although the Craft initially springs from the Land, its power, tides and seasons and She is the embodiment of this, yet She stands ever in the background of Traditional practice and belief, never fully perceived or apprehended, nor does She ever fully reveal Herself. Whereas the male Powers are very much to the fore and active in a dynamic way – generally – the female Powers are much more concerned with the "overall picture", the planning and the formation of energy flows, which the male then manifests on this level. It is She that holds the tides of Life in Her hands, be they seen as threads on a loom - the warp and weft that create the final pattern – or the tides of moon and sea that wax and wane, as does She. She is Fate, Wyrd, Doom and Destiny. It is she that stands behind the stars, in the spaces in-between, and orders their courses. If the God has the power to make and shape, to craft and make manifest, it is She that originates and inspires that power. She is and can be all things to all Mankind and is the eternal Mystery. It has been said of Her that, "No man has lifted my veil and seen my face. And in the moment that he does so he shall perish". This is still true. No one depiction of the Goddess can fully express Her powers and nature but Her essence exists in all the goddesses invented by Man – for all have been. The true Witch Goddess is beyond all forms and figures, beyond all times and tides, as these are Her tools and She cannot be known by them alone. She is the ultimate origin and source of all things, the Divine Ancestress and true Witchmother.

She can be, seemingly, cruel and capricious at one moment and wildly seductive and loving the next. She can make the knees of a man, or woman for that matter, turn to water in an instant and raise the hairs on the back of your neck in horror a moment later. She is the First Mother and Divine Ancestress of us all, the Bloodmother of W.G. Gray's Sangreal Prayer and it is from Her that we all issue and to Her that we shall all return at the end of times. This is not a simple or easy Being to comprehend. She bears little resemblance to the bright, loving and caring Goddess of modern pagan practice. She is the stern and tireless Keeper of the Mystery of Creation. It is She that heaves the innocent souls from unformed chaos and imposes upon them the order of manifestation. It is She that births them into the Light of the World. Likewise, is She, the Great Destroyer. She is the vaunted Crow Goddess of Battle and Lust, whose blood-soaked hair betokens Her insatiable desire for destruction. Her influence is found in all of the daughter "avatars", from Creatrix to Destroyer. It would be impossible to fully describe Her in a work of this size, so I shall attempt to give an impression of two aspects and hope that the interested Crafter will come to find Her somewhere in-between.

The Great Queen and the Black Goddess are Traditional titles for two very different aspects of the Witch Goddess and are sometimes viewed as Her Summer and Winter faces respectively. However, as you will see, they are much more than just this and both aspects are just as present as each other at any given time.

The Great Queen

Life, Love, Sexuality, Death and the Land - This may seem a strange way to sum up the essence of the "brighter" feminine Powers, but it is to these fundamental and archetypal basics that we must look if we are to have any chance of understanding the complex nature of this aspect. All the attributes mentioned above have one essential thing in common and that is "being alive"; yes, even Death is part of Life, being just one stage upon the journey. The Traditional Craft is essentially a practical way of conducting oneself and one's spirituality; therefore all the pre-requisites for Life are embodied in the Great Queen. She is concerned with everything from the beginning to the end of Life and all that comes in between. Thus, she is at one and the same time the sensuous maiden who entices Her lovers into both dangerous and enlightening embraces. She can lead them on a merry dance and destroy their dreams and assumptions utterly, only to open them up to a greater level of reality, awareness and understanding. Love can come at any stage of Life and is not just associated with the heady days of Youth; therefore, She is also the mature and understanding woman, who teaches by example. She is the Mother who gives birth in care and compassion and also the wrathful teacher who chastises to drive home harsh lessons, the better to equip Her children with the tools for development. She is the tender doe who cares for Her fawn and the remorseless sow that devours Her own piglets. At the end of days, She is the Queen in mourning who nurtures the souls of the dead in the Isles of Avalon, there to await rebirth from the midst of Her Castle of Roses. It must be remembered that to the Crafter, the gods are both marvellous and mysterious and we do not seek to put the perceptions of mankind onto our deities. Therefore, if the understanding and concerns of people change – feeling less comfortable than they did with certain aspects of the deities they have adored for centuries – that does not mean that the gods themselves change. As they are products and indeed part of, the natural universe around us and although they too evolve, they cannot change their basic nature, even if we happen not to find certain aspects acceptable in a changing world. The Crafter knows this and seeks to know his or her gods as they are, warts an' all! To feed and nurture her cub, the vixen must kill the fluffy bunny and present it with blood-stained muzzle.

The Great Queen is to be seen in the Land, which is held as sacred to the Witch, as this is the outer garment of the inner realities. Not just the dirt and soil of the physical realm, but in the shining light that animates its very essence, within and integral to it, for those with eyes to see. This light partakes of the same essence and origin as that of the Master of Light, the Fire within, but is different in kind, being the life energy of a complementary force – the feminine nature of divinity. To some the Great Queen is named "Sovereignty" and is the animating spirit of the countryside; Mother Earth or Nature if you like. This is true, but again She is so much more; She is the very Life in and of the Land; without Her it simply would not be. Consider Her power. She is the force that thrusts a tiny blade of grass through solid concrete. She is the strength of a twist of ivy that pulls down a building. She is the determination that makes a woodland glade re-grow after destruction by fire but She is also the power that destroys all these. This is all part of the one thing and it is something that every Crafter has to learn and experience, no matter how unpalatable it may be. The Great Queen may not seem so approachable when first you experience Her but understand even a part of Her nature and you will understand a part of yourself, which will lead you to a deeper understanding of both.

Addressing the Dame

This is less a rite and more of a continuing practice but is nonetheless valid for that. It is designed to build up a relationship over a period of time, between the Crafter and the Great Queen. Her nature is such that it would be impossible to do it otherwise, even with repeated, single rites.

Pick a time of year that feels right to you, one that you feel in tune with, to start this practice. It doesn't matter when that is, nor the phase of the Moon, as long as it resonates with you and feels right. Make a note in your diary as you will need to remember when you started. You need also to make a form of personal dedication, or vow, before you begin, that you will continue this practice for a year and a day and will make your trips out at regular, set, intervals. This may be once a day, once a week or once a month, but at no less a frequency than this last. This is not a game, nor is it flower arranging, but an attempt to make a strong and lasting link with the Goddess as manifest within the Land.

Go out into the countryside for a long walk. Again, it doesn't matter whether it is woodland, moor land, coastal or mountainous, as long as it is out in the "wilds" (as far as we can find them these days!). On your first trip, look out for some natural materials out of which you can create a rough, human shape. This could be a piece of wood that you could roughly carve, or some twigs/straw/vines that you could twist into shape; maybe some dried seaweed stalks or dried remains of a bush or creeper. Anything that catches your eye and that can be used to create a form. When you find them, take a moment to stop and make a small prayer of thanks to the Dame (another term for the Great Queen) and maybe leave behind a bit of bread, milk or honey that you will have brought as an offering to the wild. Once found, take your materials home and begin to work on them. You need to form them into a simple, humanlike form, roughly female appearing if possible. As you work, keep your mind on the thought that you are fashioning an image in which you will ask the spirit of the Dame to dwell and to which you may address petitions, prayers and requests for aid in your work. The image will become a form of fetish, or idol if you will, but one that is empowered both by your focussed intent and by the indwelling energy and spirit of the Great Queen. As you work, intone a petitionary charm, using these words or similar.

"As I work to shape this form,
This charm of craft I make,
May powers of the Dame emerge,
With every twist and snake.
I call the Great Queen here to be,
Devotion's plea addressed,
Grant presence of divine intent,
This image now be blessed."

Once you are satisfied with your initial image, cover it with a dark cloth and put it away somewhere safe, away from profane eyes. Over the next year, you will make frequent trips out into the countryside, as per your initial vow and in all weathers. On these trips you will collect items from nature that you will add to your initial image, refining and developing it over a period. You can add anything that you find, as all things partake of the essence of the Great Queen; leaves, bark, seeds, nuts, berries, creepers, feathers, fruits, bones, twigs, shells, stones, whatever you feel attracted to that can be incorporated. Add whatever you find each time you come home, using the same chant, then take some time to sit in contemplation before the image, focusing on what you are doing and calling on the Dame to indwell it. Then cover it with the cloth again and put it away securely. Over the year of creation the image will grow and develop, not just physically but magically and spiritually as well. After a while you should begin to feel a palpable sense of something 'other' around it and you may like to start using it in your rites at this point.

At the end of the year (remember your original date!), you will have created a living image of your relationship with the Great Queen. You will have learnt to appreciate and honour Her in all seasons and weathers and your knowledge of Her works will have grown immensely. Not only this but a little spark of Her being (if you are successful), will be indwelling the image and you may use it for all forms of your work. Obviously this is not a task to be entered upon lightly or taken up on a whim. Once started, this work must be carried out to the end, which will be a test of both your devotion to this path, your integrity and your perseverance. However, you may well be richly rewarded for your efforts.

The Black Goddess

Although this aspect of the feminine Power is termed "Black", it has no connotation of evil or negativity –

except as it may be perceived by the fragile human ego when coming face-to-face with the immense power and force of this Being. The term "Black" refers to the fact that She deals mainly in the realms of things secret, hidden generally from the eyes of humankind, occult in fact. Her ways are those of Night and Mystery, of Planning, Guile and Craft. For those who are able, Her presence may be felt both in the patterns of the stars above, the phases of the Moon and in the deep places below the Land. She is the keeper – and spinner – of the patterns that lead mankind on its endless quest for soul evolution and it is She that shapes, creates and dictates those patterns. She is Fate, Destiny, the Ultimate Goddess. (Perversely, this same aspect is also known as the "Pale-Faced Goddess" and represents exactly the same things).

The concept of this Power derives from some of the earliest experiences of mankind; indeed it was She that inspired them. Gazing up at the stars on a clear, cloudless night, away from city lights, can still be quite an overwhelming experience to someone who knows all the scientific explanations of what they are and where they come from. Imagine the utter awe and not a little fear as our ancestors looked up in the same way and experienced that jolt of near total insignificance that can still overwhelm us today. The thought that the Being who orders such a vast universe has Her very existence and origin out there among the stars, in the spaces in-between, but is also concerned with the intimate details of our own lives can be a very daunting and humbling one. Likewise, when our ancestors contemplated the deep, dark places of the world, caverns and caves leading deep into the unknown depths, where spiders might be the least of your worries, the same feeling of awe and insignificance came over them. This was a recognition and an inner knowing that the Being that orders and shapes all things is ultimately unknowable and we are all pretty insignificant in comparison.

However, having said that, it does not mean that we cannot have a very personal and meaningful appreciation of and relationship with this Goddess. To show you what I mean – and perhaps to illustrate something that is very difficult to put into words – I shall tell you something of a rite I once performed in which I had the honour, and shock, of coming very much into contact with Her.

The rite was a simple one, as the best ones always are and I had just finished the preliminaries and was settling down to await a response. I first became aware of being drawn upwards out of my body and away from my immediate vicinity, until I could see the surrounding countryside below me, the whole country and finally up into space, where I had a view of the planet, all blue and white, hanging against a backdrop of black space and stars. The planet drew away and for a time I just hung in space, floating. After a while I became aware of a pentagram, or I should say five stars with lines that seemed to join them like a pentagram, hanging before me. I seemed to go through the centre then, like a gateway, into more black space, like a void. I then became aware of faint stars in the background and the very bright stars of the constellation of Cassiopeia in the foreground, with a picture superimposed over it, like a lady reclining on a couch in outline, holding a distaff upright in her left hand, but I could still see the other stars through it. The constellation then began to shine very brightly and to pulse and throb with a great energy. I felt the back of my neck begin to throb and heat built up behind me. This continued for a while, and then everything began to fade away. The last thing I was aware of was a female voice in my ear, whispering like liquid honey, but chilling at the same time. I couldn't understand the words, but I shall never forget them.

This is just an example of the type of contact you might experience if you are lucky enough. What the experience means is very personal to the individual and you will have to work out your own for yourself if you are fortunate enough to have one.

As the shaper and creator of the patterns of life, She is also the supreme Sorceress and the keeper of the magic cauldron in the Otherworld; the cauldron that is perpetually bubbling away, brewing up the next shapes of force to be unleashed on the world. It is to this aspect of the Goddess that we appeal for any of the grand magics, the great life-shaping and life-changing works that we would attempt. These are not to be approached without great consideration and meditation beforehand but, when we are certain that it is the right thing to do – and Traditional Crafters *do* meddle and change things – then it is to the great Black Goddess that we apply for the permission and power to carry out the work. She will aid, or not, for Her own reasons, not ours and it may be a very long time indeed before we find out those reasons, if ever.

Watching the Stars Below

This rite has a two-fold intention. Firstly, it is intended to put you in touch with the essence of the Black Goddess, so that you may have just a small experience of the immensity of Herself. She is called upon as the Great Shaper who has Her being in the vasty depths of Outer Space and also their counterpart in the depths below the Land; the caverns in the Underworld where the Cauldron of Fate and Inspiration is kept perpetually seething. Secondly, it is intended to give you some insight into the patterns that govern your life and shape the path that you are likely to follow. It will *not* tell you your future or your fortune in life but may give you some ideas as to where your life path is taking you and what to do about it. Be open to all impressions during this rite as, when dealing with matters of Fate or Wyrd, things don't always go as we intend and they may take on a pattern of their own!

Perform this rite at the Dark of the Moon, on a cloudless night when the stars can be clearly seen. Perform it out in the open, with no obstructions, at the top of a hill if at all possible. This rite incorporates another variation on the normal compass hallowing, which you may choose to use if you wish, or continue to use your normal format; the choice is yours.

Prepare and clear your ritual area as usual. Place a Cauldron full of clean spring, well or rain water, in the centre of the area, positioned so as to reflect the stars on the surface when you are standing over/beside it. Have a Cup of similar water standing beside it and four, white stones, to mark the directions later. (You may like to use some form of natural quartz, or similar, to catch and reflect the available light). Have no other lights at all, just the light of the stars above. You will also need three bowls or pouches, containing the "makings" for marking the edge of your compass. This will involve laying 3 concentric rings of different materials, whilst you remain on the *inside* as you go round. The symbolism of each of the rings can be complex and involved and I direct the interested reader to the suggested reading list at the end of this book for more details than I can give here. However, in brief, the rings are composed as follows;

1) A ring of Salt, representing Life. All things need salt to live; it preserves and cleanses and gives continuation.

2) A ring of Ashes, representing Death and Rebirth. Different Traditions use different woods or herbs, but the most usual are the mixed ashes of burnt Willow and Birch trees. This represents the passage from one Life to another.

3) A ring of Water, Wine, Vinegar & Salt, representing the River of Time, classically the River Lethe. Water represents Time itself (and also the River). Wine represents all those good things in life that we leave behind. Salt and Vinegar represent life and all the moments of bitterness and sadness in it. When we "Cross the River" at death, we forget and leave behind all the good things of life and come to stand at the threshold of the Castle of the Goddess.

(You may wish to create your three concentric "ditches" in advance of beginning the rite, in which to pour out your symbolic items. Remember to leave enough room to walk between them and enough room inside the final ring to work your rite).

The Cauldron in the centre of your area should be positioned where the four lines of the quarter directions meet and represents the Castle of the Goddess, in this instance. At the centre of the compass, it symbolises the place of power, where this world and the Other meet, where order develops from chaos, and recognisable patterns emerge to view. Hence, it is the place of the Creatrix of All Time; the Black Goddess.

Have all things in readiness and compose yourself before you begin.

Take up your bowl/pouch of Salt and starting at the North, go round clockwise, pouring it out in the outer ditch in a fine trickle, saying words to the effect of

> *"This Salt represents all that works to preserve Life. I create the Ring of Life."*

As you go, focus intently on the meaning of the words you use. When you have come round to the North again, step back and, using the bowl of ashes, create the second ring, saying words like

> *"These ashes represent both Death and Rebirth. With the creation of this ring, I cut myself off from the world of the Living and all it entails."*

Again, focus intently on the meaning as you go round. When back at the North, step backwards to create the final ring. As you pour the liquids, use words such as

> *"This River represents Time and Memory. As I create this ring, I am severed from the cycle of Death and Rebirth. I am beyond Death itself and stand at the threshold of the Castle of the Goddess."*

Focus on these words and understand their import.

It is now time to place the four stones to mark the directions. Take the first stone to the North and place it on the inside of the inner ring. Stand and look up to the night sky, pause and say:

"Black Goddess."

Return to the Cauldron, take up the second stone and place it in the East. Look at the bright points in the dark, say:

"Lady of the Stars."

Return to the Cauldron, take up the third stone and place it in the South. Look around you and say: "Mother of All."

Return to the Cauldron, take up the final stone and place it in the West. Look down below you and say:

"Queen of the Underworld."

Return to the Cauldron and take up the Cup. Raise it up before you. From each direction of the compass, envisage a stream of fiery light, approaching from the far distance. See them approaching, like four cords or threads, snaking in from infinity. As they move towards you, become aware of intense force coming from both above and below you as well; thick cords of pulsing blue fire approaching from infinitely above and infinitely below. Envisage all these six cords of force as approaching and coming together in the Cup in your hands. Once you can see the contents of the Cup glowing with the combined force of these threads, slowly and gently pour the contents into the Cauldron before you.

Now, begin to tread the mill widdershins around it, softly intoning the following chant:

"Ancient One of Wisdom
Hidden Mistress of the Night,
Hear the Call I send you
Fill me with insight.
I reach across the darkness
In Silence Above and Below,
I seek the hidden patterns
And Will to Dare and Know."

Continue the chant until it fades away naturally and, from then on, continue the mill in silence.

When you feel that shift in consciousness that tells you the veil is parting, stop pacing and sit or kneel beside the cauldron. *Gaze* upon the surface of the waters and contemplate the reflections of the stars therein. Do not try to scry, but call now upon the Black Goddess in your own words and ask what you wish to know, whilst still looking into the waters. Await what will come with patience and fortitude; it may take some time.

When you have gained all that you feel that you can at this time, anoint your brow with some of the water and make thanks in your own words. You may celebrate a small feast here if you so wish, but many people feel that this is not the time; it is up to you.

When you have finished, rise and starting in the North, go to each stone in turn, widdershins. Bow, with a slight inclination of the head, pick up the stone and replace it by the Cauldron. Next, tip over the Cauldron, such that the outflow washes away a section of all three rings that you originally created. Collect your equipment and walk back in silence, through the gaps you have made in the rings. As you pass through, see and feel yourself crossing back over the River, the cycle of Death and Rebirth, to return to the world of the living. Walk away without looking back.

When you arrive home, go straight to bed and take especial note of any dreams on arising; they may well have something important to tell you.

Approaching the Power

Although generally approached as the God or Goddess – and often both together – ultimately, many witches consider that there is only one divine Power. Some consider that this is the Ultimate Goddess, the One behind all others and the One who birthed the Goddess that we know and have described above. Some call Her Chaos, that which was before both Fate and Night and gave both life. She is beyond understanding and apprehension and can only be dimly imagined. Some, again, simply call this Power, the Devil, and leave it at that. He is seen as a Being that is against the accepted norms of society. He is firmly linked to ideas of mayhem, civil disobedience, lack of good citizenship and ruthlessness. He is cunning in executing His will and desires and in achieving His ends. He is a being characterised by His lust for pleasure and the good things in life and also, significantly, for his knowledge of arcane secrets and power over the things of this world – His magical knowledge and ability – things that normal society, and, in particular, the Church, deems dangerous, forbidden and not to be indulged in. Witchcraft is associated with the Devil mainly because He is the symbol of opposition, the ultimate "Opposer"; *not* "evil", but in opposition to whatever is the accepted norm and, hence, frightening to most people. He is the Being who pushes and drives the individual to become more than they are, by whatever means possible.

Others, however, see this ultimate Power as a union of both God and Goddess, male and female, a conjunction and resolution of seeming opposites. This Power is sometimes imaged as the androgynous idol known as Baphomet, supposedly worshipped by the Knights Templar and given its most widespread depiction by the occultist Eliphas Levi. Shown as the horned goat-devil of the Sabbat, this Baphomet bears both breasts and a rearing phallus, combining the essential "qualities" of both male and female. It also bears between its horns, the flaming brand of divine illumination and knowledge. It is this flaming brand that is the key to this resolution, as it stands *between* the horns on the goat-devil's brow and combines the essence of both male and female but transcending them both. If we go back to look at the description given of the Stang in the first chapter of this book, we will see that this tool may also be used to depict both the masculine and feminine sides of creation and it, too, often has a lighted candle or lantern placed between the fork at the top. So the Stang already contains the symbolism of resolved opposites, however, or whatever, else it is used to represent by the individual Crafter. This is the image that gives the Witch their focus for their own, internal resolution of opposites. As essentially a Mystery path – as mentioned earlier – the ultimate goal for many Traditional Witches is the mystical union and realisation of the dual nature of the human spirit and the integration of both sides into a whole. This may be helped by many of the methods that I have already described in this book, but the process is often begun by the rite variously known as Initiation or Dedication.

Whilst there *are* various established Traditions within modern Traditional Witchcraft, each with their own acknowledged lineage and practices, historically it was more usual for the witch to be a solo practitioner. Certainly they gathered together upon occasions when fellows were known in the vicinity and certainly they swapped lore and instructed each other in their individual ways of knowledge but the path was – and is – essentially a solitary one. Certainly no other witch can bring about this resolution in another, as it is an intensely personal realisation. To begin on this path is a big step for the individual and is usually marked by a special rite, as mentioned above. Strictly speaking, one cannot initiate oneself; this must be done either by another person or by the Gods themselves, and is why this term is more often used to denote entrance into an established Tradition with its own ways of doing things. The person seeking to start out on the path of a Traditional Witch would more often than not – and certainly historically – have performed a rite of Dedication to the Powers or Power, howsoever they were viewed.

There are various traditional methods of doing this and I would like to finish here by suggesting a way of performing a Dedication for the interested reader, drawn from a combination of these traditional methods. It is intended to bring the individual to the "attention" of the One Power (although this may be altered to suit the individual's focus of practice), who may then accept the dedication, or not, as They will. This should become apparent at the time of the rite, or soon after!

I shall also describe another, final, method of creating the compass. This is a bit more formal and may be of more use to a gathering of witches, rather than for solitary use. However, it has Traditional antecedents and the individual may like to use this on important occasions – such as a Dedication rite – or for seasonal rites and observances, outside of the normal working pattern.

A Rite of Self-Dedication to the Old Power

This rite should take place at the time of the Full or Dark of the Moon, depending on the orientation of the individual. It should be performed in some wild and secret place; a deserted seashore, an abandoned heath, an ancient grove, or alternatively in a secluded churchyard or cemetery. The location will depend upon the availability of place but, more importantly, on the energetic and devotional leanings of the individual practitioner. You will need to take with you your Stang, Knife, Cord, Cauldron and the things for a small housle feast. In addition you will need some incense and a burner, a beeswax taper, a small bottle of spring water and a bowl to put it in and some salt. (These last things will represent the four classical elements of Air, Fire, Water and Earth respectively, within your rite). Aim to arrive at your chosen location while there is still some light to set up, or make sure you bring a lantern with you to provide the same, but take a lantern with you anyway. Clear away all obstructions and mark out your physical area of working. Have everything you will need within this area. Aim to start after sunset but before midnight.

Place your Stang in the centre of the area, tie one end of your cord around it and attach your Knife to the other end. Silently, from the North, go round and create the edge of your compass, marking it deeply in the earth, at the same time as seeing the blue fire fill the ditch as you go. Remember what this means and what you are doing. When you have come back to the North, untie your Knife and Stang and tie your cord around your waist. Place your Stang in the ground at the North and your Cauldron directly in front of it. (If you wish, you may fill the Cauldron with soil/stones and plant your Stang within it; I hope by now the symbolism should be obvious here). Arrange your other items before the Cauldron, to your liking, before continuing. Pour some of the water into the bowl and make the sign of the equal-armed cross over it, saying such words as:

> *"In the Name of the Ancient Providence, be this water purified, blessed and made consecrate."*

Go round the edge of the compass three times, sprinkling the water as you go.

Return to the North and take up the incense. Take this round the compass three times and return to the North. Take up the salt and sprinkle round likewise, returning to the North once more. Light your beeswax taper and, finally, take this round three times also. As you go round in each circuit, softly chant these words or similar:

"As I tread this compass round,
The Castle is raised, the Castle is bound.
Elements four I call your powers,
Secretly in these darkling hours.
As I tread this compass-stead,
The Castle is raised, the Castle is blessed."

Return to the North and place the lit taper between the "horns" of the Stang, being fully aware of the symbolism that you are creating.

Pause a few moments, before calling upon the Spirit Guardians at the directions.

At the North, use these words, or similar:

"Arise, Black Spirits of the North!
Ward, guard and watch over this rite,
With the force of the airy darkness!"

Pause for a moment, then go to the East. Use these words or similar:

"Arise, Red Spirits of the East!
Ward, guard and watch over this rite,
With the force of the fiery dawn!"

Pause for a moment, then go to the South. Use these words or similar:

"Arise, White Spirits of the South!
Ward, guard and watch over this rite,
With the force of the earthy brightness!"

Pause for a moment, then go to the West. Use these words or similar:

"Arise, Grey Spirits of the West!
Ward, guard and watch over this rite,
With the force of the misty dusk!"

Complete the circuit to the North. (These directional correspondences are from Traditional sources, but if they do not coincide with your personal associations, make the necessary substitutions in their places).

To complete the empowerment of this compass, you now need to enliven the forces that you have called. Taking a sunwise direction and using a skipping type of step as you go, chant the following with full vigour:

"Black spirits and White, Grey spirits and Red,
Come you in this compass-stead,
Around and around, throughout and about,
All good enter in and all ill keep out!"

Keep this up for as long as you feel the need but not so that you are exhausted. When you are finished, return to stand before the Stang and the Cauldron at the North and pause for a while. Collect your thoughts and prepare to make your Dedication to the Oldest Power(s) of all. When you feel ready – and this is not a light step to take, as it is utterly irrevocable – make the following invocation, or words of your choosing. Speak from the heart with all sincerity:

"Ineffable One of Ancient Providence, Formless One out of the Dark before the Dark,
Mother-Father of the Parents of all the gods, Devil, Goddess!
Ultimate Witch Father-Mother, Light of Resolution, Flame of Flames!
I stand before you in true humility and sincerity and crave thine attention!

I seek to step upon the Hidden Way of Night and Darkness, that leads forth into Light and Day,
Which is the combination and entirety of both. The Way of the Witch; the Way of the Mysteries.
Turn your unlidded eye upon me and gaze with acceptance upon my trials!
I take the spiral path to the centre, to the ever-turning Castle,
That revolves between the worlds without spinning,
There to make my Dedication of true intent.
See me and make it so."

Now, place your lighted lantern in the centre of the compass and begin to tread a widdershins mill around it, starting at the North. As you go, focus on the Dedication you are about to make and what it means to you. You may wish to make a short chant to this effect which you will intone softly as you pace. Take as long as you need over this, until you begin to feel a light trance state come on. At this point, begin to spiral in towards the centre of your compass and your lamp. You will need to make several circuits to spiral in, so do not rush this. (You may feel a slight heaviness and/or lethargy at this point - do not worry, this is entirely natural and normal and denotes the changing levels of consciousness).

Once you have reached the centre, pause. You have crossed the threshold and entered the Castle at the centre of all things; be aware of this in subsequent actions. Then, lift your lantern and blow out the candle within. This signifies the death of your old self and the return to the formless darkness from which we all come. Take your lantern and, returning to the North, place it on the ground before the Cauldron. Next, untie your cord from around your waist and place that inside the Cauldron.

Kneel down on one knee before the Stang and make your heartfelt Dedication to the Old One, the most Ancient Deity of Witchcraft. Place your right hand on the top of your head and your left under the sole of your foot; use these, or similar, words:

"O Ancient One of all Dark and Light,
Dualities Conjoined, Supreme Arbiter,
Come fill me with the Witches Might,
And I shall work with all my will.
Come take me now, and take me all,
Take lungs and liver, organs and feet,
Take me, take me, now I say!
From the brow of the head, to the tip of the toe.
Take all that's out and in of me.
Take hair and hide and all to thee.
Take heart and brains, flesh, blood and bones,
Take silence and devotion all,
In the name of the great Initiator!"

Pause for a moment for any response. Take up your knife and cut off a small piece of hair from your head and burn it in the flame of the candle between the horns of the Stang. Next, make a small cut on your left hand, between the first and second fingers, and let a few drops fall onto the ground. Say these words or similar:

> *"With these gifts of offering I seal my oath and my pledge unto thee. To this end I take the name of X* (the new witch name that you have, carefully, chosen for yourself beforehand). *I shall bear this name in secret and in pride, as a true son/daughter of the Old Faith. So mote it be."*

Take up your cord from inside the Cauldron. Tie a single knot in the centre, kiss it and re-tie it around your waist. Re-light the candle in your lantern and go to place it in the centre of the compass.

From the lantern, begin to tread a clockwise spiral outwards, until you reach the edge of the compass, then continue to tread an exuberant and joyous mill of celebration. (You can let rip here if you will; jump, shout, laugh, run, as you will; witchcraft is a celebration of Life as well as a walk into the Mysteries, so acknowledge this in your rite).

When you have finished, return to the Stang and Cauldron and celebrate a housle feast, to, with and in the Name(s) of the Power(s) that you have dedicated to. At the end, mix the remains together in one Cup or bowl and anoint your brow with the mixture, saying:

"I, X, make this anointing in the Old One's Name, as a true son/daughter of the Old Faith. So be it."

Make offerings of the remains of the feast at the base of the Stang, directly out onto the ground. In your own words, give thanks to the Power(s) that you have called upon in your rite.

Conclude your rite by addressing the Spirit Guardians at the directions, beginning at the North and working round widdershins. Use these words, or similar:

"My thanks, Black Spirits of the North,
For your ward, guard and watch over this rite.
Return now to your place of airy darkness,
For now this rite is closed."

Pause for a moment in respect, then go to the West and say:

"My thanks, Grey Spirits of the West,
For your ward, guard and watch over this rite.
Return now to your place of misty dusk,
For now this rite is closed."

Pause for a moment in respect, then go to the South and say:

"My thanks, White Spirits of the South,
For your ward, guard and watch over this rite.
Return now to your place of earthy brightness,
For now this rite is closed."

Pause for a moment in respect, then go to the East and say:

"My thanks, Red Spirits of the East,
For your ward, guard and watch over this rite.
Return now to your place of fiery dawn,
For now this rite is closed."

Return to the North, pause for a moment, then make three, widdershins circuits of the compass in silence, drawing back the essence that you used to create it. Then go to the centre, stamp on the ground or clap three times, saying:

"This rite is over. So mote it be!"

Blow out your lantern, clear all your paraphernalia away and leave the space without looking back.

Sleep in your cord that night and take note of your dreams!

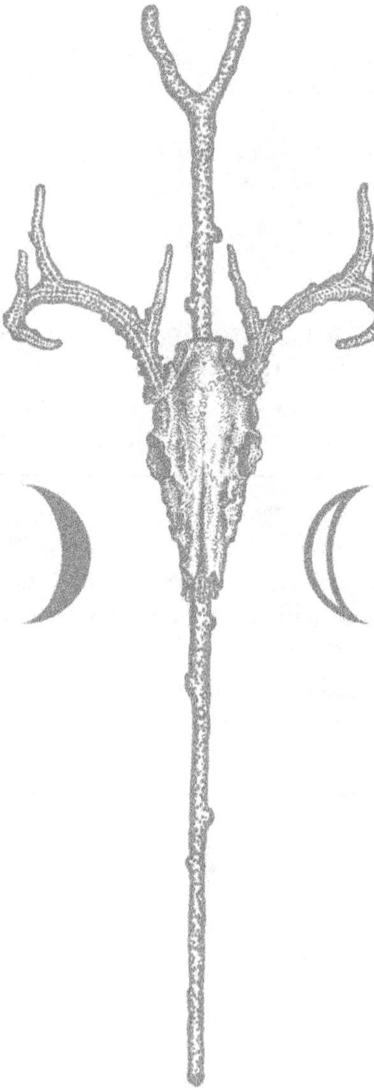

SELECTED BIBLIOGRAPHY & SUGGESTED READING LIST

13 Moons – Walker-Craven, Fiona. Ignotus Press. ISBN 1-903768-02-0.

A Deed Without a Name: Unearthing the Legacy of Traditional Witchcraft – Morgan, Lee. ISBN 978-1780995496 .

A Grimoire for Modern Cunning Folk: A Practical Guide to Witchcraft on the Crooked Path – Paddon, Peter. Pendraig Publishing. ISBN 978-0984330218 .

Anima Loci – Pennick, Nigel. Nideck.

Ask the Fellows who Cut the Hay – Evans, George Ewart. Faber & Faber. ISBN 0-571-06353-5.

Azoetia: Grimoire of Sabbatic Craft – Chumbley, Andrew D. Xoanon Publishing.

Call of the Horned Piper - Jackson, Nigel Aldcroft. Capall Bann. ISBN 1-898307-09-1.

Children of Cain – Howard, Michael. Three Hands Press. ASIN:B006XKJF2U.

Craft of the Untamed – de Mattos Frisvold, Nicholaj. Mandrake. ISBN 978-1906958114.

Cunning Folk – Davies, Owen. Hambledon & London. ISBN 1-85285-297-6.

Cunning Folk & Familiar Spirits – Wilby, Emma. Sussex Academic Press. ISBN 1-84519-079-3.

Demons & Spirits of the Land. Lecouteux, Claude. Inner Traditions. ISBN 978-1-62055-399-2.

Fauna Britannica – H.R.H. Prince Charles & Buczaki, Stefan. Hamlyn. ISBN 0-600-59867-5.

Flora Britannica – Mabey, Richard. Sinclair-Stevenson. ISBN 1-85619-377-2.

Hedge Rider – de Vries, Eric. Pendraif Publishing. ISBN 978-0979616877.

Herbcraft – Lavendar, Susan & Franklin, Anna. Capall Bann. ISBN 1-898307-57-9.

High Rise Witch – Walker-Craven, Fiona. Ignotus Press. ISBN 1-903768-07-1.

Liber Nox – Howard, Michael. Skylight Press. ISBN 978-1-908011-85-5.

Light from the Shadows – Gwynn. Capall Bann. ISBN 186163061-1.

Masks of Misrule - Jackson, Nigel Aldcroft. Capall Bann. ISBN 1-898307-67-9.

Mastering Herbalism – Huson, Paul. Madison Books. ISBN 1-56833-181-9.

Mastering Witchcraft – Huson, Paul. Pedigree Books. ISBN 0-399-50442-7.

Meeting the Other Crowd – Lenihan, Eddie. Gill & Macmillan. ISBN 0-7171-3659-0.

Mirrors of Magic – Heselton, Philip. Capall Bann. ISBN 1-89830-784-9.

Operative Witchcraft – Pennick, Nigel. Lear Books. ISBN 9-781907-614101.

Oxford Dictionary of English Folklore – Roud, Steve & Simpson, Jacqueline. Oxford University Press. ISBN 0-19-860766-0.

Root & Branch – Draco, Melusine & Harriss, Paul.

Ignotus Press. ISBN 1-903768-05-5.

Rowan Tree and Red Thread – Davidson, Thomas. Various editions.

Sacred Mask, Sacred Dance – Jones, Evan John & Clifton, Charles S. Llewellyn. ISBN 1-56718-373-5.

Secrets of East Anglian Magic – Pennick, Nigel. Capall Bann. ISBN 186163 2436.

Seidways – Fries, Jan. Mandrake Press. ISBN 978-1869928360.

Spellcraft – Skelton, Robin. Phoenix. ISBN 978-0-919345-21-8.

Stations of the Sun – Hutton, Ronald. Oxford University Press. ISBN 0-19-285448-8.

The Black Toad – Gary, Gemma. Troy Books. ISBN 978-0-9561043-7-3.

The Book of Fallen Angels – Jackson, Nigel & Howard, Michael. Capall Bann. ISBN 1-861632-36-3.

The British Book of Spells and Charms – King, Graham. Troy Books.

The Devil's Dozen: 13 Craft Rites of the Old One – Gary, Gemma. Troy Books. ASIN:B01FZIKVZU

The Devil's Plantation – Pearson, Nigel G. Troy Books. ISBN 9-781909-602113.

The Discoverie of Witchcraft – Scot, Reginald. Dover Publications Inc. ISBN 978-0486260303.

The Eldritch World – Pennick, Nigel. Lear Books. ISBN 1-095475-343-7.

The Flame in the Cauldron – Foxwood, Orion. Weiser. ISBN 9-781578-635368.

The Folklore & Witchcraft of Suffolk – Glyde, John Jun. Oakmagic Publications. ISBN 1-904330-80-.

The Forge of Tubal Cain – Finnin, Ann. Pendraig Publishing. ISBN 978-0979616839.

The Living World of Faerie – Stewart, R.J. Mercury

Publishing. ISBN 1-892-137—09-7.

The Lore of the Land – Simpson, Jacqueline & Westwood, Jennifer. Penguin. ISBN 0-141-02103-9.

The Lost Gods of England – Branston, Brian. Thames & Hudson. ISBN 0-500-11013-1.

The Pattern under the Plough – Evans, George Ewart. Faber & Faber. ISBN 0-571-08977-1.

The Pillars of Tubal Cain – Jackson, Nigel & Howard, Michael. Capall Bann. ISBN 1-861630-29-8.

The Return of the Dead – Lecouteux, Claude. Inner Traditions. ISBN 978-1594773181.

The Robert Cochrane Letters – Cochrane, Robert & Jones, Evan John. Ed. Howard, Michael. Capall Bann. ISBN 1-861632-21-5.

The Roebuck in the Thicket – Jones, Evan John & Cochrane, Robert. Ed. Howard, Michael. Capall Bann. ISBN 1-861631-55-3.

The Sacred Earth Guide – Howard, Michael. Capall Bann. ISBN 1-86163-136-7.

The Secret Commonwealth of Elves, Fauns and Fairies – Kirk, Rev Robert. Dover Publications Inc. ISBN 978-0486466118.

The Tradition of Household Spirits – Lecouteux, Claude. Inner Traditions. ISBN 978-1620551059.

The Witches Ointment – Hatsis, Thomas. Park Street Press. ISBN 978-1620554739.

Traditional Witchcraft: A Cornish Book of Ways – Gary, Gemma. Troy Books. ISBN 9-780956-104342.

Tree Wisdom – Paterson, Jacqueline Memory. Thorsons. ISBN 0-7225-3408-6.

Under the Witching Tree – Boyer, Corinne. Troy Books.

Viridarium Umbris, The Pleasure Garden of Shadow – Schulke, Daniel. Xoanon Publishing.

Visions of Isobel Gowdie: Magic, Shamanism and

Witchcraft in Seventeenth-Century Scotland – Wilby, Emma. Sussex Academic Press. ISBN 978-1845191801.

Walking the Tides – Pearson, Nigel G. Troy Books.

Witchcraft, A Tradition Renewed – Jones, Evan John & Valiente, Doreen. Robert Hale. ISBN 0-7090-4139-X.

Witchcraft Medicine – Muller-Ebeling, Ratsch & Storl. Inner Traditions. ISBN 0-89281-971-5.

Witches, Werewolves & Fairies – Lecouteux, Claude. Inner Traditions. ISBN 0-89281-096-3.

Printed in the USA
CPSIA information can be obtained
at www.ICGtesting.com
JSHW082000011023
49380JS00003B/112

9 781909 602212